northwest

food & wine

northwest
food & wine

Great Food to Serve with the
Wines of Oregon & Washington

Dan & Kathleen Taggart

SASQUATCH BOOKS
SEATTLE

To Julie and Sue, two wine lovers who get things done

Printed in the United States of America.
Distributed in Canada by Raincoast Books Ltd.
02 01 00 99 98   5 4 3 2 1

Cover design: Karen Schober
Cover photograph: Angie Norwood Browne
Interior design: Kate Basart

Library of Congress Cataloging in Publication Data
    Taggart, Dan.
        Northwest food & wine : great food to serve with the wines of Oregon & Washington /
    Dan Taggart & Kathleen Taggart.
            p.   cm.
        Includes index.
        ISBN 1-57061-147-5 (alk. paper)
        1. Cookery, American—Pacific Northwest style. 2. Wine and wine making—Washington
    (State) 3. Wine and wine making—Oregon.
    I. Taggart, Kathleen, 1951-   . II. Title.
    TX715.2.P32T34   1998
    641.5979—dc21   98-26355

SASQUATCH BOOKS
615 Second Avenue
Seattle, Washington 98104
(206) 467-4300
books@SasquatchBooks.com
http://www.SasquatchBooks.com

*Sasquatch Books publishes high-quality adult nonfiction and children's books related to the Northwest
(Alaska to San Francisco). For more information about our titles, contact us at the address above, or
view our site on the World Wide Web.*

acknowledgments

This book began as an idea that came to Kathleen one day. It became a book because Gary Luke understood the idea and guided the writing process. Joan Gregory fine-tuned the manuscript and provided moral support at critical moments. Matt Elsen and Bob Liner answered our wine questions directly and with characteristic humor. Jim and Judy Rankin tested recipes when they didn't have to. Bonnie Culberhouse and David Berger tested recipes because we knew where to find them every day; they did it with gracious honesty. David Taggart and Terry Burko converted email to evening dinners and told us what worked and what didn't. Sue and Tom Horstmann hosted dinners in their home so that wine makers could taste our food and tell us what they thought in a congenial atmosphere. We are indebted to them all.

contents

foods to pair with pinot noir

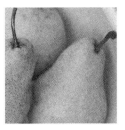

foods to pair with cabernet sauvignon

foods to pair with merlot

foods to pair with syrah

foods to pair with chardonnay

foods to pair with sauvignon blanc

foods to pair with late harvest wines

introduction

When Kathleen and I arrived in the Northwest in 1979, we had never tasted a Northwest wine. Oregon had only thirty-two wineries, and Washington only sixteen (which was a lot more than either state had only five years earlier). A blind tasting in Paris that year pitted some 330 wines from many of the best growing areas in the world against one another. To the amazement of most of the wine world, an Oregon entry—a 1975 Eyrie Vineyards Pinot Noir—placed third. The next year, the same wine placed second against six competitors from the finest of Burgundy. Northwest wine had arrived.

We are remarkably lucky to be Northwest immigrants. Over the years our appreciation of things Northwest—its people, natural beauty, climate, food, and wine—has grown steadily. The Pacific Northwest's citizens are envied by food lovers all over the world, for the incredible bounty of edibles from Mother Nature. It has been so since Native Americans' lives revolved around the ripening of huckleberries and wild blackberries, the great spawning runs of salmon and steelhead, the ebbing and flowing of tidal waters over clam beds, and the migration patterns of deer and elk herds. It was so when European settlers introduced their farmed crops of wheat and barley and watermelons and potatoes and more. They found the right climates for trees bearing peaches, apricots, apples, pears, cherries, hazelnuts, and plums, in Washington's vast Columbia Valley, in Oregon around Hood River, The Dalles, Medford, and Ashland, using irrigated water in many cases. Domesticated raspberries and strawberries, supremely sweet, candylike if the weather cooperated at harvest, became commonplace in Oregon's northern Willamette Valley. The lush grasslands of the western valleys supported large herds of dairy cattle, and became the foundation of thriving cheese industries. Those same and other grasslands nurtured sheep, allowing the growth of an important lamb meat business. Northwest food production capability became legendary for its variety in well under one hundred years.

Kathleen and I love to eat, and we love to cook. The four previous books we co-authored (with several equally passionate cooks) were all intended to make the reader want to head straight for the kitchen. We have shared the joys of the table doing countless television programs, demonstrations, and cooking classes throughout the Northwest. During those years, the world has begun to recognize the rising quality of Northwest wines.

Vitis vinifera wine grapes of European origin, now grown in the Northwest, are relative newcomers to the region. That these grapes have mostly thrived here, once their desired soil and climate has been located, is a testament to the dedication and hard work of growers who farm wine grapes rather than, say, apples or hazelnuts. Some of the growers have been bankrupted in the trying, dealt fatal blows by fickle weather at critical times. The wines from these grapes exhibit flavor characteristics remarkably similar to wines made from the same grapes some six thousand miles to the east, in Europe, at similar latitudes. Northwest microclimates, soil variations, and wine-makers' skills have resulted in wine rivaling the world's best in many categories.

This book is about enjoying the wines of Washington and Oregon (and Idaho) along with good food. Our recipes are organized into chapters according to the wine grape variety we believe makes both the food and the wine taste good. We've made the wine selections based on our experiences eating dinner together at home, nearly every night, for more than twenty-five years. That's time enough to learn a lot about your dinner partner and about how foods and wines go together.

Northwest Food & Wine is a tribute to the vineyard owners and wine makers of the Northwest. Some of them were casually involved in recipe testing for this book, in the form of having dinner cooked by us and then commenting about it and about the wines, both their own and those of others. They were universally kind while being honest.

Here's to the hard work of those in the Northwest who grow the grapes, to the knowledge and instinct of those who turn them into wine, and to the good taste of those who believe that a good meal deserves a good wine.

—*Dan Taggart*
Durham, Oregon

a brief history of northwest wine making

As you appreciate a glass of Northwest wine, ponder the short modern history that made your enjoyment possible.

A group of friends in Seattle began making wine for themselves as a hobby in the 1950s, using *Vitis vinifera* (European) wine grapes, unusual at the time. By 1967 they had incorporated as Associated Vintners and produced their first commercial vintage. That first release of Associated Vinters (now the parent company of Columbia Winery, Covey Run Vintners, Paul Thomas Winery, and others) included Cabernet Sauvignon, Gewürztraminer, Pinot Noir, and Riesling. The white wines were released in 1969 to rave Seattle-area reviews, and sold out within a week. At the time the entire state of Washington had only about four hundred acres planted to vinifera grapes. Thirty-one years later, award-winning Columbia Winery winemaker David Lake, a Master of Wine, oversees thousands of acres of vineyards.

In 1970 Wally Opdyke in Seattle met with Dr. Walter J. Clore of Washington State University's research extension, father of modern grape growing in Washington. The meeting convinced Opdyke that there was a future in Washington wine making, and he persuaded the aging owners of an old sweet wine company, American Wine Growers, to sell out. He gained their old label, Chateau Ste. Michelle, and hired legendary André Tchelistcheff of California's Beaulieu Vineyards as consultant. A financial partnership with U.S. Tobacco began in 1973, when Washington was down to two real wineries, providing Ste. Michelle with the capital to grow the new winery. In 1974 a Ste. Michelle Riesling (1972) won a tasting organized by Robert Balzer of the *Los Angeles Times*. The world took notice, and more importantly, so did Washington growers, who began to plant the vinifera grapes Dr. Clore had been telling them for years could be successful.

In Oregon, meanwhile, Richard Sommer had moved up from California in the late 1950s after gaining a degree from the University of California at Davis. In 1961 he planted vinifera grapes on a hillside in the Umpqua Valley, in southern Oregon, and in 1963 established HillCrest Vineyard winery, now the oldest continuously operating winery in Oregon. Charles Coury came north in 1965, founding Charles Coury Vineyards on a property that turned out to have been the same one Frank Reuter farmed grapes on in the 1890s. The winery lasted only a few years, but this meteorologist understood microclimates, and was convinced that vinifera grapes could be grown in the cool, damp Willamette Valley of northwestern Oregon. He claims credit for influencing several other Oregon wine-making pioneers to give the climate a try. Those pioneers include Dick Erath (Erath Vineyards, 1972, the year of his first commercial vintage), David Lett (The Eyrie Vineyards, 1970), Dick Ponzi (Ponzi Vineyards, 1974), David Adelsheim (Adelsheim Vineyard, 1978), Bill Fuller (Tualatin Vineyards, 1973), Myron Redford (Amity Vineyards, 1976), and Bill Blosser (Sokol Blosser Winery, 1977).

Twenty-five years later hundreds of Oregon and Washington wineries (and a few in Idaho) produce a great variety of wines made from the vinifera vines once thought ill-suited to Northwest microclimates. The Northwest wine-making experiment has turned out so well that some prestigious foreign wineries have bought vineyard property and are now making making wine in America.

northwest wine country

Sipping a well-made wine with a good meal is a pleasure. Having stood on the soil from which the wine originates makes the pleasure even greater. Here is an abbreviated guide to the Northwest's growing regions, called American Viticultural Areas (AVA), and an explanation of the climate affecting the grapes in those areas.

The Rogue Valley in Oregon is the southernmost wine-growing region in the Northwest. Actually a series of valleys, the area begins at the California border and stretches north and east along both sides of Interstate 5, encompassing Ashland, Medford, and Grants Pass. Three separate microclimates support vineyards that grow everything from Cabernet Sauvignon to Sauvignon Blanc grapes. Bridgeview Vineyards and Winery and Foris Vineyards are in the higher, cooler Illinois Valley. The warmer, drier Applegate Valley is home to Valley View Winery, named for a vineyard planted in 1850 by pioneer Peter Britt. The Rogue River subregion from Ashland northeast to Grants Pass is hot and dry. Ashland Vineyards and Weisinger's of Ashland are two of the area's wineries. This region is also home to acres of pear, peach, and apple orchards.

A few miles north of the Rogue Valley region is the Umpqua Valley, straddling I-5 between the Cascade Mountains and the Coast Range. Actually a series of valleys, the region is often referred to as the "Hundred Valleys of the Umpqua." Compared to the Willamette Valley, its neighbor to the north, the Umpqua has a drier climate and more pronounced swings in daily temperature. A little more than twenty inches of rain falls here annually. Oregon's first postprohibition winery, HillCrest Vineyard, was established here in 1963 by Richard Sommer. Other wineries in the area include Callahan Ridge Winery, Girardet Wine Cellars, Henry Estate Winery, and La Garza Cellars. The long list of grapes grown includes Cabernet Sauvignon, Pinot Noir, and Riesling.

Slightly south of Cottage Grove, Oregon's Willamette Valley growing region begins. It stretches from the Cascade Mountains in the east to the Coast Range in the west, and then north to the Columbia River. Most of Oregon's wine grapes are grown in this area, about sixty miles wide at best, and more than one hundred miles long. In general, it is cooler and wetter here than farther south, with about forty inches of rain annually, though it can be dry for a couple of months in the summer. The Willamette Valley is a highly productive region—the largest grass seed–growing area in the world, as well as a rich source of fruits, vegetables, and other produce, including berries, hazelnuts, corn, prunes, broccoli, and beans. Its fertile land has made it the population center of Oregon, and brought pioneering wine makers into the region in the 1960s.

The majority of Willamette Valley wineries are on its western side, many nestled into the foothills of the Coast Range or situated on south-facing slopes. At the southern end is a collection of wineries both large and small, including Hinman Vineyards, Secret House Vineyards Winery, and King Estate Winery. Farther north in the Corvallis and Albany areas are, among others, Alpine Vineyards, Tyee Wine Cellars, Springhill Cellars, Serendipity Cellars, and Airlie Winery. Willamette Valley Vineyards is slightly south of Salem, which is home to many wineries, including Stangeland Winery, Witness Tree Vineyard, St. Innocent Winery, Eola Hills Wine Cellars, Cristom Vineyards, and Evesham Wood Vineyard. Many wineries, including some of these, are situated in the Eola Hills subregion to the north and west of Salem.

The northern Willamette Valley to the southwest of Portland is where Oregon's wine making is concentrated. Pioneer wine-makers David Adelsheim, Bill Blosser, Dick Erath, Bill Fuller, David Lett, Dick Ponzi, and Myron Redford all bet the farm in the late 1960s and 1970s that Burgundian grapes like Chardonnay and Pinot Noir would thrive in the cool, damp climate. Today the region boasts more than eighty-four wineries, the greatest percentage of them in Yamhill County. The Red Hills subregion near Dundee hosts a number of big names in the business, including The Eyrie Vineyards, Sokol Blosser Winery, Lange Winery, Erath Vineyards, Cameron Winery, Brick House Vineyards, and Adlesheim Vineyard. Pinot Noir is the star grape here, but Chardonnay and Pinot Gris are quite important, too.

On the east side of the Cascade Mountains is the Columbia Valley AVA, a huge region that occupies a good portion of eastern Washington as well as a slice of northern Oregon. This is hot, dry country, but irrigation has transformed it into a rich agricultural region, as well as a primary source of wine grapes for Northwest wineries. The Oregon section has few vineyards and even fewer wineries, but has made its reputation with big, chewy Cabernet Sauvignon and Merlot wines reminiscent of those from Washington's Walla Walla area. Seven Hills Winery is the primary winery here. This land also produces wheat, barley, watermelons, and other crops in its eastern portion. Around The Dalles is irrigated orchard land, yielding apples, pears, and cherries, as well as some old-vine vineyards.

In Washington, the Columbia Valley region encompasses the broad basins and valleys of the Columbia and Snake Rivers, stretching east from the Cascades toward Spokane and the Idaho border, and north from Oregon to within about sixty miles of the Canadian border. This is Washington's agricultural and ranching heartland. Wheat fields cover rolling hills in the east, and huge sprawling ranches produce beef, pork, and lamb. Fertile farmlands and orchards in the west and south portions grow apples, pears, onions, cherries, asparagus, apricots, plums, and corn. Both red and white grape varieties come from Columbia Valley vineyards, including Chardonnay, Sémillon, Riesling, Merlot, Syrah, and Cabernet Sauvignon. Within the Columbia AVA are two separately named regions, the Yakima and the Walla Walla Valleys.

The Walla Walla Valley region is bounded by the Blue Mountains on the east, the Columbia River on the west, the Snake River on the north, and actually includes the Milton-Freewater area in Oregon. Most of the wineries here, which include Leonetti Cellar, Woodward Canyon Winery, L'Ecole No. 41, and Canoe Ridge Vineyard, are small, with focused missions. They have gained an international reputation for big, supple Cabernet Sauvignon, Chardonnay, and Merlot wines.

The Yakima Valley is the most concentrated winery region in Washington. Some eighty miles in length, extending from Yakima to slightly west of the Tri-Cities, it receives ten inches or less of rain per year. Hot days and cool nights develop full fruit flavors in the grapes, and superb wines are made from them in wineries as far away as Seattle and Oregon. Cabernet Sauvignon, Chardonnay, and Merlot occupy the most vineyard land, but other grapes include Chenin Blanc, Gewürztraminer, Lemberger, Riesling, Sauvignon Blanc, and Syrah.

Winery access is easy in the Yakima Valley either from Interstate 82 or from U.S Highway 12, the Yakima Valley Highway. Hyatt Vineyards, Covey Run Vintners, Washington Hills Cellars, Paul Thomas Estate and Winery, Chinook Wines, Hogue Cellars, Hedges Cellars, and Chateau Ste. Michelle are among the numerous wineries that have established themselves in the Yakima Valley.

In the southern part of the Columbia Valley, around the Kennewick-Pasco-Richland (Tri-Cities) area, are several wineries, including Barnard Griffin and Preston Premium Wines. On the eastern side of the region, the city of Spokane, while technically not part of the AVA, is nonetheless home to wineries such as Arbor Crest Cellars, Caterina Winery, Worden's Washington Winery, and Latah Creek Wine Cellars, among others.

West of the Cascades lies the Puget Sound region, Washington's metropolitan and population center. Because of cool, damp, marine weather, it is not home to very many vineyards, but several wineries have established themselves here, usually using grapes from the Columbia Valley. Seattle is home to a handful of wineries, including E.B. Foote. Bainbridge Island Winery, Rich Passage Winery, and Andrew Will Winery are all located on islands just west of Seattle. Cavatappi Winery is in Kirkland, on the eastern side of Lake Washington. Farther east is Snoqualmie Winery. The Woodinville area, northeast of metropolitan Seattle, hosts a group of wineries, including Columbia Winery, Facelli Winery, Silver Lake Sparkling Cellars, and the corporate offices and one of three production facilities of Chateau Ste. Michelle. In the northern part of the Puget Sound region are Mount Baker Winery, near the mountain of the same name, and Lopez Island Vineyards, in the middle of the San Juan Islands. The Olympia and Tacoma areas, in southern Puget Sound, have a few wineries, including McCrea Cellars in Rainier. Just west of Puget Sound, on the Olympic Peninsula, is Camaraderie Cellars, in Port Angeles.

Idaho's small wine industry is concentrated west of Boise, in the hills near the town of Caldwell, just across the Snake River from Oregon. Ste. Chapelle is the largest and oldest winery in the area, and by far the best known out of state. The climate is similar to the Yakima Valley's, with hot summers and cold winters. A few wineries, such as Pend d'Oreille Winery, are located north in the panhandle region, and three are scattered through the Snake River Valley between Boise and Twin Falls. In a project similar to Washington State University's extension research program at Prosser, the University of Idaho's Parma Research and Extension Center now has a program in place to develop greater knowledge of how specific wine grapes fare in Idaho's climate, and under what irrigation conditions.

wine terms made simple

ACIDITY: The sharpness necessary to balance a wine's flavor. All wines have it. If there is too much the wine will taste sour; too little, and the wine is flabby.

APPELLATION: A government-designated growing region listed on a wine label. Quite specific in Europe, it is very general in the Northwest.

BARREL FERMENTED: Wine that has been vinified (changed from grape juice into wine) in wooden barrels, rather than in tanks made of plastic, stainless steel, or any other substance that does not impart its flavor to the wine.

BODY: The way a wine feels in your mouth. Light, crisp wines often feel thin. Higher-alcohol wines are thicker in the mouth, thanks to the glycerin in the wine. Too much alcohol makes a wine feel hot.

BOTRYTIS: A fungus that attacks grapes on the vines leading to so-called noble rot, a condition in which grapes shrivel and dehydrate. Wines made from these grapes can be excellent dessert wines—and quite expensive.

BREATHING: Allowing wine to have contact with air, so that the oxygen will mix with the wine and open up its flavors faster. The quickest way is to swirl wine in your glass. Some people leave bottles uncorked for hours before tasting them, while others think the practice does very little.

BRIX: A measurement system for sugars in liquids, in this case wine grapes. Wine makers have a specific notion of what sugar concentration they want in grapes when they are picked, so a brixometer is used in the vineyards as part of testing for perfect ripeness.

CORKED: Spoiled by a cork. A certain percentage of all wines sealed with natural cork become corked. The exact cause is unknown. A corked wine smells musty, like wet wood or mold. A corked bottle should be returned to the retailer or restaurant waiter, who should replace it graciously.

DECANTING: Slowly pouring a wine into another container while taking care not to disturb visible sediment in the bottom of the bottle. Pouring stops before the sediment escapes the bottle. The sediment is a mixture of tannin and pigments that have combined to form crystals, which feel furry and taste bitter.

FERMENTATION: Natural bacterial action (assisted or controlled by the wine maker) that breaks down sugars in sweet liquids like wine grapes into carbon dioxide and alcohol. The resulting wine is no longer very sweet (unless dessert wine is being made) and may be bone dry, with no sweetness detectable in the mouth. (See also Malolactic Fermentation.)

FINING (pronounced FINE-ing): The addition of one or more natural additives which help to clarify the wine.

FINISH: The length of time a wine's flavors linger in your mouth after a sip.

FREE RUN: Juice that is allowed to drain from a press or fermenter into another vessel without the use of pumps, which can mix unwanted sediments into wine.

LEGS: The rivulets of glycerin that run down the inside of a wineglass when a wine with big body is swirled in it.

LEES (and sur lees aging): The yeast cells and other fermentation debris that accumulate at the bottom of the fermenting vessel. Wine makers looking for extra flavor will sometimes age their newly made wine in the barrel with the lees, rather than transfer it to another container. This is called sur lees aging.

MALOLACTIC FERMENTATION: A second fermentation. Harsh malic acid is converted to the softer-tasting lactic acid to create a more balanced wine. The fermentation may occur spontaneously, or it may be assisted or stopped by the wine maker.

NOSE: The assertiveness and kinds of aromas released when wine is swirled and sniffed.

OAK: The presence in a wine's flavor of those tastes commonly associated with aging in oak barrels, usually flavors such as vanilla, clove, and toast.

OXIDATION: The decline in a wine's fresh taste, resulting from age, poor sealing, poor wine-making techniques, improper storage, etc. Brown hues in white or red wines usually indicate oxidation of some degree.

RACKING: Transferring wine from one vessel to another, in order to leave behind sediments that have formed.

RESIDUAL SUGAR: Unconverted sugar left in the juice when fermentation is stopped. A level of 0.5 percent or less cannot be tasted by most people, 1 to 2 percent is called off-dry, and 3 percent or more tastes noticeably sweet. An important measure to note if you are trying to find a very dry white wine, for example.

SOMMELIER (pronounced som-mel-YAY): A restaurant's designated wine expert and server. This person should know the wine list well, be able to talk in plain English about the wines on the list, and be willing to recommend wines in various price ranges if asked.

SULFITES: Sulphur dioxide naturally dissolved in wines during fermentation, as well as that usually added to control unwanted bacterial action.

TANNIN: An astringent acid present in grape skins, seeds, and stems. It provides part of the appealing structure of bigger red wines, and is usually unwanted in white wines. Too much of it makes a wine feel furry in your mouth. Several years of bottle age will soften tannic acid to some degree.

TOAST: The amount of char on the inside of a wine barrel, which contributes to the perception of toast as a flavor ingredient in wine.

VARIETAL: The specific wine grape used to make a wine.

VINTAGE: The year the grapes were harvested and the wine made, not the year the wine was released for sale by the winery.

foods to pair with

pinot noir

Pork and Pistachio Terrine
Mushroom Crostini
Olive Bread Salad
Poached Eggs with Garlic Croutons on Mixed Greens
Northwest Mushroom Omelet
Fettuccine with Chanterelles and Crème Fraîche
Penne with Caramelized Walla Walla Onions
Seared Ahi Tuna on a Bed of Fresh Spinach
Grilled Pacific Salmon with Sweet Peppers
Smoked Chicken with Black Beans
Roast Turkey with Cornbread-Hazelnut Dressing
Cranberry-Pear Chutney
Steam-Roasted Duck with Fresh Flour Tortillas
Fresh Flour Tortillas
Rabbit Braised in Pinot Noir Sauce
Grilled Butterflied Leg of Lamb with Rosemary
Pork Fajitas with Grilled Tomato–Onion Salsa
Grilled Tomato–Onion Salsa
Pizza Kathleen
Raspberry Jam Brownie Squares

the pinot noir grape

The Pinot Noir (PEE-no NWAHR) grape is a red wine grape that can tolerate the cool, moist climate of western Oregon, where it stars. It is also grown in southern Oregon vineyards and made into good wines by Foris Vineyards Winery and Bridgeview Vineyard, among others. Some Pinot Noir grapes are also grown in Washington (ranking tenth in acres planted), as well as in the Snake River region

of Idaho, where it is made into both Pinot Noir and a nice sparkling wine. But by far the lion's share of Northwest Pinot Noir is planted in Oregon's Willamette Valley region, and it ranks as Oregon's most planted grape.

Northwest wine makers often refer to Pinot Noir as a feminine wine—seductive and flirtatious—and it is frequently called the Queen of Red Wines. It is less tannic than Cabernet Sauvignon and Merlot, with earthy overtones to balance the berry flavors. Pinot Noir is believed to have originated in what is now France's Burgundy district; it is the primary red grape there today. Oregon's latitude is nearly the same as Burgundy's, and its climate too is very similar. The early Oregon wine makers guessed that they should be able to successfully grow the grape, and their faith has been rewarded. Wineries producing Pinot Noir now dot the hills all over the Willamette Valley, the thickest concentration being in Yamhill County near Dundee. Wine-making pioneer David Lett of The Eyrie Vineyards established Oregon's primacy in Pinot Noir before the end of the 1970s by placing nearly at the top of two prestigious blind tastings in Europe. The French noticed and bought land in Oregon, where Domaine Drouhin now makes Pinot Noir side by side neighbors such as Erath, Lange, and Cameron.

The wine is famous for its ability to change character on short notice, undergoing more changes in a few weeks at the winery than other wines do in years. Wine makers are challenged by that capriciousness, and part of their art is to determine when the wine is best bottled and how—or if—to blend it. Most Pinot Noirs are quite drinkable between two and six years of age, though fuller, inky, heavily oaked versions may cellar for fifteen years or so.

Because Pinot Noir is lighter in tannin than Cabernet Sauvignon or Merlot, among other reds, it is considered by many to be a fine food wine. Lighter versions can easily pair with some poultry and many fish dishes. The old adage "Drink red wine with red meats and white wine with white meats and fish" is less true today than in decades past, thanks to modern wine-making methods. And Pinot Noir has always been a grape able to steer a middle ground at the table. Most versions are fruity, exhibiting flavors that can include currants, raspberries, strawberries, cherries, flowers, spice, toasted wood, mint, and tobacco. Bottle aging can bring out earth, mushroom, and leather notes.

Serve at cool room temperature, about 60°F.

pork and pistachio terrine

This terrine is meant to be served in thin slices after chilling and curing for one to three days. It makes an appealing appetizer or first course, or a very satisfying quick dinner when served with rustic bread from one of the Northwest's artisan bakeries. Pour a Northwest Pinot Noir, such as Grateful Red, from Redhawk Vineyard near Salem, Oregon. Wine-maker Tom Robinson is known for his quality wines.

This recipe always makes us think of Greg Higgins, owner and chef at Higgins restaurant in Portland. Greg's talent in the kitchen is amazing, especially with the pâtés, terrines, and mousses that grace his menu. If you have a classic, rectangular, enameled-iron terrine mold with a lid, about 12 x 4 x 3 inches, use that. If not, a 9 x 5-inch loaf pan will work nicely.

2¼ pounds boneless pork shoulder or boneless country-style ribs

1 large onion, cut into 1-inch pieces

1 teaspoon dried savory leaves

1 teaspoon dried oregano leaves

1 teaspoon dried thyme leaves

¼ teaspoon ground nutmeg

4 teaspoons coarse salt

1 teaspoon freshly ground black pepper

¼ cup cognac or brandy

1 cup unsalted roasted, shelled pistachio nuts

1 large egg, beaten

2 bay leaves

4 strips of bacon, preferably apple wood–smoked

FOR SERVING

> Dijon mustard
> Cornichons
> Crusty bread

PREHEAT THE OVEN TO 275°F.

IF YOU HAVE A MEAT GRINDER, grind the pork through the coarse plate and follow with the onion. If you have a food processor, remove obvious gristle from the pork but leave the fat for moisture in the terrine. Cut the pork into 1-inch cubes, put in the work bowl, and coarsely chop using the pulse button on the machine. When the pork is almost chopped, add the onion and continue pulsing to chop the pork and onion together. (Or buy ground pork at your market— coarsely ground if possible—and chop the onion by hand.) Transfer the ground or chopped pork to a large mixing bowl. Add the dried herbs, nutmeg, salt, pepper, cognac, pistachios, and egg, and stir to combine without compacting more than necessary.

PLACE THE BAY LEAVES and then 2 strips of bacon in the bottom of a terrine mold or loaf pan. Spoon the pork mixture into the pan, spread evenly, and level it across the top. Cover with the remaining 2 bacon strips. Cover with the lid or foil. Bake until an instant-read thermometer registers 170°F when inserted into the middle of the terrine. Cooking time can be as short as 1 hour 20 minutes, if baked in a long, thin terrine mold, or as long as 3 hours, if baked in a loaf pan. Cool in the pan for two hours. Do not pour off the juices; they will be reabsorbed. Refrigerate for 1 to 3 days.

RUN A KNIFE AROUND THE EDGES of the pan to loosen the terrine, then turn it upside down on a carving board. Blot excess juices with paper towels. Serve chilled or at room temperature, sliced ¼ to ½ inch thick, with mustard, cornichons, and bread slices.

> Serves 8 to 12 as a first course or 40 or more if cut into small pieces
> as an appetizer

ken wright

Ken Wright was the co-founder and wine maker at Panther Creek Cellars in McMinnville, Oregon, from 1986 until 1994, when he founded Ken Wright Cellars. His passion for making good wine quickly gained Panther Creek a reputation for quality, and that same reputation has continued at Ken Wright Cellars. Wright's approach to grape growing is to let someone else do it, with strict controls. He was an early pioneer of the system of leasing space in carefully selected vineyards, and establishing long-term relationships with growers. Wright wants it done his way, and pays growers by the acre, not by the ton.

Ken Wright's philosophy of wine making starts in the vineyards. Once a grower has produced a crop that meets Ken's standards, a single, experienced person determines the moment of harvest in each particular vineyard. Those grapes are harvested, and identified both by site and by clone. They are kept separate throughout the entire wine-making process, which often includes a pre-fermentation soak to increase color and flavor intensity without extracting excess tannin. Wright stresses winery sanitation to avoid contamination that could lead to off-flavors, and grapes are sorted by hand before going into the crusher. After wine making and initial aging, Wright blends the wines from various clones, and from some of the vineyards. Single vineyard wines are his specialty.

Ken Wright Cellars in located in Carlton, Oregon. Wright is also consulting wine maker at Domaine Serene.

mushroom crostini

The forests of the Northwest are legendary for their wild mushrooms, such as chanterelles and morels. Commercial growers also raise oyster mushrooms as well as the brown cremini or white variety called for in this recipe, which also uses porcini mushrooms. Dried porcini mushrooms are a very special ingredient, worth a trip to a specialty market. The flavor is often described as earthy. Although the price per pound is eye popping, you buy them by the ounce, not the pound. And once they're stored in a tightly covered jar, dried porcini mushrooms will last long enough for you to forget the price. Given a choice, buy larger, lighter-colored pieces for best flavor. This mushroom spread for crostini, a recipe that Kathleen's sister, Marianne Barber, created for this book, is a perfect match for Northwest Pinot Noir. Tualatin Vineyards, located in Washington County, Oregon, makes Pinot Noir, as well as several well-regarded white wines. Tualatin was one of the earliest wineries in the state, dating back to 1973.

MUSHROOM SPREAD

1 ounce dried porcini mushrooms

2½ tablespoons olive oil

8 ounces cremini or white mushrooms, brushed or wiped clean, and finely chopped

1 large clove garlic, minced

2 tablespoons grated imported parmesan cheese

¼ cup (lightly packed) parsley leaves, finely chopped

1 teaspoon coarse salt

Freshly ground black pepper

CROSTINI

20 thin (¼-inch) slices of baguette-type bread

Olive oil

SOAK THE PORCINI MUSHROOMS for 30 minutes in warm water to cover. Drain in a paper towel–lined wire strainer, saving the liquid. Rinse to remove any sand, squeeze dry, and chop finely. Heat the olive oil in a 10-inch skillet over medium heat. Add the porcini mushrooms, cremini mushrooms, and garlic, and sauté, stirring, until the mushrooms have released their liquid and it has evaporated. Remove the pan from the heat and stir in 1 tablespoon porcini soaking liquid, the parmesan, salt, and pepper to taste. Spoon into a small serving bowl or ramekin.

PREHEAT THE OVEN TO 400°F.

LIGHTLY BRUSH BOTH SIDES of bread slices with olive oil and arrange on a baking sheet. Bake for about 4 minutes on each side, or until bread is lightly browned.

PLACE THE BOWL of mushroom spread in the center of a large platter and arrange the crostini around it. Provide a small spreader or butter knife for guests to serve themselves.

Makes 20 pieces

olive bread salad

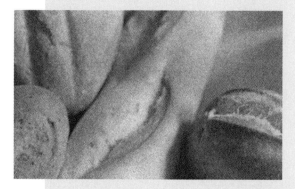

Several wineries are located in the Dundee, Oregon, area, among them Domaine Drouhin, the U.S. extension of the famous Maison Drouhin of the Burgundy region of France, which saw the potential in the land and purchased more than one hundred acres in 1987. The winery is not open to the public except for special events. Domaine Drouhin wines are considered among the very finest produced in Oregon. They are made by Véronique Drouhin, who clearly inherited her father's wine-making skills. In one memorable meal, we paired the Domaine Drouhin 1992 Pinot Noir with this humble, but full-flavored and filling salad, accompanying it with slow-roasted beef ribs as a meaty accent. A country-style loaf of dense, thick-crusted olive bread, available from many artisan bakeries in the Northwest, forms the backbone of this salad.

1 pound olive bread

2 heads garlic

1 teaspoon vegetable oil

4 medium tomatoes

½ teaspoon coarse salt

4 scallions, thinly sliced

½ red bell pepper, cut into ½-inch dice

½ cup (lightly packed) basil leaves, chopped

¼ cup extra virgin olive oil

1 tablespoon red wine vinegar

Freshly ground black pepper

PREHEAT THE OVEN TO 475°F.

CUT THE OLIVE BREAD into 1- to 1½-inch cubes. Place the cubes on a baking sheet and toast in the oven for 5 to 7 minutes, or until cubes are golden brown. Remove cubes from oven and reduce heat to 375°F.

CUT THE TOP QUARTER off each whole garlic head to expose the flesh. Rub the exposed ends with vegetable oil and place the garlic on a baking sheet. Roast for 40 minutes.

TRANSFER THE BREAD CUBES to a large salad or mixing bowl. Cut one of the tomatoes in half crosswise and squeeze the juice out onto the bread cubes. Add salt and toss well. Let stand for 15 minutes.

SLICE THE REMAINING 3 TOMATOES into thin wedges and add to the bread cubes. Squeeze the garlic cloves out of their skins and add. Add the scallions, red pepper, and basil. Whisk the oil and vinegar together, add to salad, along with pepper to taste, and toss thoroughly. Serve.

Serves 4

poached eggs with garlic croutons on mixed greens

The first time we visited France, we came across this salad in nearly every restaurant we ate in. It is built around "spring mix," a mixture of baby salad greens whose makeup varies but commonly includes mizuna, tatsoi, arugula, baby green and red romaine, lolla rosa, red swiss chard, baby green and red oak, tango, and baby green and red leaf lettuces. Many inventive versions of mixed baby greens are available from Northwest producers. The resulting salad can be a light dinner, or a first course. Either way it is elegant in its simplicity, allowing the wine to shine. We think it is an excellent match for a Pinot Noir, a red wine of noble flavor.

Pinot Noir is a wine maker's challenge, able to be something tomorrow that it was not today. Because of the climate, many Oregon wineries growing Pinot Noir grapes have been—and will continue to be—award winners on the world stage. One of the more recent stars has been Chehalem Winery, in Newberg, Oregon. Chehalem absorbed the former Veritas Vineyard, and has other vineyards coming along.

CROUTONS

¼ cup extra virgin olive oil

2 cloves garlic, crushed

12 thick slices (about ½ inch) of baguette-type bread, fresh or day-old

SALAD

> 10 ounces spring mix (baby salad greens), cleaned
>
> ½ cup extra virgin olive oil
>
> 2 tablespoons red wine vinegar
>
> ½ teaspoon Dijon mustard
>
> 2 cloves garlic, minced
>
> Coarse salt
>
> Freshly ground black pepper
>
> 12 large eggs
>
> ½ cup parsley leaves, chopped, for garnish

PREHEAT THE OVEN TO 325°F.

TO MAKE THE CROUTONS, pour olive oil into a small saucepan over medium heat. Add the crushed garlic and cook until it begins to color lightly, 3 to 5 minutes. Discard the garlic. Brush oil on both sides of the bread slices and arrange in a single layer on a baking sheet. Bake 10 minutes. Turn and bake for 10 minutes more.

POUR 1½ TO 2 INCHES of water into a 12-inch sauté pan or skillet and bring to a simmer while you prepare the salad.

PUT THE SALAD GREENS in a large mixing bowl. In a small bowl or jar, whisk together the olive oil, vinegar, mustard, garlic, and salt and pepper to taste. Pour over the greens and toss thoroughly. Arrange greens on dinner plates. Arrange 3 croutons on top of salad on each plate. Crack the eggs into the water, six at a time, cooking until whites are just set and yolks are soft. Gently remove with a slotted spoon, blot dry with paper towels, and lay on croutons. Sprinkle with parsley. Repeat with the remaining 6 eggs. Serve immediately.

Serves 4

pinot noir

northwest
mushroom omelet

Omelets are easier to make than many cooks believe. And, depending on the omelet's filling, they partner with all manner of wines. Wild and cultivated mushrooms and Pinot Noir are good friends, and the Northwest is a major source of both. Northwest forests yield several types of mushrooms during different growing seasons, fungi so valuable that people actually have lost their lives contending for mushroom turf. The U.S. Forest Service issues permits to pick for commercial purposes, but with some mushrooms worth more than $150 a pound in Asian markets, the picking disputes still smolder.

Not in dispute is the popularity of Brick House Vineyards Pinot Noir. Brick House is one of the newest Northwest wineries, located on Ribbon Ridge, northwest of Newberg, Oregon. Organic growing methods and winemaking emphasizing concentrated flavor are the standards that drive the popularity of this small producer.

MUSHROOM FILLING

2 tablespoons unsalted butter

½ cup finely chopped onion

1 pound wild mushrooms, such as chanterelles, shiitakes, oysters, or a combination, wiped or brushed clean, and coarsely chopped

2 tablespoons chopped fresh thyme leaves, about 10 sprigs

½ teaspoon coarse salt

Freshly ground black pepper

OMELET

12 large eggs

4 tablespoons (½ stick) unsalted butter

½ teaspoon coarse salt

TO MAKE THE MUSHROOM FILLING MIXTURE, melt the butter in a 12-inch non-stick skillet over medium heat. Add the onion and cook for about 1 minute. Add the mushrooms and thyme and cook, stirring occasionally, until the mushrooms have released their liquid and it has evaporated. Add salt and pepper to taste. Scrape the mixture out of the pan into a bowl or onto a large plate. Wipe the skillet clean.

TO MAKE THE OMELETS, have serving plates slightly warmed but not hot in a very low oven. Divide the eggs between 2 medium mixing bowls, add ¼ teaspoon salt to each bowl, and beat. Make the omelets one at a time. Heat 2 tablespoons of the butter in the skillet. When the butter melts and the foam subsides, add the eggs from one of the bowls. When a skin has formed on the pan's bottom, use a fork to remix the eggs. Allow a second skin to form, tilting the pan while raising an edge of the egg mixture with a rubber spatula, to allow uncooked eggs to run under the skin. When the eggs are mostly but not quite completely set on top, add half of the mushroom mixture. Push-jerk the pan to fold the omelet over on itself, or use a large rubber spatula to fold it over. Lightly brown, then gently turn and lightly brown the other side. Use the spatula to cut the omelet in half in the pan, then slide out onto 2 plates. Keep finished portions barely warm while you repeat the process. Serve at once.

Serves 4

fettuccine with chanterelles
and crème fraîche

One of the crown jewels of the kitchen, chanterelle mushrooms can be smaller than your thumb or larger than your hand. They often come to market decorated with the needles of the fir trees that tower over them in Northwest forests. A gentle brushing or wiping with a paper towel is usually enough to make them presentable. Crème fraîche, a cultured milk product with a tangy flavor, is available at many specialty markets, but it can be made easily at home. Though this dish is meatless, the chanterelles can stand up to a Pinot Noir that has backbone. An unusual brand is Firesteed Cellars, which is actually a label created to market reasonably priced wines. The wines are made at a winery on contract in sufficient quantity to allow a friendly price point.

2 pounds chanterelle mushrooms

Coarse salt

4 cups chicken stock or low-sodium canned broth

3 tablespoons soy sauce

1⅓ cups crème fraîche (see page 15)

Freshly ground black pepper

2 cups (lightly packed) parsley leaves, chopped

1 pound fresh fettuccine

1 tablespoon vegetable oil

BRUSH MUSHROOMS AS CLEAN AS POSSIBLE. Cut them into uniform wedges if large. Leave whole if small. Set aside.

BRING 6 QUARTS OF WATER TO A BOIL in a pot over high heat. Add 1 tablespoon salt and reduce to a simmer while you prepare the mushroom sauce. Bring the stock to a boil in a large, wide pan over medium-high heat. Add the mushrooms and maintain a vigorous boil until the mushrooms have cooked down and liquid has been reduced by half. Stir in the soy sauce and crème fraîche. Add pepper and taste for seasoning; if canned broth has been used, salt will probably not be required. Stir in the parsley.

BRING PASTA WATER BACK TO A ROLLING BOIL. Add fettuccine and cook, stirring often, until al dente, about 3 minutes. Drain, return to pot, and toss with the oil. Divide among 4 large soup or pasta bowls. Divide the mushrooms among them, then ladle out equal amounts of mushroom liquid. Serve.

Serves 4

to make crème fraîche

Make crème fraîche the day before you plan to use it. Stir 2 tablespoons plain yogurt or buttermilk into 2 cups whipping cream. Cover and let stand at room temperature overnight. Refrigerate. (Crème fraîche will keep for 1 week or more, covered, in the refrigerator.) Makes 2 cups.

penne with caramelized walla walla onions

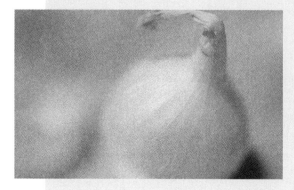

Onions have a remarkable chameleonlike ability to change their raw assertiveness into a soft, rich sweetness if cooked long and slowly enough. Certain onions, such as those from the Walla Walla region of southeastern Washington, have a "sweet" taste even in their raw state, which makes them quite popular. In concert with hot pasta, heavy cream, and grated cheese, caramelized Walla Walla onions give a meatless dish enough substance to pair well with Pinot Noir.

Secret House Vineyards Winery, in Veneta, Oregon, west of Eugene, is known for its Pinot Noir as well as for its several interesting sparkling wines. Its reputation has been built on good wines at real-people prices.

4 tablespoons (½ stick) unsalted butter

2 large Walla Walla onions, halved and cut in ¼-inch slices

Coarse salt

1 pound penne or mostaccioli

1¼ cups chicken stock or low-sodium canned broth

1¼ cups whipping cream

1 cup grated imported parmesan cheese

Freshly ground black pepper

1 cup (lightly packed) parsley leaves, chopped

2 medium tomatoes, peeled, seeded, diced (10 to 12 ounces total)

HEAT THE BUTTER IN A HEAVY 12-INCH SKILLET or sauté pan over medium heat. Add the onions and cook, covered, for 10 minutes. Uncover, add ¼ teaspoon salt, and cook, stirring occasionally, until the onions have begun to color. Then stir more often and cook until onions are a very dark brown. They will look burned but will taste sweet and be slightly chewy. Cooking time depends on how much water is in the onions, but will likely be at least 20 minutes after uncovering.

MEANWHILE, BRING 6 QUARTS OF WATER TO A BOIL in a large pot over high heat. Add 1 tablespoon salt. Add the pasta and cook until al dente. Drain, and return the pasta to the pot. Add the stock, cream, and parmesan, and warm over medium heat for one or two minutes. Taste for salt. Grind pepper over the top, add the parsley and tomatoes, and give everything a big stir.

Serves 4

walla walla sweets

Sweet onions, such as those from the Walla Walla, Washington, growing area, are prized by cooks who crave onion flavor but prefer to skip the eye-watering intensity of other onions. The soil in that region of southeastern Washington and northeastern Oregon has less sulfur than some other soils. The onion seed is a special variety as well, and the result is onions with a pleasing sweetness. They should be used within two or three weeks of purchase, or be refrigerated; they have a high water content and spoil more rapidly than other onions.

seared ahi tuna
on a bed of fresh spinach

One of the many compelling reasons to drink a Pinot Noir is that firm-fleshed, oil-rich tuna pairs so well with light- to medium-bodied red wine. Bigeye ahi and yellowfin ahi are two kinds of tuna that are particularly moist, and they are frequently available in the Northwest. Albacore is also quite flavorful, though drier in texture.

Many believe Oregon's cool, moist Willamette Valley nurtures Pinot Noir vines as well as any place in the world, producing wines that can be complex and world class. One Oregon Pinot Noir producer with an interesting history is Laurel Ridge Winery, near Forest Grove. Its vineyard site was first planted in 1883 as Reuter's Hill Winery, which sold Riesling and Zinfandel. It was replanted by Oregon wine pioneer Charles Coury in 1966. The age of those replanted vines means some of them are different from today's standard clones, and subtle flavor differences may result. Finn Hill, a separate vineyard in Yamhill County, also produces grapes for Laurel Ridge.

SAUCE

¾ cup chicken stock or low-sodium canned broth

1 tablespoon red wine vinegar

⅓ cup finely chopped red onion

1 teaspoon anchovy paste

½ cup whipping cream

Coarse salt

Freshly ground black pepper

1 bag (10 ounces) prewashed spinach, thick stems cut off

2 cups (lightly packed) parsley leaves, chopped

2 tablespoons extra virgin olive oil

½ teaspoon red wine vinegar

Freshly ground black pepper

1 to 1½ pounds ahi tuna steaks, 1 to 2 inches thick

Vegetable oil for coating fish

Coarse salt

Loaf of crusty bread

IN A 2-QUART NONREACTIVE SAUCEPAN, combine the stock, vinegar, onion, and anchovy paste over medium-high heat and bring to a boil. Boil until liquid is reduced to about ¼ cup. Whisk in the cream. Taste for seasoning, adding salt and pepper to taste. Remove from heat and keep warm.

PUT SPINACH AND PARSLEY IN A LARGE MIXING BOWL. Combine oil and vinegar in a small bowl and set aside while you cook the tuna.

CUT TUNA INTO 4 MORE OR LESS EQUAL PIECES, if not purchased that way. Dry with paper towels. Lightly brush both sides of each piece with vegetable oil. Place a cast-iron or enameled cast-iron skillet over medium-high heat until a bead of water dropped in the pan dances across the surface. Place tuna in the pan and sprinkle with salt. Turn tuna when a crust has formed and tuna can be loosened from pan, 2 to 3 minutes. Sprinkle with salt and repeat process for second side. While tuna is cooking on its second side, whisk together the oil and vinegar. Pour dressing onto spinach, toss thoroughly, and season to taste with pepper. Arrange a bed of spinach on each of 4 gently warmed plates. Place the fish pieces on top of the spinach and spread sauce equally over them. Serve with crusty bread.

Serves 4

grilled pacific salmon
with sweet peppers

There is not a more classic Northwest meal than grilled Pacific salmon. And in the Northwest, the salmon–Pinot Noir combination is also becoming a classic. Drinking red wine with fish can work out quite well as long as the wine is not too tannic, since the tannin can combine with fish oils to produce an unpleasant metallic taste. Luckily, Pinot Noirs typically are not heavily tannic, making them ideal companions for grilled salmon. The choice of salmon will depend partly on the season, and partly on your fish preference. Some consider chinook (king) the fish to buy, while others prefer coho (silver) or other varieties. Farm-raised fish, now imported from several places around the world, help to maintain a supply when the Northwest stocks are not running.

Oregon's Willamette Valley growing region offers abundant choices in Pinot Noir wines. Archery Summit, owned by the Andrus family, who also own Pine Ridge Winery in Napa, is a recent addition to the growing list of Yamhill County wineries. Archery Summit occupies some of the choicest vineyard real estate in Oregon and is producing wines to match.

1 tablespoon vegetable oil

1 red bell pepper, halved, seeded and cut lengthwise into
  ¼-inch slices

1 yellow bell pepper, halved, seeded, and cut lengthwise into
  ¼-inch slices

½ cup chicken stock or low-sodium canned broth

1 to 1½ pounds salmon fillet, pin bones, if any, removed with needle-
   nose pliers (buying tail pieces is smart because they are boneless)

Coarse salt

Freshly ground black pepper

PREPARE A MEDIUM-HOT CHARCOAL FIRE or preheat a gas or electric grill.

HEAT A WIDE SKILLET OR SAUTÉ PAN over medium-high heat. Add the oil, then the peppers, and sauté, stirring often, until the peppers have softened and browned lightly. Add the stock and boil down until the pepper mixture is moist but not runny. Taste for salt. Cover and keep warm.

SPRINKLE THE FLESH SIDE OF THE SALMON with salt and pepper. Fish may be cut into serving pieces before or after grilling. Place the fish skin-side down on the grill, cover, and cook without turning fish unless it is a thick center-cut fillet. Timing for cooking the salmon will depend on how thick it is and how hot your grill is. Start checking it after 7 or 8 minutes. Fish is done when an instant-read thermometer registers 120°F for very moist salmon. Cook it to 140°F for a drier, flakier texture. Remove the fish from grill; some skin may stick to the grill, which is good. Peel off any skin that is still attached to the fish. Divide fish among 4 warmed dinner plates, top with the peppers, and serve.

Serves 4

smoked chicken
with black beans

Spanking fresh, Northwest-raised chicken is easily available in local markets, often less than a day after processing. And if a roast chicken is simple, elegant eating—and it is—then a smoked chicken is just a little closer to hen heaven. Add a plate of black beans for an irresistible combination. A King Estate Pinot Noir and smoked chicken make a fine pair. The King family, of aircraft electronics fame, founded King Estate Winery in 1992 near Eugene. The 110,000-square-foot winery was designed for volume production of quality wines, with state-of-the-art equipment.

2 cups dry wood chips, such as alder, apple, hickory, maple,
    mesquite, or oak

1 whole chicken (3½ to 4½ pounds)

Coarse salt

Freshly ground black pepper

BLACK BEANS

1 pound dried black beans

8 ounces bacon strips, cut crosswise into 1-inch pieces

1 medium onion, coarsely chopped

1 bay leaf

1 teaspoon celery seeds

Coarse salt

4 scallions, thinly sliced

1 cup (lightly packed) mixed fresh herbs, such as parsley, thyme, oregano, sage, and/or rosemary, chopped

Freshly ground black pepper

PLACE THE WOOD CHIPS in the center of a 12-inch square of aluminum foil. Fold the foil over the top of the chips to make a square envelope. Use a two-tined fork or metal skewer to punch holes all over the top of the foil packet, to allow smoke to escape easily. If you are using a charcoal grill, build a medium fire on one side the foil packet directly on the coals. If you are using a gas grill with 2 burners, place the foil packet directly on the lava rocks or metal burner cover of 1 burner. Sprinkle the chicken with a little coarse salt and pepper. Place the chicken on the side of the grill opposite from the heat source, and close grill cover. After a few minutes the foil packet will begin to issue smoke, which will flavor the bird. After awhile the smoke will subside. Continue to cook, adding more charcoal as necessary, until an instant-read thermometer registers 170°F when inserted between the thigh and body of the bird, or until the thigh juices run clear when pricked with the point of a small, sharp knife, about 2 hours. Cooking time will vary depending on your equipment and the outside temperature.

WHILE THE BIRD IS BEING SMOKED, pick over the beans, discarding any foreign material, and rinse. Sauté the bacon in a 4-quart saucepan over medium heat until not quite crisp. Add the onion, and cook, stirring occasionally, until the onion is softened, about 5 minutes. Add 8 cups of water, the bay leaf, celery seeds, and 1 tablespoon salt. Increase the heat to medium-high, and bring beans to a boil. Reduce the heat and simmer, covered, until beans are tender, 1½ to 2 hours, adding water if necessary to keep the beans covered. Use a slotted spoon to lift out about 1 cup of beans. Mash them in a shallow bowl with a fork, then stir back into pot to thicken the beans.

CARVE THE CHICKEN INTO QUARTERS. Stir scallions, herbs, and pepper into the beans, and taste for seasoning. Spoon about 1 cup beans onto each of 4 dinner plates or wide soup plates. Arrange a chicken quarter on top of or next to the beans and serve.

Serves 4

roast turkey with cornbread-hazelnut dressing

Pinot Noir is a noble accompaniment to a roast turkey. On more than one occasion, we have found the Torii Mor Pinot Noir, created by wine-maker and general manager Patty Green, a welcome addition to our table. We've also picnicked outside Torii Mor's tasting room in the hills near Dundee, Oregon, passing through a large gate (torii) to a small yard (mor) beneath the fir trees, where visitors can enjoy the surroundings. The area around Dundee is also the source of much of the Willamette Valley's hazelnut crop.

The turkey is brined before roasting, which results in more uniform seasoning and increased moistness. If you follow our cooking instructions, your turkey will roast in one and a half hours or so. Allow an additional half-hour resting period. You will need two large oven bags or a twelve-quart or larger stockpot to brine the turkey in. The dressing has a crumbly texture, similar to a grain pilaf, flecked with sausage meat and coarsely chopped toasted hazelnuts. It is cooked in its own pan, which is both quicker and safer than cooking it stuffed inside the bird.

2 cups coarse salt, or 1 cup table salt
1 whole turkey (10 to 12 pounds), thawed if frozen
Freshly ground black pepper

DRESSING

About 5 cups diced (½ inch) stale cornbread

2 cups hazelnuts (filberts), roasted and skinned (see page 110)

1 pound mild (not hot) bulk Italian sausage

4 tablespoons (½ stick) unsalted butter

2 large carrots, coarsely chopped

2 large onions, coarsely chopped

4 ribs celery, trimmed and coarsely chopped

2 tablespoons fresh rosemary leaves, finely chopped

¼ cup chopped fresh sage leaves

1 tablespoon fresh thyme leaves

½ cup chopped parsley leaves

2 large eggs, beaten

1½ cups chicken stock or low-sodium canned broth

⅓ cup bourbon whiskey

Coarse salt

Freshly ground black pepper

Cranberry-Pear Chutney (see page 27)

BRINE THE TURKEY FOR AT LEAST 8 HOURS but not more than 24 hours before roasting. Dissolve the salt in 2 gallons of water. (An easy method is to bring 1 quart of water to a boil, add the salt and stir well, then pour the salt water into the remaining 7 quarts water.) Remove the turkey from its wrapper. Remove the bag containing giblets and trim off the tail. (Reserve giblets, neck, and tail for making a pan gravy in your favorite fashion.) Place the bird in a 12-quart or larger nonreactive stockpot and cover with brine. Or place the turkey in a doubled large-size plastic roasting bag and hold upright while pouring brine over the bird. Expel air from the bag and attach a wire twist, then place turkey upright in a 5-gallon plastic bucket or large nonreactive roasting pan. Refrigerate the turkey 8 to 24 hours.

PREHEAT THE OVEN TO 275°F.

TO MAKE THE DRESSING, thoroughly dry out the cornbread cubes in the oven. Transfer to a large mixing bowl. Add the hazelnuts to the mixing bowl. Sauté the sausage in a 12-inch skillet or sauté pan over medium-high heat until lightly browned. Add the sausage to the mixing bowl. Melt the butter in the same pan, then sauté the carrots, onions, and celery until soft but not browned, 5 to 10 minutes. Scrape the vegetables into the mixing bowl. Add the rosemary, sage, thyme, and parsley. Blend the eggs with the stock and bourbon and add to the cornbread mixture. Season with 1 teaspoon salt and ½ teaspoon pepper. Toss well and spoon into a greased 9 x 13-inch baking dish. If the turkey roasting pan and dressing pan don't fit together in the oven, bake the dressing first, then reheat it while the turkey rests.

PREHEAT THE OVEN TO 500°F with the rack in the lowest position.

TO ROAST THE TURKEY, drain the brine and rinse the turkey thoroughly inside and out for a couple of minutes. No brine should remain. Pat dry with paper towels and place on a roasting rack in a baking pan. Tie the legs with kitchen twine if you like. Sprinkle with pepper. Place the pan in the oven and roast 30 minutes.

REDUCE THE OVEN TEMPERATURE to 350°F. Place the dressing pan in the oven if there is room. Roast the turkey for 60 minutes more and check for doneness—an instant-read thermometer should register 170°F when inserted into the thigh meat next to the body of the turkey without touching the bone. (Don't rely on the pop-up thermometer that may be present in the turkey unless you have to—they are notoriously inaccurate and usually result in an overcooked, dry turkey.) Remove the turkey from the oven, cover with foil to keep warm, and allow it to rest for at least 30 minutes before carving. Rewarm the dressing now if previously cooked. Carve and serve with dressing and Cranberry-Pear Chutney.

Serves 10

cranberry-pear chutney

It is no secret that the Northwest is a major producer of apples. Not so well known is that pears and cranberries also call the Northwest home. Pear trees thrive as far south as the Rogue Valley region near Medford, Oregon, and are found in the Willamette Valley, the Hood River Valley, in the hills above The Dalles, and in Washington's vast Columbia Basin. Many of the same orchardists who raise apples and cherries also harvest pears. Cranberries are raised in bogs in such diverse locations as Bandon, on the Oregon coast, and Long Beach Peninsula, on the Washington coast.

The cranberry-pear combination in this chutney provides a bright counterpoint to the roast turkey; the hazelnuts, without doubt from the Willamette Valley, contribute their buttery taste and addictive crunch. Few accompaniments to a meal are packed as full with the Northwest's bounty!

1 bag (12 ounces) fresh or frozen cranberries, picked over and rinsed

1 cup maple syrup

1 piece orange zest, about 3 x ¾ inches

1½ teaspoons ground cardamom

¼ teaspoon coarse salt

2 Anjou or Bosc pears, peeled, cored, and cut into ½-inch dice

½ cup golden raisins

1 cup hazelnuts (filberts), roasted and skinned (see page 110)

COMBINE CRANBERRIES, 1 cup water, maple syrup, orange zest, cardamom, and salt in a 4-quart or larger nonreactive saucepan over medium heat. Bring to a boil, then immediately reduce to a simmer. A few berries will pop. Add pears and raisins and simmer for 10 minutes more. Allow to cool in the pan. When cool, stir in the hazelnuts, then refrigerate. The chutney will keep, covered in the refrigerator, for at least 3 weeks.

Makes about 8 cups

steam-roasted duck with
fresh flour tortillas

Duck has a thick layer of fat that needs to be removed one way or another. Long roasting, about two hours, is one way. Another, which is easy on the cook, is steam-roasting. The duck, covered with a foil tent, is oven-steamed on a rack in a pan. Most of the duck fat melts away. The skin is discarded, and the meat picked off the bones. It can then be wrapped in flatbreads such as tortillas or nan, for example, topped with yogurt, salsa, or chutney, and served with a cabbage slaw or Spicy Corn Relish (see page 165) on the side. Sweet Walla Walla onions would be a great choice in the salsa. Pinot Noir complements the flavor of duck. Just be sure the condiments used are not blazingly spicy.

1 duckling (about 5 pounds), thawed if frozen

Coarse salt

Freshly ground black pepper

12 flour tortillas, homemade (see page 31), or store-bought

4 scallions, thinly sliced

2 cups plain yogurt

Grilled Tomato–Onion Salsa (see page 39), or bottled chutney

PREHEAT THE OVEN TO 350°F.

REMOVE THE GIBLETS from the duck cavity. Sprinkle the duck with salt and pepper. Place 4 small ramekins, or clean empty tuna cans, in the corners of a 9 x 13 x 2-inch pan. Set a roasting rack on the ramekins or cans. Place the duck on the roasting rack. Pour hot water into the pan to a depth of 1 inch. Make a foil tent to cover the duck, tightening the foil against the sides of the pan. Set the pan on a rimmed baking sheet to catch any drips, and place in oven. Steam-roast for 2 hours. Remove duck from the oven.

REDUCE THE OVEN TEMPERATURE to 200°F. Allow duck to cool until it can be handled. Pull off the skin and discard. Pull the meat off the bones, and cut across the grain into 1½ x ¼-inch pieces. Place the meat in a shallow, covered casserole and keep warm in the oven. Place tortillas in a similar container. Warm them in the oven for 10 minutes before serving. Mix the scallions into the yogurt and put in a small serving bowl. Pour the salsa in a small serving bowl. Place all ingredients on the table. Take one warm bread at a time, spread with yogurt mixture and salsa, and add some duck pieces.

Serves 4

fresh flour tortillas

Packaged tortillas are a real convenience, but until you've made your own you'll never know how much better homemade flour tortillas are.

1⅛ teaspoons coarse salt

4½ cups bleached all-purpose flour

6 tablespoons vegetable shortening

1 cup plus 2 tablespoons boiling water, or more if needed

MIX THE SALT INTO THE FLOUR in a medium mixing bowl. Use your fingertips, or 2 table knives, or a pastry blender to cut the shortening into the flour, until bits of shortening are the size of a pea or smaller. Pour in the boiling water and mix with a wooden spoon or rubber spatula. The mixture should hold together and be slightly sticky. Add more water if necessary. Turn out onto a floured countertop or board and knead for 2 minutes, pressing, folding, and turning the dough until it is lightly resilient. Cover with plastic wrap and allow to rest for 30 minutes.

DIVIDE DOUGH INTO 12 PIECES. Roll each one out on a floured countertop or board into a very thin round, no more than ⅛ inch thick. Heat a 12-inch griddle or cast-iron skillet over medium to medium-high heat until a bead of water dropped into the pan evaporates on contact. Cook each round for 30 to 40 seconds on each side, until light brown spots appear. Remove to a plate and cover, and keep warm.

Makes 12 tortillas

rabbit braised
in pinot noir sauce

Rabbit is a delicious alternative to the ubiquitous chicken. It is similar in taste, lean, and increasingly available in specialty markets and better supermarkets. Its mild flavor makes it a good candidate for saucing with light- to medium-bodied red wines. In this dish, the sauce may be left quite liquid to serve over noodles or rice, or thickened enough to serve with a vegetable and mashed potatoes.

Rabbit goes especially well with Pinot Noir. We enjoyed this dish for Christmas dinner in 1997, accompanied by an Erath 1995 Pinot Noir. Another winery with a fine reputation is Panther Creek Cellars, owned by Ron and Linda Kaplan. Many single-vineyard wines of real complexity come from their winery, crafted by Mark Vlossak.

6 thick strips of bacon (about 8 ounces)

½ cup all-purpose flour

4 rabbit hindquarters (leg/thigh combination), skinned

¼ cup olive oil

1 large onion, coarsely chopped

½ small carrot, finely diced

1 rib celery, finely diced

5 large cloves garlic, thinly sliced crosswise

1 bottle (750 ml) Pinot Noir

1 cup chicken stock or low-sodium canned broth

1 bay leaf

12 sprigs fresh thyme, leaves only

Coarse salt

Freshly ground black pepper

¼ cup cold water

1 cup (lightly packed) parsley leaves, chopped

Cooked noodles, for serving (optional)

CUT BACON CROSSWISE INTO ¼-INCH PIECES. Cook the bacon, uncovered, in a 12-inch sauté pan with a tight-fitting lid over medium heat until it is not quite crisp. Remove from pan with a slotted spoon and set aside. Pour off all but about 2 tablespoons of the fat. Spoon ¼ cup of the flour into a dry plastic bag. Add a piece of rabbit and shake the bag while holding it closed, to coat the rabbit in flour. Repeat with the remaining rabbit pieces. Heat bacon fat over medium heat. Sauté rabbit pieces until well browned on both sides, about 5 minutes per side. Set the rabbit aside on a plate and pour off the fat from pan.

ADD THE OLIVE OIL, onion, carrot, celery, and garlic. Cook, stirring occasionally, until the vegetables are soft but not browned, about 5 minutes. Return the rabbit to the pan and add the reserved bacon, the wine, stock, bay leaf, and thyme. Bring to a boil, reduce heat and simmer, covered, until the rabbit is tender when tested with the point of a small knife, about 30 minutes. Transfer the rabbit pieces to a platter and keep warm. Taste sauce for salt, and add pepper. Combine the remaining ¼ cup flour and the water in a small jar with a tight-fitting lid and shake thoroughly to blend. Use a small whisk to break up any lumps. Immediately pour about half the mixture into the simmering rabbit sauce, stirring constantly for 1 minute to keep lumps from forming. When the sauce has thickened for 2 or 3 minutes, decide whether you want it thicker. If you are serving the dish over noodles or rice, it should be gravy-thick. If you are serving the rabbit as a stand-alone portion on a plate, the sauce should be stew-thick—add more of the flour-water mixture, shaking the jar well before adding. Cook, stirring to keep lumps from forming, for 3 minutes. Stir in the parsley. Serve rabbit pieces with sauce, over noodles if desired.

Serves 4

grilled butterflied
leg of lamb with rosemary

The Ellensburg region of the north Columbia Valley in Washington, and the Willamette Valley south and southwest of Portland, Oregon, are two of the most notable lamb-raising areas in the United States. As it happens, both are also the sites of wineries producing red wine. Serve this simple grilled leg of lamb with a Pinot Noir, from Cooper Mountain Vineyards, perhaps. Like Ponzi Vineyards, it is located in Beaverton, Oregon, and it enjoys a rapidly growing reputation for quality.

1 boned and butterflied leg of lamb (3½ to 4½ pounds)

6 sprigs of fresh rosemary, leaves only, minced

½ teaspoon coarse salt

½ teaspoon freshly ground black pepper

ABOUT TWO HOURS BEFORE COOKING, trim the fat and skin from the outside of the lamb if necessary. Dry the meat with paper towels. Combine the rosemary, salt, and pepper in a small bowl. Sprinkle the mixture over both sides of the lamb and press the seasonings into the meat. Wrap snugly in plastic and refrigerate. Remove from refrigerator 30 minutes before cooking.

PREPARE A HOT CHARCOAL FIRE or preheat a gas or electric grill.

PLACE THE LAMB ON THE GRILL AND COOK, covered, for about 7 minutes. Turn the lamb and cook, covered, until an instant-read thermometer inserted on an angle into thickest part of meat registers 120°F; for medium-rare doneness, cook about 7 minutes more. Place lamb on a platter or carving board and allow to rest for 5 minutes, covered with foil, before carving. Cut into very thin slices across the grain and serve immediately.

NOTE: Leg of lamb is made up of several muscles in which meat fibers go in different directions. When carving, try to find the "average" direction, then carve across it.

Serves 10

pork fajitas with grilled tomato-onion salsa

Pork tenderloin is flavorful, very tender, and quite simple to cook. Fajitas combine that ease of preparation with the nearly universal appeal of the inviting, warm flavors of Mexican-style foods. The fajitas are completed with onions, bell peppers, tomatoes, sour cream, and a homemade salsa.

Warmth is not particularly abundant in Oregon's Willamette Valley, source of most of the Pinot Noir for which the state is famous. But farther south, in the Rogue Valley, warmer climes prevail and wines of a slightly different character are produced from the same grapes. Cave Junction, about fifteen miles north of the California border, is home to both Bridgeview Vineyard and Foris Vineyards Winery, Oregon's southernmost wineries. Both produce a variety of award-winning wines.

1 pork tenderloin (about 1 pound)

1 clove garlic, split lengthwise

3 tablespoons vegetable oil

Coarse salt

2 large onions, halved and cut into ¼-inch slices

3 red bell peppers, halved, seeded, and cut into ¼-inch slices

12 flour tortillas, about 9 inches in diameter, homemade
 (see page 31), or store-bought

Grilled Tomato–Onion Salsa (see page 39)

6 ripe tomatoes, cut in 8 wedges each

1 cup sour cream

1 cup (lightly packed) cilantro leaves, chopped

PREHEAT THE OVEN TO 450°F.

TRIM THE TENDERLOIN of its surface gristle, if any, by inserting a sharp boning knife between the meat and the gristle and, with the knife angled slightly toward the gristle, cutting along the length of the tenderloin to free the gristle. Rub the meat with the cut side of the garlic pieces. Rub 1 tablespoon of the oil all over the meat. Sprinkle with coarse salt.

HEAT A HEAVY, OVENPROOF SKILLET, preferably cast-iron, over medium-high heat for 2 to 5 minutes, until you can feel the heat when you hold your hand 1 or 2 inches above the pan. Place the tenderloin in the pan, reduce the heat to medium, and cook, uncovered, for 5 minutes. Turn the meat, and place the pan in the oven. Cook until an instant-read thermometer inserted on an angle in the middle of the meat registers 145°F, about 9 minutes. The meat should be slightly pink in the center.

MEANWHILE, heat the remaining 2 tablespoons of oil in a 12-inch or larger skillet or sauté pan over medium-high heat. Add the onions and bell peppers, toss them in the oil, and sprinkle with salt. Sauté, stirring often, until vegetables are limp but still slightly crisp, about 10 minutes. Remove the pan from the heat and cover to keep warm.

WHEN PORK IS DONE, transfer it to a carving board and allow to rest for 5 minutes before carving. Turn off the oven. Place tortillas in a covered ovenproof container, and place the container in the oven.

PLACE THE SALSA, tomatoes, sour cream, and cilantro in serving bowls on the table. Using a sharp carving or chef's knife, cut the pork across the grain into ¼-inch slices. Place the pork slices on a warmed platter and transfer the vegetables to a warmed serving bowl. Place both on the table. Place the tortilla container on the table, on a heatproof trivet if necessary. Diners help themselves to 1 tortilla at a time, spread it lightly with sour cream, add a few pork slices, some vegetables, 4 tomato wedges per fajita, a sprinkle of cilantro, and one or two spoonfuls of salsa. Knives and forks are less mess, but the adventurous can pick up their fajitas if they like.

NOTE: The meat and vegetables may be grilled over a hot fire if desired. Toss vegetables with oil and salt before spreading them on the hot grill.

Serves 4

five great northwest pinot noirs

Adelsheim Vineyard, Newberg, Oregon

Beaux Frères, Newberg, Oregon

Domaine Drouhin Oregon, Dundee, Oregon

Ken Wright Cellars, Carlton, Oregon

Rex Hill Vineyards, Newberg, Oregon

grilled tomato-onion salsa

Homemade salsas are justifiably popular in the Northwest, especially when tomatoes are ripening on the vine in backyard gardens. This one depends on just a few charred fresh vegetables for its appeal, and takes little time to make. It is spicy, but not blazingly hot. You will enjoy it with your Pork Fajitas (see page 36) as well as with the Steam-Roasted Duck with Fresh Flour Tortillas (see page 29). We also suggest you try some with scrambled eggs.

2 pounds ripe red or yellow tomatoes

1 jumbo or 2 medium onions (about 16 ounces total), cut in
    ½-inch slices

3 serrano chilies

1 cup (lightly packed) cilantro leaves, chopped

1 tablespoon red wine vinegar

PREPARE A HOT CHARCOAL FIRE or preheat a gas or electric grill.

WHEN THE FIRE IS VERY HOT, grill the tomatoes until their skins split. Set them aside. Add the onion slices and the chilies, and grill until the chili skins are blackened, turning as needed. Coarsely chop the onions, and the tomatoes with their skins, and place in a medium bowl. Split and seed the chilies, mince them with their skins, and add to the bowl. Add the cilantro and vinegar, and toss to combine. Cover and refrigerate.

Makes about 3 cups

pizza kathleen

Good food is often simple food. In our minds, there is nothing on earth more satisfying than good bread joined with savory accompaniments, precisely the description of Pizza Kathleen, our variation of Pizza Margherita. Make the dough yourself; it isn't difficult. Then reward yourself with some Northwest Pinot Noir.

One of the Northwest's more unusual wineries, Golden Valley Vineyards is located inside a brewery of the same name in McMinnville, Oregon. The vineyards are up in the Red Hills near some prestigious neighbors, and most of the grapes go to other wineries. Enough grapes are held back to make a few barrels down at the brewery.

DOUGH

1 cup warm water, about 105°F

Pinch of sugar

1 tablespoon or 1 package active dry yeast

3 tablespoons olive oil

2½ cups unbleached all-purpose flour, plus more if needed

½ cup cornmeal, yellow or white, plus some for dusting pan

1 teaspoon coarse salt

TOPPING

4 ounces extra-sharp aged cheddar (preferably Tillamook White, aged over 15 months), shredded

4 ounces whole-milk mozzarella, shredded

¼ cup grated imported parmesan

1 pound tomatoes, peeled, seeded, and cut into ¼-inch strips

Freshly ground black pepper

About 15 whole basil leaves

TO MAKE THE DOUGH, pour the water into a small bowl or 2-cup glass measure and whisk sugar and yeast into water. When the mixture bubbles vigorously, about 5 minutes, whisk in the olive oil.

TO MIX THE DOUGH, combine the 2½ cups flour, cornmeal, and salt in the work bowl of a food processor fitted with the metal blade. (See page 68 for how to make dough by hand; page 192 for how to make dough in a stand mixer.) Process for 10 seconds to blend. Switch to the plastic dough blade if available. Whisk the yeast mixture again and, with the machine running, pour the yeast mixture through the feed tube into the dry ingredients. If you hear a sloshing sound, you are pouring too quickly. When a ball of dough forms, let it rotate in the machine for 60 seconds to knead. Add 1 or 2 additional teaspoons of flour at a time if the dough is too sticky for machine to run without straining. Add 1 tablespoon of water at a time if dry bits of dough are loose in the processor. Remove the dough, gather into a ball, and place on a floured work surface. Cover with a large glass bowl. (Or, place the dough in a gallon-size plastic bag, squeeze out all the air, and close with a wire twist at the very top of the bag to allow room for expansion.) Allow dough to rise until about double in bulk, about 45 minutes.

PREHEAT THE OVEN TO 500°F and adjust the rack to the middle level. Liberally sprinkle a 12- to 14-inch pizza pan or other round baking sheet with cornmeal and set aside.

DEFLATE DOUGH, loosen from the work surface (if necessary) with a pastry scraper or plastic spatula, and pull into a ball with your hands. Roll out on a lightly floured surface into a round about 1 inch wider than the pan. Lightly flour the top of the dough, using your hands to spread the flour. Roll the dough around a rolling pin, then unroll over the top of the pan. Use your hands to nestle the dough into the pan, folding the extra edges over to form a thicker crust around the edge. Top evenly with the cheeses, add the tomatoes, and sprinkle with pepper. Arrange the basil leaves evenly over the top.

BAKE UNTIL THE CHEESES ARE BUBBLY and edges of crust are golden brown, 10 to 12 minutes. If bubbles form in the crust during baking, poke them with a skewer or other sharp instrument. Allow to rest for 3 minutes to allow cheese to set. Cut into wedges and serve.

Serves 4

raspberry jam
brownie squares

*Brownies satisfy a serious choco-
late craving, and can be quite an
elegant mouthful to enjoy with a
red wine. The chocolate and red
wine match is often a good one,
especially if the dessert is straight-
forward, without lots of oversweet bric-a-brac. You could try a Pinot Noir
from Maresh Red Hills Vineyard with your chocolate. Legendary Jim
Maresh raises grapes on land that once produced prunes, near Dundee, Oregon. His organic, limited-yield crop is purchased by several big-name wineries in the area, who make wines for him to sell under his own label only in
his tasting room.*

16 tablespoons (2 sticks) unsalted butter

4 ounces unsweetened chocolate

1½ cups granulated sugar

4 large eggs

1 teaspoon real vanilla extract

1 cup bleached all-purpose flour

Pinch salt

1½ cups (about 6 ounces) walnut pieces, roasted (see page 69)

½ cup raspberry (or other good-quality berry) jam

PREHEAT THE OVEN TO 350°F.

LINE THE BOTTOM AND SIDES of a 9 x 13-inch baking dish with aluminum foil. Press the foil gently into the corners to avoid tears. Greasing the foil is unnecessary.

MELT BUTTER AND CHOCOLATE over very low heat in a large, heavy-bottomed saucepan, stirring occasionally. Add the sugar and then the eggs, one at a time, stirring well after each addition. Add vanilla, flour, salt, and walnuts, blending just until all white streaks are gone. Scrape the batter into the prepared pan. Put dollops of jam over the brownie mixture in a random pattern. Using a table knife, swirl the jam through the batter, being careful to get some into the corners of the pan.

BAKE UNTIL A CAKE TESTER or toothpick inserted in the center comes out barely clean, about 35 minutes. Let cool completely. When cool, refrigerate for 2 to 3 hours. Turn upside-down on a board and peel the foil away from the brownie. Cut into 4 strips lengthwise, and 8 crosswise, to form 32 small pieces. The brownies freeze quite well.

Makes 32 brownies

foods to pair with

cabernet sauvignon

Sautéed Goat Cheese on Greens with Caper Dressing

Chanterelle and Mixed Greens Salad with Grilled Sausages

Rigatoni with Blue Cheese, Onions, Peppers, and Peas

Spaghetti Carbonara with Apple Wood–Smoked Bacon

Cabernet Sauvignon Risotto

Roast Beef Tenderloin with Red Wine Butter Sauce

Salt and Pepper Grilled Northwest Lamb Chops

Pear, Bacon, and Blue Cheese on English Muffins

Tillamook Cheddar Cheeseburgers

Tomato, Basil, and Gruyère Biscuit Pie

Focaccia with Walnuts and Oregon Blue Cheese

Dark Chocolate Hazelnut Torte

the cabernet sauvignon grape

The Cabernet Sauvignon (CAB-er-nay SO-veen-yon) grape is the third most planted wine grape in Washington, and the fifth most planted in Oregon. Its modern history in the Northwest dates back to the early 1960s at HillCrest Vineyards near Roseburg, Oregon, and the long, hot summer days and cool nights of the Columbia Valley region have made it the source of nearly 90 percent of the North-

west's crop. Nearly every winery in the Columbia Valley makes some Cabernet, but huge amounts of the grape are trucked over the Cascade Mountains to be crushed and vinified at Puget Sound–area wineries. These include Columbia Winery, an award-winning pioneer of the Washington winery industry, and Chateau Ste. Michelle, another pioneer of great renown. (Chateau Ste. Michelle makes its red wines at its new Canoe Ridge Estate Winery near Paterson, Washington, and its white wines in Woodinville, near Seattle.)

Cabernet Sauvignon was native to the Mediterranean region, most likely, and achieved superstar status as the primary grape of France's Bordeaux district and in California's Napa Valley. Northwest wine drinkers love it for its full-fruit, food-friendly characteristics. The wines are usually dry, and range from light and fruity to medium bodied to full flavored, tending toward the fuller end of the spectrum. The fullest-flavored versions tend to be tannic when young, and may need ten years or more aging in the bottle to soften to the point of maximum appeal. Most are best with five to ten years bottle age.

Cabernet Sauvignon leans toward herbal and vegetal flavors when grown in cooler climates like Oregon's Willamette Valley. In warmer regions like southern Oregon, the Columbia Valley, and Walla Walla, the grapes become fruitier and more full bodied. Often Merlot and/or Cabernet Franc are blended with Cabernet Sauvignon to soften and round out the wine.

Common flavors and aromas of Cabernet Sauvignon include those of currants, blackberries, herbs, toasty wood, spice, and tobacco. Heavier, younger, and more tannic wines are good paired with foods that have rich flavors that coat the tongue, such as well-marbled beef, lamb, sausages, and strong cheeses. Older Cabernets, or lighter bodied versions, can pair well with less assertive meals.

Serve at cool room temperature, about 60°F.

sautéed goat cheese on greens with caper dressing

Goat cheese, such as that made by Juniper Grove in central Oregon, or Sally Jackson in Washington, has a fresh, tangy flavor that balances its natural richness. One of the wines made in the Northwest, Cabernet Sauvignon, has a natural affinity for foods with some richness. The tannins in a Cabernet are neutralized, to some extent, by the butterfat in cheese, making the wine seem softer. We once served this dish at a fund-raiser for the Maryhill Museum, located on the Columbia River Gorge. One of the wines offered that evening was Proprietor's Red, a blend of Cabernet Sauvignon, Merlot, and Cabernet Franc made by wine-maker Joel Tefft, of Tefft Cellars in Outlook, Washington. A Northwest cheese and a Northwest wine complemented each other nicely that evening, as they often do.

DRESSING

¼ cup red wine vinegar

2 tablespoons Dijon mustard

½ teaspoon salt

Freshly ground black pepper

½ cup extra virgin olive oil

¼ cup finely diced red onion

2 tablespoons small capers, or coarsely chopped large capers, rinsed and drained

cabernet sauvignon

8 to 10 cups mixed torn salad greens, such as romaine, butter lettuce, leaf lettuce, or curly endive

4 small, ripe tomatoes, cut into ¼-inch slices

Olive oil for sautéing

8 slices rustic bread (crusty, slow-rise, full-flavored), about ½ inch thick

1½ cups dry medium-size bread crumbs

10 to 12 ounces goat cheese, preferably log shape, cut or patted into 8 or more rounds ½-inch thick

WHISK TOGETHER THE DRESSING INGREDIENTS, or shake them together in a jar with a tight-fitting lid. Toss the dressing with the salad greens and spread the salad out on each of 4 dinner plates. Arrange the tomato slices around the edge of each plate.

HEAT ¼ CUP OLIVE OIL in a large skillet over medium heat. Lightly brown each bread slice on both sides in the oil, adding more oil as necessary. Arrange 2 slices of toasted bread side by side on top of the greens on each plate, without covering up the tomatoes. Place the crumbs in a shallow bowl or on a plate. Gently press the cheese rounds into the crumbs on both sides. Sauté cheese 1 to 2 minutes on each side, or until lightly browned. Arrange cheese rounds on the bread slices and serve at once.

Serves 4

alex golitzin

Most wineries make wines from several different kinds of grapes, in order to offer as broad a selection on the retail shelves as possible. Rare is the wine maker who is willing to bet the winery on just one grape variety. A few miles northeast of Seattle in Snohomish, Washington, is just such a winery. Quilceda Creek Vintners, open only by appointment, is hidden by an emerging subdivision on the side of a hill. The owners, Alex and Jeanette Golitzin, are widely renowned as producers of Cabernet Sauvignons of very high quality. Their son Paul is now the primary wine maker, maintaining a tradition that began with Alex's uncle and mentor, the late legendary wine maker at Beaulieu Vineyards in the Napa Valley, André Tchelistcheff. In a style that is repeated in some other limited-production Northwest wineries, the winery itself is in the Golitzin's backyard. The mountain view seen through the window of their living room is repeated on the wine labels.

There is nothing homemade about the wines, however. The Golitzins buy their grapes from several of the finest vineyards in Washington, including Ciel du Cheval, Kiona, Mercer Ranch, and Klipsun, all located around Prosser and Benton City in the eastern end of the Yakima Valley. After fermentation, Quilceda Creek wines receive a twenty-two month nap in new French oak before bottling. They are blended, an about-face from the single-vineyard approach used by some other wine makers, because Alex is convinced that blending brings out the best characteristics from each vineyard. They spend at least another twelve months in the bottle before release. The resulting wines are expensive but packed with flavor, with the potential to age well for a couple of decades if you have the patience—and if you can find the wines. They can be so difficult to obtain that restaurant patrons have been known to buy bottles at restaurant prices to take home and cellar. This from a winery that the Golitzins started as a hobby in the 1970s while Alex was a chemical engineer with a major paper company.

cabernet sauvignon

chanterelle and mixed greens salad with grilled sausages

Northwest chanterelles are trumpet-shaped mushrooms full of unusually pleasing flavor. Mix them with prewashed baby salad greens (lettuces of varying color and texture, sometimes called mesclun or spring mix), and add Italian sausage for a satisfying salad that meat eaters will appreciate. The mushrooms are sautéed just before you serve them on the salad, so the salad greens don't have time to wilt before you eat them. This kind of dish pairs quite well with Cabernet Sauvignon, as well as with Cabernet-Merlot blends, such as those produced by Paul Thomas Winery.

The Paul Thomas Winery is hidden in the fields near Zillah, Washington. Wine-maker Mark Cave conceived the design of the winery himself. (The winery itself is not open to the public, but there are tasting rooms located off-site.) Cave creates a wide variety of white and red wines, which are usually well priced and deliver good value for the dollar. We have savored his Paul Thomas 1995 Cabernet-Merlot with this hearty salad.

12 cups mixed baby salad greens, washed and dried
¼ cup very thin slivers of onion
1 cup (lightly packed) parsley leaves, chopped

4 mild Italian sausages

DRESSING

2 teaspoons Dijon mustard

2 teaspoons red wine vinegar

¼ cup extra virgin olive oil

½ teaspoon coarse salt

Freshly ground black pepper

*

2 tablespoons olive oil

1 pound chanterelle mushrooms, brushed or wiped clean, cut in half
    top to bottom, if small, or quartered if large

PLACE THE SALAD GREENS in a large salad or mixing bowl. Add the onion slivers
and parsley. Mix the dressing ingredients in a small jar with a tight-fitting lid
and set aside.

GRILL THE SAUSAGES ON A CHARCOAL, gas, or electric grill, or sauté them in a
skillet until an instant-read thermometer inserted into the center of a sausage
reads 160°F. Place the sausages at the side of each of 4 dinner plates. Shake the
dressing jar and pour the dressing onto salad greens. Toss well and divide among
the plates.

HEAT A WIDE, HEAVY-BOTTOM SKILLET or sauté pan, not nonstick, over
medium-high heat until you can feel the heat when you hold your hand 1 or 2
inches above the pan. Add the olive oil and swirl to coat the pan, then add the
chanterelles. Sauté, stirring and tossing, until the mushrooms give up their
moisture and it evaporates in the pan. Arrange the mushrooms on top of the
greens and serve immediately.

Serves 4

rigatoni with blue cheese, onions, peppers, and peas

A creamy blue cheese, such as an Oregon Blue from the Rogue River Valley, and mascarpone set the stage for a Northwest Cabernet Sauvignon. Mascarpone is a lightly flavored cream cheese usually sold in plastic tubs in specialty markets. You could substitute a Northwest-made goat cheese for the mascarpone, giving the dish slightly sharper flavors.

The Cabernet Sauvignon could come from Oregon's Rex Hill Vineyards. Although located smack in the middle of Willamette Valley Pinot Noir country, Rex Hill offers Cabernet along with its impressive assortment of other wines. Wine-maker Lynn Penner-Ash, the mother of two young children, is one of a handful of female wine makers in the nation. She came to the Northwest after early experience at five different California wineries.

1 tablespoon salt

4 tablespoons (½ stick) unsalted butter

¼ cup all-purpose flour

1 can (14½ ounces) low-sodium chicken broth

½ teaspoon hot pepper sauce

1½ cups milk, or more if needed

2 ounces blue cheese, such as Oregon Blue, crumbled (about ½ cup)

½ cup mascarpone or goat cheese

½ medium onion, cut into ¼-inch wedges

1 large red bell pepper, seeded, deveined, and cut in ¼-inch strips

1 tablespoon olive oil

1 pound rigatoni

1½ cups frozen petite peas

Coarse salt

Freshly ground black pepper

BRING 6 QUARTS WATER TO A BOIL in a large pot over high heat. Add 1 tablespoon salt and reduce to a simmer while you prepare the sauce.

MELT THE BUTTER in a 3-quart or larger saucepan over medium heat, then whisk in the flour. Cook, stirring, until the flour colors slightly, about 3 minutes. Add the broth and hot pepper sauce, and whisk briskly, breaking up any lumps. Add the milk and bring to a simmer, whisking. Add blue cheese, and mascarpone or goat cheese. Simmer, uncovered, whisking regularly and adjusting heat so that the sauce barely bubbles.

SAUTÉ THE ONION and bell pepper in the olive oil in a 10-inch skillet or sauté pan over medium heat for about 5 minutes. Reduce the heat to low, cover, and continue to cook for 10 minutes.

BRING THE PASTA WATER BACK TO A ROLLING BOIL. Add the rigatoni and cook, stirring often, until al dente. About 2 or 3 minutes before you believe the pasta will be done, stir the pepper mixture into the sauce. Add the peas. If the sauce seems too thick, stir in more milk as needed. Taste for salt and pepper, and adjust the seasoning.

DRAIN THE RIGATONI AND RETURN IT TO POT. Pour the sauce over the pasta and toss until well coated. Serve immediately.

Serves 4

cabernet sauvignon

spaghetti carbonara with apple wood-smoked bacon

The first winery you encounter when you enter Washington's Yakima Valley wine region from the west is Staton Hills, in Wapato. Its Cabernet Sauvignon turned out to be perfect for our version of spaghetti carbonara, a dish having just a few simple, rich ingredients. Bacon that has been dry-cured and smoked with apple wood is available in some specialty markets. We use it because of its distinctive flavor and firm texture.

8 medium-thick strips of bacon, preferably apple wood–smoked

1 tablespoon salt

1 pound spaghetti

1 egg

1 cup whipping cream

¼ cup milk

1¼ cups grated imported parmesan cheese

Freshly ground black pepper

½ cup (lightly packed) parsley leaves, chopped

COOK THE BACON until not quite crisp. Drain on paper towels. When cool, cut crosswise into ¼-inch strips.

BRING 6 QUARTS OF WATER TO A BOIL in a large pot over high heat. Add the salt. Stir in the spaghetti and cook, stirring frequently, until al dente. Meanwhile, in a small bowl beat the egg with ¼ cup of the cream and set aside. Combine the remaining cream and milk. Bring cream-milk mixture almost to a simmer, and keep hot. Drain the pasta and place in a very large pasta serving bowl or mixing bowl. Sprinkle the bacon, cheese, and lots of pepper on the spaghetti. Pour the hot cream-milk mixture on top, then add the egg-cream mixture. Toss immediately; the egg will cook as it comes into contact with the hot pasta and will thicken the sauce. Add more hot milk if the sauce seems too thick. Sprinkle with parsley and serve.

Serves 4

six great northwest cabernet sauvignons

Andrew Will Winery, Vashon, Washington

Chaleur Estate, Woodinville, Washington

Chateau Ste. Michelle, Woodinville, Washington

Leonetti Cellar, Walla Walla, Washington

Seven Hills Winery, Milton-Freewater, Oregon

Woodward Canyon Winery, Lowden, Washington

cabernet sauvignon risotto

Risotto is a rice dish of Italian origin, made by slowly adding simmering liquid to Arborio rice (a special variety) until it is cooked but still has a noticeable bite in the center of each grain. (If Arborio is unavailable, substitute California Pearl rice.) Risotto makes a fine first course or a main course when served with a salad. In this recipe the liquid is three-quarters chicken stock and one-quarter Northwest Cabernet Sauvignon, which together produce a wine-colored risotto.

Most Washington Cabernet Sauvignon is grown in the Yakima Valley, but the Walla Walla region, in southeastern Washington, is responsible for a small share of the volume—and an increasing share of the accolades. Wineries in the area are mostly small, and they target a relatively elite wine buyer. Among the newest commercial producers is Walla Walla Vintners, a tiny winery on a hill east of Walla Walla, not far from Glen Fiona Winery. Three wine-making friends pooled their talents for some fifteen years as a hobby. The 1995 release (sold out, at the winery and by mail) was their first commercial wine.

3 cups chicken stock, or low-sodium canned broth

4 tablespoons (½ stick) unsalted butter

1 large onion, coarsely chopped

1½ cups Arborio rice

1 cup Cabernet Sauvignon

¾ cup grated imported parmesan, plus more for the table

¼ cup whipping cream

Coarse salt

Freshly ground black pepper

POUR THE STOCK INTO A SMALL SAUCEPAN and bring to a boil over medium-high heat. Reduce the heat and keep at a bare simmer. Melt 3 tablespoons of the butter in a 3-quart or larger nonreactive saucepan over medium heat. Add the onion and cook, stirring occasionally, until soft, about 5 minutes. Add the rice, and stir to coat with butter. Add the wine and cook until it is reduced to a syrup. Add about ½ cup of the stock and cook, stirring often, until it has been almost completely absorbed by the rice. Repeat the process until the rice grains have swollen and lost their opaque centers and raw taste but still have a bit of bite in the center, about 25 minutes. You may have broth left when the risotto is done. Add the cheese, cream, remaining 1 tablespoon butter, and salt and pepper to taste. Add enough stock or hot water, if necessary, to thin the risotto to the consistency of very soft mashed potatoes. Serve immediately.

Serves 4

roast beef tenderloin
with red wine butter sauce

Roast tenderloin of beef is quite easy to prepare and usually cooks in forty-five minutes or less. It is wonderful served unsauced, and even better with a red wine butter sauce. Here is a sauce similar to that served in many Northwest area restaurants, but slightly thickened to help prevent its separating on the plate. Cabernet Sauvignon wines pair very well with sauces like this one, since their tannins (natural compounds that give some red wines a slightly tea-like feel in the mouth) are balanced by the richness of the sauce.

1 whole tenderloin of beef, roast ready (about 3½ pounds)

Coarse salt

Freshly ground black pepper

4 cups chicken stock or low-sodium canned broth

4 cups Cabernet Sauvignon or other dry red wine

8 cloves garlic, whole

16 tablespoons (2 sticks) unsalted butter, cut into 8 pieces, at room temperature

4 teaspoons cornstarch mixed with 2 tablespoons cold water

PREHEAT THE OVEN TO 400°F.

TRIM SILVERY GRISTLE, if any, by inserting a sharp boning knife between the meat and the gristle and, with the knife angled slightly toward the gristle, cutting along the length of the gristle. Place the meat on a rack on a roasting pan lined with foil to make cleanup easier. Fold the tail under so the whole roast looks about the same thickness and tie the tail with kitchen string. Sprinkle with salt and pepper. Roast until an instant-read thermometer inserted in the center of the roast registers 110°F to 120°F for medium rare, 130°F to 140°F for medium, about 35 to 45 minutes, depending on the size of the roast. Set the roast aside, covered, for 10 minutes, to allow juices to set.

MEANWHILE, in a nonreactive 3-quart saucepan over medium-high heat, combine the stock, wine, and garlic. Boil down to about 2 cups. Shortly before serving add the butter to the bubbling liquid. As soon as it has melted, reduce the heat to low, stir the cornstarch slurry, and pour half of it into sauce. Whisk to blend well. Sauce should be syrupy, but not gummy. Add the remaining thickener only if necessary. Keep sauce barely warm while carving the beef.

PLACE THE BEEF on a carving board and use a very sharp knife to cut across the grain into ½-inch slices. Ladle about ¼ cup of sauce onto each plate, overlap 2 slices beef on top of sauce. Serve.

Serves 8 to 12

salt and pepper grilled northwest lamb chops

Prime lamb, particularly that produced in Oregon's Willamette Valley and Washington's Ellensburg area, is a Northwest specialty. Lamb comes to market at between five and ten months of age, when it is still tender. One of the quickest, simplest, and most satisfying meals you can prepare is grilled lamb chops. They need almost no preparation, just a quick fat trim—if that—and a little salt and pepper.

The natural richness of lamb means that a red wine is in order. Cabernet Sauvignon pairs very well with foods that have natural fat, such as steaks and chops. One Northwest producer of Cabernet Sauvignon is Chinook Wines, located across the Wine Country Highway from Hogue Cellars and Thurston Wolfe Winery, at the east edge of Prosser, Washington. The wines made in the old barn gather praise from near and far.

8 loin or rib lamb chops, cut 1½ to 2 inches thick
Coarse salt and freshly ground black pepper

PREPARE A HOT CHARCOAL FIRE or preheat a gas or electric grill.

TRIM CHOPS OF NEARLY ALL VISIBLE FAT, to prevent flare-ups on the grill. Grill the chops, seasoning each side with salt and pepper. Turn when the first side is browned, about 6 minutes, and cook until an instant-read thermometer registers about 110°F for medium-rare chops. Transfer to warmed plates and serve.

Serves 4

pear, bacon, and blue cheese on english muffins

English muffins with pears and bacon and a blue cheese make a flavorful knife-and-fork open-faced sandwich, at once fruity, salty, and creamy—flavors against which a Cabernet shines. Northwest pears such as Anjou or Bosc have wonderful flavor, as well as a firmer texture than other varieties. They make a sandwich with better bite.

Pears are a major crop in the Rogue Valley of southern Oregon, as are wine grapes. The southernmost winery in the state is Foris Vineyards Winery, located near Cave Junction. It grows grapes on some seventy acres, making everything from Sparkling Brut to Cabernet Sauvignon, and plenty others in between, many of which are award-winners.

4 English muffins, split

Dijon mustard

8 medium-thick strips of bacon, preferably apple wood–smoked, crisp cooked

2 ripe Anjou or Bosc pears, peeled, cored, and quartered, each quarter cut into 3 slices

4 ounces blue cheese

½ cup (lightly packed) parsley leaves, chopped

PREHEAT THE OVEN TO 400°F.

LIGHTLY SPREAD THE CUT SIDE of each muffin with mustard and lay muffins, cut side up, on a baking sheet, preferably nonstick. Cut the bacon strips in half and place 2 pieces on each muffin. Arrange 3 pear slices on each muffin. Use a thin knife to cut blue cheese slices, running it under hot water between each slice. Top the pears with the cheese. Bake until the cheese has melted down into the pears, about 10 minutes. Sprinkle with parsley and serve.

Serves 4

northwest pears

One of the premier products of Northwest farms are pears. The same warm days and cool nights that develop ripe flavors and acid balance in wine grapes also result in high-quality pears, prized by U.S. residents and consumers in many other countries. Northwest farmers grow more than 21 million boxes worth of pears a year, accounting for a significant percentage of the nation's crop. In Oregon, the major pear-growing areas are near Medford and around Hood River, White Salmon, and The Dalles near the Columbia Gorge; in Washington, they are in the Yakima Valley and near Wenatchee.

Northwest pears are harvested from July through October, depending on the variety. They are picked when the pears are fully developed, but usually before they are actually ripe, to prevent overripe and grainy fruit from reaching the market. After being sorted according to size and quality, they are placed in cold storage for up to nine months until shipped.

A pear is considered ripe when it yields slightly to thumb pressure at the stem end. A ripe pear should be eaten that day or refrigerated. To ripen pears as quickly as possible, place them in a paper bag and let stand at room temperature. Color change is not a reliable indicator of a pear's ripeness, regardless of the variety, since many do not change color as they ripen.

The most popular cultivated pear varieties include Yellow Barlett, Red Bartlett, Green Anjou, Red Anjou, Bosc, Comice, Seckel, and Forelle. Bosc pears have especially dense flesh, which makes them good for cooked dishes. Comice pears can be quite large, very sweet, and creamy textured. A 6-ounce pear contains practically no fat and but has a higher percentage of nature's sweetest sugar than any other fruit. Little wonder that Northwest pears are so popular.

cabernet sauvignon

tillamook cheddar cheeseburgers

If you live where you can easily find Northwest wine, then you should be able to find an aged cheddar from Tillamook Creamery, one of the several quality producers of cheese in the North-west. Tillamook is located within a stone's throw of the Pacific Ocean, on the central Oregon coast, surrounded by thousands of acres of dairy land. A slice of sharp Tillamook cheddar or, even better, extra-sharp reserve, aged over fifteen months, will turn that traditional grilled burger into something special, as will pairing its natural richness with a glass of Cabernet Sauvignon.

Washington's Columbia Valley includes several key vineyard areas growing Cabernet grapes, many of which are trucked into the Seattle area to wineries both large and small. The large include Chateau Ste. Michelle and Columbia Winery, the early pioneers among modern wineries in Washington. Both are noted for consistency and quality, and both have tasting rooms not to be missed.

2 pounds ground beef, preferably 20 to 23 percent fat
1 teaspoon coarse salt
Worcestershire sauce
Freshly ground black pepper
4 thick slices Tillamook extra-sharp cheddar
Sweet-hot mustard, such as Beaver brand
4 hamburger buns or soft rolls

4 thin slices red onion

Thick-sliced, lightly salted potato chips

PLACE MEAT IN A LARGE GLASS OR STAINLESS BOWL and loosen the strands with a fork. Sprinkle the salt all over the meat and toss well with the fork, trying not to compact the meat. With wet hands, form into 4 patties ¾ to 1 inch thick. Set on a plate, cover with plastic wrap, and refrigerate.

BUILD A HOT CHARCOAL FIRE, or preheat a gas or electric grill, or select a heavy skillet for indoor cooking. Preheat the oven to 175°F to warm both the plates and buns.

GRILL OR PANFRY THE PATTIES ON ONE SIDE, sprinkling with Worcestershire sauce and pepper, until they are lightly browned, about 3 minutes. Turn, season the other side, and cook until red drops of juice appear on top of patties, 2 to 3 minutes. Add cheese slices to lightly melt while burgers finish cooking. Remove burgers from grill or pan when an instant-read thermometer registers 110°F for red in the middle, 130°F for pink in the middle, or 160°F for very well done. Spread mustard lightly on the bun tops and bottoms, place onion slices on bottoms, and set cooked patties on top of onions. Put each burger on a plate, add a handful of potato chips, and serve at once.

NOTE: if you are concerned about bacterial contamination of ground meats such as hamburger, be sure to cook them to at least 160°F.

Serves 4

tomato, basil,
and gruyère biscuit pie

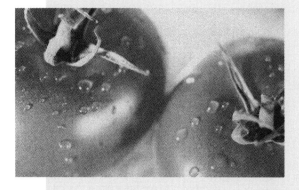

When we were new to Oregon, a version of this pie was very popular with customers who stopped by our catering kitchen to pick up a ready-to-eat dinner. That was some years ago, but the pie hasn't lost its appeal. Formed in large ramekins or ovenproof glass dessert bowls, the pies have a richness that stands up to a Cabernet Sauvignon.

BISCUIT CRUST

2 cups bleached or unbleached all-purpose flour

1 tablespoon baking powder

1 teaspoon coarse salt

¼ cup (lightly packed) whole basil leaves

4 tablespoons (½ stick) unsalted butter, well chilled

½ cup milk

Nonstick cooking spray

10 Roma tomatoes

2 tablespoons pesto, homemade (see page 228), or store-bought

½ teaspoon coarse salt

½ teaspoon freshly ground black pepper

4 ounces gruyère cheese, grated (generous 1½ cups)

¾ cup crème frâiche (see page 15)

6 small sprigs of basil (optional)

PREHEAT THE OVEN TO 400°F.

COMBINE THE FLOUR, baking powder, salt, and basil leaves in the work bowl of a food processor and process for 15 seconds. Cut the butter into cubes and add. Process again, pulsing, until the mixture is the texture of coarse meal. With the machine running, quickly pour the milk through the feed tube. Process until mixture just begins to hold together. Do not let it form a ball. Transfer to a floured countertop and gather the mixture together. Divide into 6 equal portions. Roll each into a 5-inch disk. Spray six 10-ounce ramekins or ovenproof glass dessert bowls with nonstick cooking spray. Lift each pastry round with both hands and nestle gently down into the ramekins, pressing dough into the bottom and up the sides. Set aside.

CORE THE TOMATOES and cut them in half horizontally. Squeeze to remove the seeds and juice. Coarsely chop the tomatoes and put them in a medium mixing bowl. Toss with the pesto, salt, and pepper. Divide the tomatoes among the biscuit crusts. Mix the grated gruyère with the crème frâiche and spread over the top of the tomatoes. Place the pies on a baking sheet to catch any drips. Bake for 20 minutes. Reduce the heat to 350°F and continue to bake until well browned, about 15 minutes more. Remove from the oven and allow to set for at least 5 minutes before serving. Garnish each with a sprig of basil, if desired.

Serves 6

focaccia with walnuts and oregon blue cheese

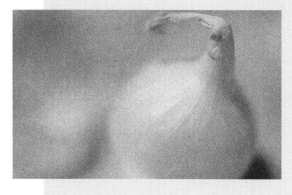

This is a pillowy bread to serve with a medium-bodied Cabernet. The fat in the cheese and olive oil makes a mellow match with the wine. You could use Oregon Blue, a cheese that comes from southern Oregon, on the eastern edge of the Rogue Valley growing area, and your Cabernet Sauvignon choice could be of the region, too. Wineries close by include Ashland Vineyards, Valley View, and Weisinger's of Ashland.

1 tablespoon or 1 package active dry yeast

2¼ cups lukewarm water (105° to 115°F)

1 tablespoon coarse salt

2 tablespoons extra virgin olive oil

5½ to 6 cups bleached or unbleached all-purpose flour

TOPPING

8 ounces sweet onions, preferably Walla Wallas, thinly sliced

¾ cup walnuts, roasted and coarsely chopped (see page 69)

8 ounces blue cheese, such as Oregon Blue, crumbled

2 tablespoons extra virgin olive oil

PLACE THE YEAST and ¼ cup of the water in a large mixing bowl. Allow to proof for 5 minutes, or until the mixture is bubbly. Add the remaining 2 cups water, salt, and olive oil. Add 4 cups of the flour and mix well with a wooden spoon. Add additional 1½ to 2 cups flour. Blend as well as possible, then turn out onto a floured work surface. Knead until smooth and elastic, adding more flour as necessary but keeping the dough soft and slightly sticky. Place in a large, well-oiled bowl. Cover with plastic wrap and let rise until double in bulk, 1 to 2 hours.

OIL TWO 10-INCH CAKE or springform pans generously with olive oil. Punch down the dough on a floured surface. Divide in half and place each half in an oiled pan. Press the dough out to the sides of the pan. Cover with plastic wrap and let rise again until soft and fluffy, but not quite doubled, about 45 minutes.

ABOUT 30 MINUTES BEFORE BAKING, preheat the oven to 400°F.

MAKE SEVERAL INDENTATIONS in each bread with your fingertips. Top each loaf with onion slices, walnuts, and blue cheese. Drizzle with additional olive oil. Place the pans in the oven and spray the oven walls with water from a spray bottle. Spray again after 4 minutes, then again after 8 minutes. After 10 minutes, reduce the oven temperature to 375°F. Continue to bake until golden brown, 10 to 15 minutes more. Allow to cool in the pans for 10 minutes, then remove the focaccias from the pans and transfer to cooling racks.

Makes two 10-inch focaccias

to roast walnuts

Preheat the oven to 325°F. Spread the walnuts on a baking sheet. Roast until lightly browned, about 10 minutes. Cool thoroughly before chopping.

oregon blue cheese

Just north of Medford in Central Point, Oregon, is the Rogue River Valley Creamery, home of Oregon Blue, a legend in the world of blue cheese. Purchased in 1935 by Italian-born Thomas Vella, patriarch of the Vella cheese-making family of Sonoma, the creamery made cheddar and cottage cheese for Kraft and Borden.

Then, more than forty years ago, Borden persuaded Vella to make blue cheese. He and his wife spent time in Roquefort, France, learning the tricks of the trade. The result was Oregon Blue, which RRVC still makes. In fact, it represents about half of the company's weekly production of six thousand or so pounds of cheese.

The high-protein milk for Oregon Blue comes exclusively from Noble Dairy's herd of brown Swiss cows, which are given no growth hormones. Milk is warmed (not pasteurized), mixed with an Iowa strain of blue mold, and dosed with a bacterial starter. A special French rennet is added when the proper acidity level is reached. As a very large curd forms, it is sliced both vertically and horizontally to form smaller curds, which are agitated by hand—but not too much, or the cheese would firm too quickly for proper flavor development. The whey separates out and drains. The curds are inoculated with blue mold, and then packed into metal sleeves for more draining overnight. The sleeves are turned several times to prevent the developing cheese from sticking inside them. The following day the wheels are salted, aged for two days, salted again, and aged for the remainder of the week. A multi-needle perforating machine makes holes in the cheese to supply oxygen to the developing mold inside. After three weeks and many turnings to maintain the proper shape, the cheeses are washed, dried, and coated with wax to kill bacteria. The cheese then ages as long as ninety days before the wax is removed and it is packaged for sale. This labor-intensive process produces an award-winning cheese much appreciated by lovers of blue.

dark chocolate
hazelnut torte

Red wine and chocolate? We love the combination, provided certain elements are in place. The chocolate should be dark and the dessert fairly unadorned. Gooey creations can really fight a wine, but this simple, not-too-sweet chocolate torte makes an elegant partner with a Cabernet Sauvignon. A Cabernet-Merlot blend would work well too, such as the one from Hedges Cellars in Benton City, Washington. A tasting room is located southeast of Seattle, in Issaquah, where you can also try their unusual blend of Chardonnay and Sauvignon Blanc. If it's the right season, make this torte even more special by topping it with raspberries or strawberries fresh from a Northwest berry farm.

7 ounces bittersweet chocolate, broken into pieces

12 tablespoons (1½ sticks) unsalted butter, plus more for buttering pan

6 large eggs, separated

½ cup plus 1 tablespoon granulated sugar

4 ounces hazelnuts (filberts), roasted, skinned, and finely chopped (see page 110)

1 tablespoon all-purpose flour

Pinch of salt

Unsweetened Dutch process cocoa powder, for dusting

1 cup whipping cream

1 teaspoon framboise (optional)

1 tablespoon sugar (optional)

2 pints fresh raspberries or strawberries (optional)

PREHEAT THE OVEN TO 350°F. Butter a 10-inch springform pan and line with parchment paper. Butter the parchment.

MELT THE CHOCOLATE and the 12 tablespoons of butter in a small, heavy-bottomed saucepan over very low heat. Stir frequently. Set aside.

BEAT THE EGG YOLKS with ½ cup sugar in a large mixing bowl until they lighten and form a ribbon. With the mixer on low, add the warm chocolate. Blend well. Add the hazelnuts, flour, and salt. Combine on low speed until flour almost disappears.

BEAT THE EGG WHITES until foamy. Add the remaining 1 tablespoon of sugar and continue to beat until soft peaks form. Add one third of the egg whites to the chocolate mixture and mix completely. Add the remaining egg whites and beat on low speed until almost all the white has disappeared. Pour into the pan.

BAKE UNTIL A CAKE TESTER or toothpick barely comes out clean, about 35 minutes. Remove the cake from oven. Let stand for 10 minutes. Run a table knife around the edges of the pan and release the springform. Gently turn the cake over and remove the bottom of the pan and the parchment paper, then turn right side up onto a cooling rack. When completely cool, dust generously with cocoa, using a strainer.

JUST BEFORE SERVING, beat the whipping cream with framboise or 1 tablespoon sugar until it just begins to hold its shape. Serve each piece of torte with a dollop of cream and berries, if desired.

Serves 12

foods to pair with

merlot

Roast Chicken Bread Salad
Sautéed Duck Breast with Dried-Cherry Sauce
Roast Quail with Barley, Prune, and Hazelnut Stuffing
Veal Chops with Roasted Garlic, Rosemary, and Merlot
Sautéed Calf's Liver with Slow-Cooked Walla Walla Onions
Lamb Satay over Basmati Rice
Dill-Coated Grilled Pork Tenderloin

the merlot grape

Merlot (mer-LOW) occupies more acres of vineyards than any other fine wine grape in the world. In the Northwest, 95 percent of the crop comes from the Columbia Valley, where the plantings make it the number two grape in Washington (after Chardonnay). Oregon's acreage is far lower, and Merlot vines rank sixth in the state. Many wineries make and sell Merlot wine, or blend it into Cabernet

Sauvignon. Among them are Hyatt Vineyards, in Zillah, Washington; Washington Hills Cellars, in Sunnyside, Washington; Chinook Wines, in Prosser, Washington; and Seven Hills Winery, in Milton-Freewater, Oregon.

Probably originally from the Balkans, Merlot is prized for its cherry-like fruitiness and velvety texture. It has been the primary grape blended with Cabernet Sauvignon in Bordeaux wines (which are often more Merlot than Cabernet). The Northwest Merlots are usually less tannic than its Cabernet Sauvignons. They can be soft to medium to very full bodied. Producers such as Leonetti Cellar and Andrew Will Winery have built their reputations in part on making full, robust Merlots with strong influences from the oak barrels in which the wines are aged. Some Merlots can bottle-age ten to fifteen years, but most are best between about three to eight years.

As with most wine grapes, cooler temperatures and shorter daylight hours result in wines that are less intense but often very good indeed. The Columbia Valley's long, hot summer days and cool nights help preserve acids in the grape, balancing flavor in the wine and leading to the big, dark wines that have become the most popular reds in the Northwest.

Common flavors and aromas of Merlot wine include those of berries, herbs, wood, spice, and tobacco. Merlots pair well with red meats and full-flavored poultry dishes, but lighter, less tannic versions could be carefully paired with fish like salmon or tuna. (Beware the tannin in red wine when serving fish, as it can easily produce a bitter, metallic taste in your mouth.)

Serve at cool room temperature, about 60°F.

roast chicken bread salad

Many Northwest restaurants prepare variations of this salad. It is a hearty and colorful dish that depends on rustic bread with a thick crust and chewy texture. A Northwest Merlot would make an excellent accompaniment. One of the major wineries in the Merlot world is Hyatt Vineyards, in the Yakima Valley in Zillah, Washington. Known especially for Merlot production, Hyatt's former wine makers have included such respected names as Wade Wolfe (now with Hogue Cellars and owner of Thurston-Wolfe Winery) and Joel Tefft (owner of Tefft Cellars). Ray Sandidge accepted the challenge in late 1994, following his award-winning experience at the Georg Breuer estate winery in Germany's Rheingau district as well as at Washington Hills, in Sunnyside, Washington. We enjoyed a pleasant visit to the handsome and well-stocked tasting room during crush in 1997.

1 whole chicken (3½ to 4½ pounds)

Coarse salt

Freshly ground black pepper

1 sprig of rosemary

DRESSING

¾ cup extra virgin olive oil

3 tablespoons unseasoned rice vinegar

1 tablespoon Dijon mustard

2 cloves garlic, minced

1 sprig rosemary, leaves only, minced

½ teaspoon coarse salt

Freshly ground black pepper

SALAD

1 large head romaine, torn into pieces

2 medium tomatoes, cut into 8 wedges each

1 small onion, halved and thinly sliced

1 red bell pepper, cored, seeded, and cut into thin strips

½ large cucumber, peeled, halved lengthwise, seeded, and cut crosswise into ⅛-inch slices

8 ounces rustic-style bread (chewy crust, fairly dense texture), cut into 1-inch cubes

Freshly ground black pepper

PREHEAT THE OVEN TO 375°F.

PLACE CHICKEN ON A RACK in a roasting pan breast side up, and sprinkle with salt and pepper. Place rosemary sprig in the cavity. Roast until an instant-read thermometer inserted between the thigh and the body registers 170°F, or until thigh juices run clear when pricked with a small, sharp knife, about 1 hour. Set aside to cool.

VIGOROUSLY WHISK or shake together the dressing ingredients in a 2-cup glass measure or jar with a tight-fitting lid. Put the salad ingredients in a very large mixing bowl and toss. Just before serving, give the dressing another whisk or shake, pour over salad, and toss thoroughly. Divide among 4 dinner plates.

CUT THE LEG/THIGH QUARTERS OFF THE CHICKEN, and cut through the middle of the breast, leaving wings on. Top each salad with a quarter of chicken.

Serves 4

top ten
washington wine grapes

Grapevine planting has exploded in Washington State. Almost four thousand acres were planted in the years 1995, 1996, and 1997. Those new plantings account for nearly 25 percent of all Washington wine grapes. The ten most popular grape varieties in the vineyards in order of acres planted are:

Chardonnay

Merlot

Cabernet Sauvignon

Riesling

Sémillon

Sauvignon Blanc

Cabernet Franc

Chenin Blanc

Gewürztraminer

Pinot Noir

Chardonnay, Merlot, Cabernet Sauvignon, and Riesling make up more than 75 percent of Washington's acreage.

sautéed duck breast
with dried-cherry sauce

Duck meat is marvelously fla-vored, darker and richer than chicken, and suitable for several kinds of cooking. Many specialty markets sell boneless duck breast ready to cook. You can also thaw a frozen duck (the way they are generally sold) and use a sharp boning knife to lift off the breast pieces, reserving the legs and thighs for another use, such as roasting or grilling. Expect to find more fat under the skin than on a chicken; the proper cooking technique will eliminate most of it. Since duck is dark meat, red wine is often a good match. Merlot, being full of fruit fla-vors and not usually heavily tannic, is appealing with this not-too-sweet cherry sauce.

The same growing region that provides most Northwest Merlot, Washington's Columbia Valley, also produces a huge cherry crop. Fresh cher-ries such as Rainier and Bing find their way even into international mar-kets, thanks to their quality. Northwest producers also sell dried cherries as well as dried cranberries, many from the southern Washington coast.

¼ pound shallots, thinly sliced

1½ cups dried cherries or dried cranberries (about 6½ ounces)

2 cups chicken stock or low-sodium canned broth

4 boneless duck breasts, skin on

2 tablespoons red wine vinegar

½ cup whipping cream

Freshly ground black pepper

Coarse salt

COMBINE THE SHALLOTS, dried cherries, and chicken stock in a nonreactive 2-quart saucepan and bring to a boil over medium-high heat. Reduce the heat to a simmer and cook, uncovered, for 15 minutes. Using a slotted spoon, lift ¼ cup of the cherries out of sauce and set aside. Purée the remaining sauce in a blender or food processor.

USE A SHARP KNIFE to cut slits through the duck skin and fat about every ½ inch, without cutting into the meat. Turn the breast and cut across the slits to create a diamond pattern. Place a heavy, nonreactive skillet or sauté pan large enough to hold all the duck in a single layer over medium-high heat. When the pan is quite hot, add the duck, skin side down. Cover with a spatter shield if you have one, reduce the heat to medium, and cook until the skin is crisp, thoroughly browned, and most of the fat has melted from under the skin, about 10 minutes. Turn and cook meat side down until the duck is pink in the center and an instant-read thermometer registers about 135°F, or the juices run slightly rosy when the meat is pricked with the point of a small, sharp knife. Set aside on a warm plate.

POUR THE FAT OUT OF THE PAN. Increase the heat to medium-high. Add the vinegar to the pan, loosening browned bits with a wooden spatula. Add the puréed cherries, the reserved cherries, cream, and pepper to taste, and bring to a boil. Taste for salt. Spoon some sauce on each of 4 warmed dinner plates and place the duck breasts skin side up in the pools of sauce. Serve at once.

Serves 4

roast quail with barley, prune, and hazelnut stuffing

Quail are tiny birds; two make an elegant dinner serving. The fine flavor of farm-raised birds is somewhere between chicken and duck. Specialty markets sometimes have quail available, but you usually have to special order them. Ask for them to be boned with the rib, breast, and back bones removed, for easier stuffing. The stuffing includes three famous Northwest products—hazelnuts, prunes, and wine. The quail are treated to a saltwater brine before cooking to increase flavor and moisture. They can be served with mashed potatoes or a purée of sweet potatoes, a green vegetable, and Cranberry-Pear Chutney (page 27). Pour a Merlot, such as Sineann, whose grapes enjoy the hot sunshine in vineyards near The Dalles, Oregon. Part of far north central Oregon actually lies within the Columbia Valley wine region, and has a climate much like that in Washington's Yakima Valley.

1½ cups coarse salt or ¾ cup table salt, for brine

8 boned quail

STUFFING

½ cup pearl barley

1 cup chicken stock or low-sodium canned broth

20 pitted prunes

1 cup dry red wine, such as Merlot

Coarse salt

Freshly ground black pepper

2 strips of bacon, preferably apple wood–smoked, cut into
¼-inch dice

1 small onion, finely chopped

¼ cup hazelnuts (filberts), roasted, skinned, and coarsely chopped
(see page 110)

1 cup (lightly packed) parsley leaves, chopped

12 sprigs of thyme, leaves only

1 large egg, beaten

SAUCE

4 tablespoons (½ stick) unsalted butter

¼ cup finely chopped onion

1 cup chicken stock or low-sodium canned broth

Freshly ground black pepper

2 tablespoons cornstarch mixed with 3 tablespoons cold water

DISSOLVE THE SALT in 3½ quarts cold water in a nonreactive pot deep enough to hold the quail. (An easy method is to bring 2 cups of the water to a boil in a saucepan, add the salt and boil until salt is dissolved, then pour the salt water into the remaining 3 quarts cold water.) Immerse the quail in the brine and refrigerate for 3 hours.

COMBINE THE BARLEY AND STOCK in a 1-quart or larger saucepan over medium-high heat and bring to a boil. Reduce the heat, cover, and cook at a bare simmer until tender, 30 to 35 minutes. Set aside to cool. Combine the prunes and wine in a 1-quart or larger nonreactive saucepan and bring to a boil. Turn off the heat, cover the pan, and allow to soak 1 hour or more. Drain the prunes through a strainer set over a bowl, reserving the wine and pressing lightly on prunes to extract any excess wine. Coarsely chop the prunes. Set aside.

SAUTÉ THE BACON IN A SMALL SAUCEPAN or skillet over medium heat until it is nearly crisp and has rendered some fat. Add the onion and cook until soft but not brown, 3 to 5 minutes. Combine the barley, prunes, bacon and onion mixture, hazelnuts, parsley, thyme, and egg in a large mixing bowl. Mix thoroughly.

merlot

81

PREHEAT THE OVEN TO 425°F.

DRAIN QUAIL, discarding brine, rinse well, and pat dry with paper towels. Using a small spoon, stuff the quail, packing the stuffing not quite tight, since it will expand during cooking. Put any extra stuffing into a small ovenproof ramekin or bowl. Tie the drumsticks with kitchen twine for best appearance, if you like. Set the quail on a rack in a roasting pan, preferably nonstick. Sprinkle with salt and pepper. Roast the quail and any extra stuffing until the birds are lightly browned and the stuffing in quail is hot (160°F on an instant-read thermometer), about 30 minutes.

MEANWHILE, make the sauce by combining butter, onion, stock, and wine from soaking the prunes in a 1-quart nonreactive saucepan. Bring to a boil and reduce to about half the original volume. When the quail are done, scrape the browned bits from the bottom of the baking pan into the sauce. Add pepper to taste. To thicken sauce, whisk the cornstarch slurry, then pour about 1 tablespoon of the mixture into the simmering wine sauce, whisking constantly. Add more only if you wish the sauce to be thicker. Serve 2 quail per person, ladling some sauce over the quail.

Serves 4

mark cave

One of the Northwest's foremost wine makers is Mark Cave of Paul Thomas Winery. He practices his art near Zillah, not far from Sunnyside, Washington, in a large concrete building on a hillside, hidden in the midst of hundreds of acres of vineyards. Mark, who in a past life learned useful skills as a roofer and restaurant chef, among other jobs, worked his way up from cellar rat to wine maker. That experience was put to good use when Paul Thomas Winery undertook the construction of a new facility. Mark sketched the outline of his imagined winery building and required systems for an architect friend, who converted the ideas into drawings. The result is a 500,000-gallon winery that includes total gravity-feed design, low labor requirements even during crush, temperature-controlled stainless steel fermenting tanks, barrel aging capability (coupled with an oak-chip technique for certain wines), and room for expansion. Cave's wines are known for being both well made and affordable, thanks to the efficiency of the winery. Cabernet Sauvignon, a Cabernet/Merlot blend, and Chardonnay are some of the wines he is best known for.

veal chops with roasted garlic, rosemary, and merlot

Because veal contains less fat than mature beef, it tastes less rich. You might decide that a softer red wine, a Merlot rather than a Cabernet Sauvignon, is a good match. Merlot, the most popular of Northwest red wines, is produced in large volume in Washington, and to a lesser degree and in a lighter style in Oregon. A certain amount comes from Idaho wineries, such as Ste. Chapelle, which is located on a hill a few miles outside of Caldwell, across the Snake River from Oregon. We found its 1996 Canyon Merlot soft and nicely balanced.

1 whole head garlic

½ teaspoon olive oil

1 cup chicken stock or low-sodium canned broth

1 cup beef stock, or canned beef broth, or broth from beef base
  (see Note)

1 teaspoon tomato paste

1 tablespoon Merlot

2 springs of rosemary, leaves only, finely chopped

4 rib or loin veal chops, 1 to 1¼ inches thick

8 tablespoons (1 stick) unsalted butter

½ cup (lightly packed) parsley leaves, chopped

1 medium tomato, cut crosswise in half, seeded, and cut in small dice

Freshly ground black pepper

PREHEAT THE OVEN TO 375°F.

CUT THE TOP QUARTER OFF the whole head of garlic, so that each clove is exposed. Rub the cut edge with the olive oil. Place on a piece of foil or small baking pan and bake for 40 minutes. Remove from the oven and let cool. Squeeze the garlic out of the skin of each clove, and finely chop. Set aside.

PREPARE A HOT CHARCOAL FIRE or preheat a gas or electric grill.

COMBINE THE CHICKEN AND BEEF STOCKS, tomato paste, Merlot, and half of the chopped rosemary in a 2-quart nonreactive saucepan over medium-high heat and bring to a boil. Boil, uncovered, until the liquid has reduced to about ¾ cup. Set aside. Grill the chops until they are medium rare, about 4 minutes per side. An instant-read thermometer should register 120° to 130°F. After turning the chops to cook on the second side, bring the sauce back to a boil, and add the butter and the garlic. When the butter has completely melted, take the pan off the heat. Stir in the remaining rosemary, the parsley, tomato, and pepper to taste. Taste for salt. Place a chop on each of 4 warmed dinner plates and spoon sauce over the top. Serve.

NOTE: Canned beef broth and bouillon cubes are almost uniformly of poor quality. For an acceptable instant broth buy Better Than Bouillon Beef Base, from Superior Quality Foods. (After being opened it has a shelf life of two months if unrefrigerated, or 1 year if refrigerated.)

Serves 4

sautéed calf's liver with slow-cooked walla walla onions

A good plate of properly cooked liver and onions, with mashed potatoes if you're in the mood, is a full-flavored meal well worth eating—and worth accompanying with a Northwest Merlot.

Use Washington Walla Walla sweet onions, slow-cooked to maximize their flavor, and you've moved this classic dish into the realm of the special.

Most Northwest Merlot is grown in Washington, in the warm, sunny summer climate of the Columbia Valley. Sunnyside is the location of Washington Hills Cellars, where high quality and good value go hand in hand. That goes especially for its Merlots. We savored the 1995 bottling. Another respected vineyard in Washington is Kiona Vineyards and Winery, in Benton City, at the southeast end of the Yakima Valley. This was the first vineyard on renowned Red Mountain, and still sells grapes to other producers. It also makes its own wines, including fine Merlot.

4 tablespoons (½ stick) unsalted butter

4 large Walla Walla or other sweet onions, cut in half, then into ¼-inch slices

Coarse salt

½ cup all-purpose flour, for dredging

Freshly ground black pepper

3 tablespoons vegetable oil

1 to 1½ pounds calf's or beef liver, sliced about ½ inch thick
  (see Note)

MELT THE BUTTER in a wide Dutch oven or sauté pan over medium heat, then add the onions. Cover and steam the onions for about 10 minutes. Uncover and cook, stirring often, until onions are quite limp, the juices have evaporated, and onions begin to color slightly, 10 to 30 minutes more. Sprinkle with salt. Cover and keep warm.

PREHEAT A HEAVY-BOTTOMED SKILLET or sauté pan over medium-high heat for 2 to 3 minutes. Combine the flour, 1 or 2 pinches of salt, and pepper to taste, on a plate or in a dry plastic bag. Dry liver with paper towels if not frozen, and coat both sides with flour. Shake off the excess and lay on a baking sheet or on a platter. Add the vegetable oil to the pan, swirling to coat the pan. Quickly place the liver pieces in pan. As soon as red drops of moisture appear on top, turn liver with tongs or a metal spatula. Brown on the second side until red drops of moisture just start to appear, probably 30 to 45 seconds. The liver should be pink in the middle. Quickly remove from the pan and serve with the onions.

NOTE: Restaurants can buy 4-ounce, neatly sliced, frozen pieces of beef liver. If you find them where you shop, keep them frozen until you are ready to cook them.

Serves 4

lamb satay over basmati rice

Thai and Vietnamese dishes are among the Southeast Asian foods that have enjoyed steadily increasing popularity in the Northwest. One particularly popular dish is satay (or saté), the Southeast Asian form of meat kabobs. Satay takes different forms in different countries. Everything from goat to turtle qualifies somewhere as satay, depending on local custom. In the United States, the peanut–coconut milk type sauce that accompanies the lamb in our recipe has come to symbolize satay dishes, skewered or not, meat or vegetable. The lamb to use depends mostly on your budget. The most tender cut is boneless loin, which is easy to cut into pieces and famously tender. The price is high, but there is no waste. Leg of lamb is more commonly used and delivers fine flavor, though not quite the tenderness of boneless loin.

Merlot's fullness in the mouth provides a smooth backdrop for lamb satay. Cooking is best done on a charcoal grill, but a broiler can also be used. You will need up to sixteen skewers, six inches or longer, metal or bamboo. If using bamboo, soak the skewers in water for fifteen minutes before using.

SAUCE

1 large clove garlic

2 quarter-size slices unpeeled fresh ginger

1 cup canned unsweetened coconut milk

¼ cup peanut butter, preferably nonhomogenized, unsweetened, and unsalted

3 tablespoons fish sauce

¼ cup (lightly packed) cilantro leaves

2 teaspoons hot chili sesame oil

◦ℓℓ⌐

1 pound boneless lamb loin, or well-trimmed leg

2 cloves garlic, minced

3 tablespoons vegetable oil

◦ℓℓ⌐

1½ cups basmati rice

2½ cups water

1½ teaspoons coarse salt

◦ℓℓ⌐

Freshly ground black pepper

¼ cup (lightly packed) cilantro leaves, chopped

DROP THE GARLIC AND GINGER into a food processor work bowl (be sure it is dry) with the machine running, and process to mince. Add the remaining sauce ingredients and process for 15 seconds. Scrape down the bowl, and process again for 10 seconds. Or, finely chop the garlic, ginger, and cilantro by hand, and stir into the remaining sauce ingredients in a medium mixing bowl. Scrape the sauce into a small serving bowl, gravy boat, or pitcher.

PREPARE A HOT CHARCOAL FIRE or preheat a gas or electric grill.

IF USING LOIN, cut it into ¼-inch slices. If using leg, note the average grain direction and cut across it in ¼-inch slices. Then cut those slices so they are about 2 inches long. Thread as many lamb pieces on each skewer as will fit. Mix the garlic and oil and brush onto the skewered lamb. Set lamb aside on a platter or baking dish until the fire is ready and the rice is cooked.

COMBINE THE RICE AND 2½ CUPS WATER in a 2-quart saucepan over medium-high heat and bring to a boil. Add the salt, and reduce the heat to a bare simmer. Cover tightly and cook 15 minutes over low heat without lifting the lid. Allow to stand, covered, until ready to serve.

BRUSH THE LAMB AGAIN with the garlic and oil if it has been standing a few minutes. Grill the lamb, turning once, just until it has browned slightly but is still pink in the center, about 1½ minutes per side. Stir the rice with a chopstick or skewer to loosen the grains, and spoon out onto 4 dinner plates. Arrange skewered lamb on top. Sprinkle with pepper, then drizzle with sauce. Garnish with chopped cilantro and serve at once. Pass extra sauce at the table.

Serves 4

dill-coated
grilled pork tenderloin

Coating a tender cut of meat with herbs and then grilling or roasting it is a sure-fire ticket to culinary success. Pork tenderloin lends itself to this treatment. While white wine is often recommended with pork, several reds, in this case Merlot, also complement it well.

Several miles north of the Yakima Valley Highway near Granger, Washington, Joel and Pam Tefft of Tefft Cellars produce Merlot as well as a variety of other red and white wines, plus a blush and, on occasion, Muscat ice wine. The winery is located a hundred yards or so off the highway in the middle of the vineyards, where Pam can often be found behind the tasting room counter.

1 pork tenderloin (about 1 pound)
2 tablespoons vegetable oil
½ teaspoon coarse salt
Freshly ground black pepper
1 cup (lightly packed) fresh dill, finely chopped

BUILD A HOT CHARCOAL FIRE or preheat a gas or electric grill.

TRIM THE TENDERLOIN OF THE SILVERY GRISTLE, if any, by inserting a sharp boning knife between the meat and the gristle and, with the knife angled slightly toward the gristle, cutting along the length of the tenderloin to free the gristle. Brush the meat with the oil and sprinkle evenly with salt and pepper. Place the dill on a large plate and roll the meat in it, coating evenly. Grill for about

7 minutes, turn, and grill until an instant-read thermometer inserted at an angle in the center of the tenderloin registers 145°F, about 7 minutes more.

LET THE MEAT REST for 5 minutes, covered with foil, to allow the juices to set. Carve slices on a slight angle so they present a larger appearance, and serve.

Serves 4

five great northwest merlots

Andrew Will Winery, Vashon, Washington

Chateau Ste. Michelle, Woodinville, Washington

Columbia Winery-David Lake, Woodinville, Washington

Leonetti Cellar, Walla Walla, Washington

Woodward Canyon Winery, Lowden, Washington

foods to pair with

syrah

Barbecued Spareribs
Mole-Simmered Chicken Thighs
Cassoulet
Braised Lamb Shanks with Almonds and Dates

the syrah grape

The Syrah (sir-RAH) grape has little vineyard space in the Northwest wine so far, but it looks as if that is going to change. In 1997 more acres were planted than existed in prior years. Syrah now covers more Washington vineyard land than Pinot Noir, and almost as much as Gewürztraminer. Expect to see more Syrah on wine merchants' shelves as the Columbia Valley vines mature over the next several years.

The grape has lots of ready-made Northwest fans, because it is the backbone of wines from France's Rhone Valley and from Australia, where it is called Shiraz. Depending on climate, it can produce big, tannic, purple, and complex wines that need a long time to mellow, or it can be made into wine that is much softer, with berrylike qualities. The middle ground is made up of wines that aren't huge but are peppery and herby. Lighter-style wines should be good for three to five years in the bottle, while really big versions can last for more than ten years. Ask your wine merchant's advice on the label you choose. Washington's offerings have been limited to a few producers so far, among them Columbia Winery, Glen Fiona Winery, Hogue Cellars, Hyatt Vineyards, and McCrea Cellars.

Syrah is a good choice when the meal includes the substantial flavors typical of heavier meat dishes, sausages, hard cheeses, duck, and goose. Common flavors and aromas include berries, pepper, smoke, and licorice.

Serve at cool room temperature, about 60°F.

barbecued spareribs

People from the Northwest love to cook outdoors, and the meat eaters among them usually love pork ribs. This recipe includes a mildly hot, tart, not very sweet sauce meant for serving on the side. Spareribs have more connective tissue and fat than back ribs, meaning that with proper barbecue-style cooking—low heat, long smoke-cooking— they can be extraordinarily tender and succulent. They are also a fine match with a big red wine, something with tannin, pepperiness, and purple enough to almost stain a wineglass. Syrah, in other words. Acreage planted to Syrah is quickly increasing in the Columbia Valley region, particularly around Walla Walla and near Benton City, Washington. We paired these ribs with a 1994 Syrah-Grenache blend from McCrea Cellars, labeled Tierra del Sol.

1 rack spareribs, preferably 3 pounds or under

¼ cup soy sauce

Freshly ground black pepper

2 cups dry wood chips, such as alder, apple, hickory, maple, mesquite, or oak

SAUCE

4 cloves garlic, sliced

1 large onion, halved and sliced

1 can (6 ounces) tomato paste

2 cups water

syrah

1 cup cider vinegar

1 tablespoon chipotle purée (see page 97)

¼ cup (lightly packed) brown sugar

¼ cup mild paprika

2 teaspoons coarse salt

½ teaspoon freshly ground black pepper

USING A SHARP BONING KNIFE, trim excess fat from ribs. Turn the ribs membrane side up. Use the knife to loosen a small bit of the clear membrane at the tip of the bone at small end of the rack. Grasp the membrane with a paper towel and pull it away from the bones, removing as much as you can. Brush both sides of ribs with soy sauce, and generously grind on some pepper.

PLACE 1 CUP OF THE WOOD CHIPS in the center of each of two 12-inch squares of aluminum foil. Fold the foil over the top of the chips to make a square envelope. Use a two-tined fork or metal skewer to punch holes all over the top of the foil packet, to allow smoke to escape easily. If you are using a charcoal grill, build a low fire on one side and place one foil packet directly on the coals. If you are using a gas grill with 2 burners, place the foil packet directly on the lava rocks or metal burner cover of the lighted burner. Place the ribs on the side of the grill opposite from the heat source, and close grill cover. After a few minutes the foil packet will begin to issue smoke, which will flavor the ribs. After a while the smoke will subside. Cook for 2 hours, adding more charcoal as necessary, maintaining 200° to 225°F if you can manage it. An oven thermometer is good for gauging heat if your grill does not have a reliable thermometer. Turn ribs, remove the used foil packet, and replace with the second foil packet. Cook until ribs are very tender, about 2 hours more. Ribs may be cooled, then refrigerated, and rewarmed as much as 5 days later. Just before serving, crisp the ribs lightly on a medium-hot grill. Ribs may also be baked uncovered in a 225°F oven for 4 to 5 hours, until very tender, then crisped quickly under a broiler.

WHILE THE RIBS ARE COOKING, combine all the sauce ingredients in a 2-quart, nonreactive saucepan and bring to a boil. Reduce the heat and simmer, covered, for 1 hour. Purée sauce in a blender or food processor. Serve the spareribs with sauce on the side. Store extra sauce in a glass jar, covered. (Sauce will keep in the refrigerator for 2 months.)

Serves 2

to make chipotle purée

Purée the chilies from 1 can chipotle chilies in a blender or food processor. Pack in a small glass jar, cover, and refrigerate. Purée will keep for months in the refrigerator.

syrah

mole-simmered chicken thighs

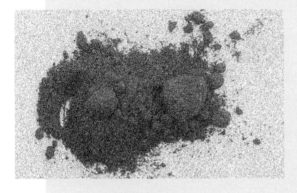

Chicken thighs, with their natural light richness, are one of the many poultry dishes that go well with Syrah. This version of the famous Mexican mole sauce is spicy, but balanced by the hidden richness of semisweet chocolate. The chicken could be grilled and the sauce brushed on during grilling, but even more intense mole flavor comes from simmering the pieces in the sauce until they are ready to fall off the bone.

MOLE SAUCE

8 dried chilies, preferably 4 anchos and 4 New Mexicos

⅓ cup raisins

Boiling water

4 Roma tomatoes

1 tablespoon vegetable oil or chicken fat

2 cloves garlic, peeled

½ cup whole blanched almonds

1 cup chicken stock or low-sodium canned broth

1 tablespoon chipotle purée (see page 97), or finely chopped canned chipotle chilies

1 tablespoon ground cinnamon

¼ teaspoon ground cloves

½ teaspoon freshly ground black pepper

3 ounces semisweet chocolate, melted

1 teaspoon coarse salt

2 tablespoons butter or chicken fat

8 chicken thighs, skinned

3 cups cooked rice, for serving

CUT THE STEMS OFF THE CHILIES and shake out the seeds. Place chilies in a 12-inch heavy skillet or sauté pan over medium heat. Toast the chilies, turning once, until fragrant, 3 to 5 minutes. Transfer chilies to a medium mixing bowl, add raisins, cover with boiling water, and let soak for 20 minutes. Meanwhile, add the tomatoes to the hot skillet to char the skins, turning them often. Remove the pan from the heat for a couple of minutes to cool somewhat. Return the pan to medium heat, add the oil, garlic, and almonds, and sauté, stirring often, until the garlic and almonds are lightly colored, 2 to 3 minutes. Remove the pan from the heat and add the stock, chipotle purée, cinnamon, cloves, pepper, melted chocolate, and salt.

DRAIN THE CHILIES and raisins and transfer to the work bowl of a blender or food processor. Add tomatoes, including skins, and the contents of the skillet. Process to a smooth purée. Pour through a wire strainer into a medium bowl, pressing down with a wooden spoon to extract as much liquid as possible. Discard the solids. Heat the butter in a 3-quart saucepan over medium heat. Add the sauce, and bring to a boil. Reduce the heat and simmer, uncovered, until the sauce thickens enough to coat a spoon, about 25 minutes. Taste for salt. The sauce may be cooled and refrigerated or used immediately to cook chicken.

TO COOK THE CHICKEN, pour the mole sauce into a nonreactive pan wide enough to hold chicken in a single layer. Pour the sauce over the chicken and bring to a simmer over medium heat. Simmer, partly covered, until chicken is very tender and no longer rosy inside, 30 to 40 minutes. Serve chicken and sauce over rice.

Serves 4

cassoulet

In southern France, there is an area defined more or less by the cities of Toulouse, Castelnaudary, and Carcassonne, which is world famous for a baked white bean dish called cassoulet. Recipes vary by area and by chef, the common thread being white beans and a rich mixture of meats and poultry. There is usually some confit—duck or goose meat that has been simmered for several hours in its own fat. This recipe uses ingredients available in most supermarkets or specialty meat markets, with steamed duck substituted for the classic duck confit, because it is easier to make and has less fat. It's best to prepare the dish over two days. This is a filling meal, flavored with the juices of several kinds of meat. A fitting wine would be a big Northwest Syrah. Substitute a Cabernet Sauvignon if necessary.

2 pounds Great Northern or navy beans, picked over and rinsed

4 smoked ham hocks

6 sprigs of thyme, tied with string

½ bay leaf

1 large onion, quartered

6 whole cloves garlic, peeled

1 teaspoon freshly ground black pepper

1 pound boneless lamb, from shoulder or leg, cut into 1-inch pieces

1 large onion, coarsely chopped

4 cloves garlic, sliced

1 tablespoon tomato paste

1 teaspoon coarse salt

2 mild Italian or French garlic sausages

2 ducklings, thawed if frozen, steam-roasted (see page 29), and
    refrigerated overnight

COMBINE THE BEANS, ham hocks, thyme, bay leaf, quartered onion, whole garlic,
½ teaspoon pepper, and 8 cups water in a 5-quart or larger pot over medium-
high heat and bring to a boil. Reduce the heat and simmer, partially covered, for
2 hours. Using a slotted spoon, transfer ham hocks to a plate to cool. Remove
and discard the thyme stems and as much onion as possible. When the hocks are
cool enough to handle, remove as much meat as possible and discard the bones.
Cut the meat into small pieces and return to the bean pot. Cool the beans, then
refrigerate overnight.

BROWN THE LAMB on all sides in a sauté pan over medium to medium-high heat.
Add the chopped onion and sliced garlic, and cook until softened, 3 to 5 minutes. Add 2 cups water, the tomato paste, salt, and ½ teaspoon pepper, and bring
to a boil. Reduce the heat and simmer, covered, for 20 minutes. Add the sausages
and simmer for 10 minutes more. Cool, then refrigerate overnight.

THE DAY YOU WANT TO SERVE, preheat the oven to 250°F.

BRING THE BEANS TO A SIMMER over medium-low heat. Remove the sausages
from their pot and set aside. Bring lamb mixture to a simmer.

SELECT A CASSEROLE or baking dish of at least 6 quarts capacity, with 4-inch or
higher sides. Ceramic is traditional, but enameled cast iron or stainless will also
do. Layer half the beans into the pan. Spread the duck over the beans. Cut the
sausages into ½-inch pieces and arrange on top of the beans. Spread the lamb
mixture over the beans, and spread remaining beans on top. Bake, uncovered,
for about 6 hours, pressing any crust that forms down into the beans about
every hour. Add water from time to time if beans appear dry. They should be
neither soupy nor pasty. Serve in wide soup plates or on dinner plates.

Serves 8 to 10

syrah

braised lamb shanks
with almonds and dates

The sexy cuts of lamb, the racks with frenched bones, the loin and rib chops, and the whole legs, are usually handsomely displayed where they are hard to miss in the meat case. Look a little farther, however, and you will usually find more humble cuts, such as breast, shoulder chops, and shanks. Shanks, with visible silverskin and lots of gristle, look tough—and they are. Tough, that is, until moist heat is applied for a couple of hours. Then the connective tissues become soft and melt into a mouthwatering pan sauce. Despite their lowly origins, braised lamb shanks are a meal of real distinction and a good reason to open a Syrah. Washington has taken the lead in Syrah plantings, but vineyards in Oregon are beginning to experiment with the grape as well.

ALMOND–CHILE SEASONING PASTE

1 jumbo onion

1 tablespoon vegetable oil

1 teaspoon whole cumin seed, dry roasted in a medium-hot pan until fragrant, and ground in a spice grinder or with a mortar and pestle

10 pitted dates

2 tablespoons sherry vinegar

1 tablespoon chipotle purée (see page 97), or minced canned chipotles in adobo sauce

¼ cup olive oil

½ teaspoon ground cinnamon

½ teaspoon coarse salt

½ teaspoon freshly ground black pepper

½ cup whole blanched almonds, roasted and chopped (see page 104)

LAMB SHANKS

2 tablespoons vegetable oil

4 lamb shanks

8 whole cloves garlic

1 can (28 ounces) whole tomatoes or crushed or diced tomatoes
  in juice

⅓ cup red wine

3 cups chicken stock or low-sodium canned broth

TO MAKE ALMOND-CHILE PASTE, peel and coarsely chop the onion and divide in half. Heat the 1 tablespoon vegetable oil in a 10-inch skillet over medium heat. Add half the chopped onion and sauté until onion is soft, about 5 minutes. Transfer to a food processor and add cumin, dates, vinegar, chipotle purée, olive oil, cinnamon, salt, and pepper. Process to blend, scraping down the work bowl as needed. Add prechopped almonds and pulse just to blend—do not purée the almonds. Set aside. You will have about 1½ cups.

TO PREPARE THE LAMB SHANKS, select a heavy sauté pan large enough for the shanks to fit in a single layer, with a lid. Place over medium-high heat and add the vegetable oil. Add the shanks and brown well on all sides. Remove shanks to a platter, reduce the heat to medium-low, and add the reserved chopped onion. Cook, stirring, until onion is browned lightly, about 5 minutes. Add ¼ cup of the almond-chile paste, the tomatoes (break up whole tomatoes with a wooden spoon or spatula) and their juice, red wine, and stock. Return the shanks to the pan. Raise the heat to medium-high until the liquid boils, then reduce it and cover. Cook shanks at a bare simmer until they are fork tender, about 1½ hours. Remove the shanks from the pan and set them aside in a warm oven. Raise the heat to medium-high and boil down the pan juices by about half. Taste for salt and pepper. Spoon off the fat. Place a shank on each dinner plate, top with about ¼ cup of the almond-chile paste, and ladle on some pan sauce. Serve.

Serves 4

to roast almonds

Preheat the oven to 350°F. Spread the almonds on a baking sheet. Roast until golden, about 10 minutes. Cool thoroughly before chopping or grinding.

doug m^ccrea

Doug McCrea lives with his wife, Kim, and children, Kevin and Kalen, near Rainier, Washington, southeast of Olympia. Doug and Kim have an extremely short commute to work, because McCrea Cellars, like some other Northwest wineries, is also their home.

Doug trained as a classical clarinetist, had a jazz performance career, and came to wine making as a hobby in the early 1980s. By 1988 he had worked in a couple of Puget Sound–area wineries, taken some wine education courses, and founded McCrea Cellars, now one of the most respected wineries in Washington. In addition to barrel-fermented Chardonnay, Doug and Kim make a southern Rhône–style blend of Grenache and Syrah labeled Tierra del Sol, a powerful Syrah, and expect to be the first Washington winery to introduce Viognier.

Like most other western Washington wineries both huge and small, McCrea Cellars does not sit in the middle of vineyards. The fruit is trucked from the Columbia Valley region three hours to the east. And, like other wine makers who purchase their grapes, Doug McCrea pays a lot of attention to vineyard practices and has agreements with his grape growers about standards to be maintained. That this sort of long-distance vineyard management works is reflected in the quality of the wines McCrea Cellars produces. Vineyards may be designated on the label in exceptional years. Barrel fermentation of McCrea Chardonnay has been the norm, in tight-grain barrels so that the oak is a spice rather than the backbone of the wine. Stainless steel cold fermenters were added recently, allowing the production of a crisper sort of Chardonnay to add to the McCrea repertoire of wines.

rainfall in northwest wine country

If you ask someone who doesn't live in the Northwest what the climate is like, you will probably be told that it rains all the time in Oregon and Washington. Not quite. Pinot Noir or Pinot Gris grapes growing in the Willamette Valley get perhaps 40 inches of rain per year, and much more in some years. But Cabernet Sauvignon or Chardonnay grapes growing in Washington's Yakima Valley get so little rain that they would be raisins without regular irrigation courtesy of the Yakima River. In general, vineyards west of the Cascade Mountains get the rains produced by the marine air off the Pacific Ocean; vineyards east of the Cascades mostly depend on irrigation to grow grapes in the hotter, drier climate.

Wine grapes must have enough moisture to thrive, but when rain arrives at the wrong time—just when the grape is ripe, its sugar content is at its highest, and it is ready or almost ready for picking—it is a potential disaster. The water dilutes the sweetness and acidity of the grape, resulting in wine with lower alcohol levels and less intense flavors. The grapes may swell to the point that skins split, allowing bacterial contamination and leading to the possible loss of the crop. Under such less than ideal conditions, a few wineries spend money on the extra labor it takes to sort grapes by hand on a conveyor so that rotten or shriveled fruit does not find its way into the wine.

foods to pair with

chardonnay

Rosemary-Roasted Hazelnuts
Northwest Clam Chowder with Oyster Mushrooms
Roasted Beet, Blue Cheese, and Walnut Salad
Chicken-Basil Salad
Spinach Fettuccine with Mushrooms and Tarragon
Northwest Cobb Salad
Cracked Whole Fresh Dungeness Crab
Scallop Sauté on Soft Polenta with Hazelnut Butter
Pan-Seared Tuna with Sherry Vinegar Sauce
Salmon Patties on Lightly Dressed Mixed Greens
Chicken in Turkish-Style Walnut Sauce
Veal Scaloppine with Apple-Brandy Sauce
Cold Sliced Pork Tenderloin with Tuna Mayonnaise

the chardonnay grape

The Northwest is fertile territory for Chardonnay (SHAR-doh-NAY), the most popular white wine grape in the world. It occupies more space in Washington vineyards than any other grape, and is the second most planted in Oregon.

Chardonnay grapes are believed to have originated in the Middle East, and so it is no surprise that the hot, dry climate of the Columbia Valley has proven  agreeable to the grape. In the Willamette Vally, the grapes ripen more slowly and tend to be more acidic. In general, Washington Chardonnays tend toward the buttery, big side, while Oregon's are typically more crisp and complex. Both styles have their many fans. Woodward Canyon Winery, near Walla Walla, Washington, takes advantage of the sun to produce consistently big, mouth-filling wines. Other notable Washington producers include Chinook Wines and Covey Run Vintners, in the Yakima Valley, and McCrea Cellars in Rainier, which uses Columbia Valley fruit. In the Willamette Valley, Adelsheim Vineyard, Bethel Heights Vineyard, Evesham Wood Vineyard, and Lange Winery are some of the many quality makers of Oregon Chardonnay.

Chardonnay wines can be blended, but better versions usually come from a single variety of grape. The wines are often aged (and sometimes fermented) in oak, which produces a viscous feel in the mouth and adds vanilla and toast flavors. Other versions are fermented and briefly aged in stainless steel, which produces a crisper wine. In both cases the depth of flavor and aroma coming from the glass depends in part on something you do yourself—control the temperature at which you serve the wine. A common mistake is serving white wines ice cold, which makes them refreshing and quaffable. Unfortunately, the esters that evaporate from wine to produce the aroma your nose appreciates don't evaporate very well at 38°F to 40°F. You will get far more flavor from white wine if you serve it at 50°F or even 60°F.

Common flavors and aromas in Chardonnay include green or yellow apples, pears, melons, bananas, pineapple, honey, citrus, toasted wood, nuts, and herbs. They drink well from the time of bottling, for lighter versions, to around five years of age for average wines; a few benefit from aging longer.

Food pairings with this grape cover a great deal of territory, since the style of the wine varies so much. Big, oaky specimens take well to assertive flavors—pepper, mustard, garlic, green olives—such as those in many Mediterranean-style dishes, not to mention buttery or creamy sauces. Crisper, lighter bodied Chardonnays partner well with lighter pastas, uncomplicated fish and shellfish dishes, and simple roast chicken.

Serve at 50° to 60°F.

rosemary-roasted hazelnuts

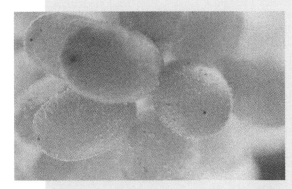

For an elegant appetizer that's easy on the cook, serve Oregon hazelnuts, roasted in butter or oil and herbs, along with a Northwest Chardonnay. Hazelnuts have a buttery quality, especially when roasted in this manner, and the rosemary adds a piney scent. Northwest Chardonnay usually has pleasing acidity to balance its butteriness, so it is a good complement to the richness of the nuts. Yamhill Valley Vineyards, near McMinnville, Oregon, makes a variety of wines in its hillside winery, including the Chardonnay we served with these hazelnuts.

2 tablespoons unsalted butter

1 pound hazelnuts (filberts), roasted and skinned (see page 110)

¼ teaspoon hot pepper sauce

¼ cup chopped fresh rosemary leaves

1 tablespoon coarse salt

PREHEAT THE OVEN TO 325°F.

PLACE BUTTER ON A RIMMED BAKING PAN and put the pan in the oven long enough to melt the butter. Toss the nuts, hot pepper sauce, rosemary, and salt together in a medium mixing bowl. Spread on the baking pan, turning with a metal spatula to coat the nuts with butter. Roast the nuts 5 minutes, stir again, then roast for 5 minutes more, or until they are nicely toasted but not burned. Cool. Store leftover nuts in a tightly covered container in the freezer, and refresh for 5 minutes in a 250°F oven before serving.

Makes 4 cups

to roast and skin hazelnuts

Preheat the oven to 350°F. Spread hazelnuts on a baking sheet. Roast for 15 minutes and check. The skins should be very dark, even smoking very lightly. Roast 1 or 2 minutes more if necessary. Place the nuts in the middle of a clean kitchen towel and wrap the towel around the nuts. Allow to rest for 20 minutes. Rub the nuts briskly between the towel layers to loosen skins. Not all skins will come off.

doug tunnell

Doug Tunnell retired from a seventeen-year career as a foreign correspondent for *CBS News* to return to his native Oregon, where he founded Brick House Vineyards in 1989. During his time with CBS, Tunnell was based in Paris for more than seven years. There, he fell in love with the wines of France. Today Tunnell lives on Ribbon Ridge, northwest of Newberg, and grows organic wine grapes on about twenty-six acres of land.

Tunnell's grapes have enough personality that part of his crop is bought by Achery Summit, Cameron, Cristom, and St. Innocent wineries—all known for making wines of considerable depth. The rest of the crop is made into big Pinot Noirs and Chardonnays under the Brick House label.

Raised in West Linn, Oregon, when it was less of a Portland suburb than it is today, Tunnell produces Oregon wines that are appreciated for their intense flavors. The etching on the label of a Brick House wine is a rendition of his house.

northwest clam chowder
with oyster mushrooms

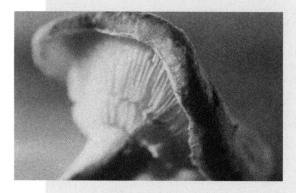

The Washington and Oregon coasts are home to many different types of clams, from the small, hardshell "steamers" used in this chowder, to the giant geoduck. This chowder also includes a Northwest wild mushroom, the oyster mushroom, named for the shape of its cap, which vaguely resembles an oyster shell. Oyster mushrooms are commercially cultivated in the Northwest and are available in better supermarkets year round.

Chardonnay is a natural choice to accompany the lightly creamy broth of this chowder. Among the many quality Chardonnay producers in the Northwest is Woodward Canyon, in Lowden, just west of Walla Walla, Washington, in an area with about ten wineries of various sizes. Woodward Canyon has a well-deserved reputation for quality, and a bottle of their Chardonnay would be a great match with the chowder.

3 pounds Manila, Pacific littleneck, Washington butter, or other
  small hardshell clams

6 strips of bacon, cut crosswise into ½-inch pieces

1 medium onion, diced

12 sprigs of thyme, leaves only, chopped

1¼ pounds waxy potatoes, such as Yukon Gold, White Rose, or
  Yellow Finn, peeled and cut in ½-inch dice

2 cups half-and-half

1 teaspoon freshly ground black pepper

1 tablespoon coarse salt

1 cup (lightly packed) parsley leaves, chopped

4 ounces oyster mushrooms, separated into individual pieces, thick
    stems (if any) sliced

RINSE THE CLAMS, discarding any that do not close when handled. Place them in a 6-quart pot or wide sauté pan, add 4 cups of water, and cover. Bring the water to a boil over medium-high heat. Cook clams until their shells pop open, about 5 minutes. Remove from the heat and, using a slotted spoon, remove the clams to a large bowl. When they are cool enough to handle, remove the clam meats from the shells, returning any juices to the pot. Coarsely chop the clams and set aside. Strain the clam cooking liquid through a paper towel–lined sieve and set aside.

SAUTÉ THE BACON in a 4-quart or larger saucepan over medium heat until crisp. Using a slotted spoon, transfer the bacon to a small bowl. Pour off all but 2 tablespoons bacon fat and return the pan to the heat. Add the onions and thyme, stir to coat, and cook until the onions soften, about 5 minutes. Add the potatoes, 3 cups of the clam cooking liquid, the half-and-half, pepper, and salt and bring to a boil. Reduce the heat and simmer, covered, for about 7 minutes or until the potatoes are just barely tender. Add the bacon, parsley, chopped clams, and mushrooms. Stir, taste for seasoning, and serve in wide soup or pasta bowls.

Serves 4

roasted beet, blue cheese,
and walnut salad

Combine beets with an Oregon cheese for this rich and hearty salad. As with most root vegetables, roasting the beets concentrates their sweetness and gives them a firmer texture than boiling or steaming. Allow about an hour to cook the vegetables. Walnuts add considerably to this salad, and a glass of Chardonnay will complement both the nuts and the cheese very well. At Witness Tree Vineyard, situated in the Eola Hills near Salem, Oregon, and named for a mighty oak that early surveyors used as a reference point, wine-maker Bryce Bagnall creates Chardonnays in various styles from vineyards on the property.

2 bunches beets, trimmed (about 1 pound)

DRESSING

    2 tablespoons fresh lemon juice

    6 tablespoons olive oil

    ¼ teaspoon coarse salt

    Freshly ground black pepper

8 cups mixed baby salad greens, washed and dried

3 ounces blue cheese, crumbled (about ¾ cup)

3 scallions, thinly sliced

1 cup (lightly packed) parsley leaves, chopped

8 ounces (about 2 cups) walnut halves and pieces, roasted and
    coarsely chopped (see page 69)

Coarse salt

Freshly ground black pepper

PREHEAT THE OVEN TO 400°F.

PLACE THE BEETS on a baking sheet lined with foil or a nonstick baking sheet.
Roast until a wire cake-tester or thin knife blade slides into a beet with only a little resistance, about 55 minutes—they will not feel as soft and fluffy as a baked
potato. Remove the beets from the oven and place them on a plate to cool. When
beets can be handled, use a paring knife to strip off the skin. Cut each beet into
about 6 wedges. Place in a medium mixing bowl. Mix together all the dressing
ingredients, and toss 2 tablespoons of the dressing with the beets. Combine the
salad greens, cheese, scallions, parsley, walnuts, salt, pepper, and remaining
dressing in a large mixing bowl and toss thoroughly. Divide among 4 salad plates
and top with the beets. Serve right away.

Serves 4

chicken-basil salad

Big dinner salads can be a creative way to use foods that are on hand in the refrigerator. Chardonnay should also be on hand at all times. A Chateau Benoit from Carlton, Oregon, not far from Ken Wright Cellars, would be a good choice with this salad. Don't serve white wine ice cold, as that diminishes the aromas a great deal. Cool room temperature is better than ice cold when it comes to tasting and smelling the wine maker's magic.

1 whole chicken (about 3¾ pounds), roasted (see page 76), and cooled enough to handle

1 pound small potatoes, cooked until barely tender, cooled, and quartered

8 ounces mushrooms, wiped clean, and cut into wedges about size of cut potatoes

3 Roma tomatoes, cut into wedges about size of potatoes and mushrooms

1 cup (lightly packed) basil leaves, whole if small, halved if large

3 scallions, thinly sliced on the diagonal

Coarse salt

Freshly ground black pepper

2 heads butter lettuce, leaves separated, washed, and dried

DRESSING

1 cup mayonnaise

2 tablespoons Dijon mustard

⅓ cup buttermilk, or more if needed

½ teaspoon coarse salt

Freshly ground black pepper

PULL OFF THE SKIN OF THE CHICKEN, then pull or cut the meat off the bones, discarding the skin and bones. Slice the meat across the grain into strips about ½-inch wide and set aside. Combine the potatoes, mushrooms, tomatoes, basil, and scallions in a large mixing bowl. Sprinkle lightly with salt and pepper.

STIR THE DRESSING INGREDIENTS TOGETHER. Dressing should be slightly thick but pourable; add a little more buttermilk if necessary. Arrange the lettuce on 4 dinner plates. Toss ½ cup dressing with the salad mixture and arrange on top of the lettuce. Arrange chicken strips on top of salad mixture and drizzle with the remaining dressing. Serve.

Serves 4

spinach fettuccine with mushrooms and tarragon

This dish includes butter and cream, two things that most Chardonnays are happy with, and is further enhanced by fresh tarragon. It calls for grilled chicken, but you can sauté it if you prefer. One of the Northwest's many Chardonnays, which remain the most popular white wines in the Northwest, will do nicely to balance and complement the rich flavors of the dish.

Many Northwest wineries produce estimable Chardonnays. Among them is Ken Wright Cellars in Carlton, Oregon. Owner–wine maker Ken Wright's reputation for producing memorable wine goes back to the eight years he was at Panther Creek. His Celilo Vineyard Chardonnay, using grapes from the legendary Columbia River–area vineyard near White Salmon, Washington, is an example of fine single-vineyard wines, which show off the growing qualities of a single plot of grapes.

3 cups chicken stock or low-sodium canned broth

2 cups whipping cream

¼ cup dry white wine, such as Chardonnay

¼ cup finely chopped red onion

2 tablespoons chopped fresh tarragon or 2 teaspoons dried tarragon

3 tablespoons unsalted butter

1 pound fresh mushrooms, white or brown, halved through the stems, then cut into ⅛-inch slices

Coarse salt

2 whole or 4 half skinless and boneless chicken breasts

Freshly ground black pepper

1½ pounds fresh spinach fettuccine

BUILD A HOT CHARCOAL FIRE or preheat a gas or electric grill.

COMBINE THE STOCK, cream, wine, onion, and dried tarragon, if using, in a 4-quart or larger nonreactive saucepan and bring to a boil over medium-high heat. Adjust the heat so that the liquid boils, but does not boil over the top of the pan—watch it carefully during the first few minutes. Cook the liquid until it has reduced to about 2½ cups, about 15 minutes.

MEANWHILE, melt the butter in a heavy 12-inch skillet or sauté pan over medium-high heat. Add the mushrooms and brown them well, evaporating any moisture that may form in the pan. Add the mushrooms to the sauce when it has finished reducing.

BRING 6 QUARTS OF WATER TO A BOIL in a large pot over high heat. Add 1 table-spoon coarse salt. Sprinkle the chicken with salt and pepper, and grill until an instant-read thermometer registers 160°F when inserted into the center of the thickest part. Remove chicken from the heat and let cool for 5 minutes. If using whole breasts cut into halves, then cut breasts across the grain into thin slices. Set aside and keep warm. Add the fettuccine to the boiling water and cook, stir-ring often, until al dente, 2 to 3 minutes. Drain, return to the pot, add the sauce and the fresh tarragon, if using. Divide among 4 wide soup plates or pasta bowls, top with the chicken, and serve.

Serves 4

northwest cobb salad

Long a favorite on restaurant menus, cobb salad is full of contrasting colors and flavors. This version really satisfies as a main course, and the necessary ingredients are easy to buy almost anywhere. Look for salmon that has been brine cured and well smoked—perhaps with Northwest alder wood—for firmest texture and robust flavor. Remember that tail pieces are naturally boneless. Serve the salad with a fresh baguette and a bottle of Chardonnay.

2 hearts of romaine

2 hard-cooked eggs, shelled and grated or chopped

1 avocado, halved, pitted, peeled, and diced (see page 121)

8 ounces tomatoes, peeled, seeded, and diced

2 scallions, thinly sliced

2 ounces blue cheese, such as Oregon Blue, crumbled or grated (about ½ cup)

4 ounces smoked salmon, boned if necessary, coarsely chopped

8 ounces cooked boneless chicken or turkey, diced

½ cup hazelnuts (filberts), roasted, skinned, and coarsely chopped (see page 110)

1 cup (lightly packed) parsley leaves, minced

Salt to taste

Freshly ground black pepper

¾ cup extra virgin olive oil

3 tablespoons red wine vinegar

DICE THE LETTUCE by cutting into ¼- to ½-inch ribbons in one direction, then turning and cutting in the other direction, and place in a shallow 14-inch bowl or large platter. Arrange mounds of egg, avocado, tomato, scallion, blue cheese, smoked salmon, and chicken or turkey in rows across the top of the lettuce. Top with the hazelnuts, parsley, and salt and pepper. Combine the olive oil, vinegar, a pinch of salt, and black pepper to taste in a small jar with a tight-fitting lid. Shake vigorously to blend, pour over the salad, and toss thoroughly. Divide among 4 dinner or lunch plates and serve.

Serves 4

to pit an avocado

If you are going to dice an avocado, choose one that yields only slightly when lightly squeezed; it will be much easier to dice than a softer one that is better used for guacamole-type preparations. Using a sharp knife, slit the avocado through to the pit all the way from the thin end around the large end and back to the thin end; leaving the knife in the fruit twist it to separate the halves. Holding the half with the pit in your hand, carefully press the knife blade (not the point) into the pit and twist it out of the fruit. Use a serving spoon to scoop the fruit out of the skin in one piece.

cracked whole
fresh dungeness crab

One of the purest joys of North-west eating between December and July is coming face to face with a whole Dungeness crab that that has been cooked and cracked. One large crab can feed two people; if you add a loaf of crusty bread you have enough food for din-ner. Each person will need a small seafood fork to extract meat from the crab shell. Northwest seafood markets sell chilled, cooked whole crabs ready to take home; they may also have live crabs if you would prefer to cook your own. Often, the same markets also sell wine, sometimes even chilled, making shopping for dinner a five-minute affair. A Northwest Chardonnay's slight—or sometimes pronounced—butteriness makes a good companion to the richness of the crabmeat.

2 cooked Dungeness crabs, cleaned

1 crusty, baguette-style loaf of bread
Unsalted butter

PREPARE THE CRABS by removing the legs and making a cut through each leg, from where it was attached to the body to the tip. A small pair of kitchen scissors or shears is a good tool to use. Arrange the legs on a platter. Break the body in half and use the scissors to cut through the cartilage of each piece to separate the top and bottom shells, so the meat is accessible. Arrange on the platter. Heat bread in a 250°F oven for 5 minutes before serving. Dig in.

Serves 4

five great northwest chardonnays

Adelsheim Vineyard, Newberg, Oregon

Brick House Vineyards, Newberg, Oregon

Cameron Winery, Dundee, Oregon

Covey Run Vintners, Zillah, Washington

Ponzi Vineyards, Beaverton, Oregon

scallop sauté on soft polenta with hazelnut butter

Italian cooking teacher Marcella Hazan points out that polenta was the sustainer of life in certain parts of Italy long before pasta came on the scene. Whether served soft and creamy, as in this recipe, or allowed to cool and later be sliced and grilled, polenta brings to the table a feeling of comfort not unlike mashed potatoes. In this recipe scallops are quickly sautéed, spread over a bed of polenta, and drizzled with hazelnuts toasted briefly in butter. It is fine food with which to sip a Northwest Chardonnay.

On Bonair Road, outside Zillah, in Washington's Yakima Valley, Gail and Shirley Puryear produce an assortment of red and white wines, some of which are quite imaginatively named for selling in the tiny tasting room, which is how most of their wine is sold. Postcards and letters from all over the world paper the walls of the room, which Shirley runs. Gail is the wine maker, and he has a way with his Bonair Winery 1995 Reserve Chardonnay, our choice for this meal.

Coarse salt

3 cups coarse white or yellow cornmeal (polenta)

6 tablespoons (¾ stick) unsalted butter

½ cup all-purpose flour for dredging

Freshly ground black pepper to taste

1 pound sea scallops

⅔ cup hazelnuts (filberts), roasted, skinned, and coarsely chopped
(see page 110)

½ cup (lightly packed) parsley leaves, chopped

BRING 8 CUPS OF WATER TO A BOIL in a heavy-bottomed 4-quart saucepan over medium-high heat. Add 2 teaspoons salt. With the water steadily boiling, slowly pour the polenta into the pan in a steady stream while whisking. Reduce the heat enough so that spattering is not excessive. Stir with a wooden spoon for 2 minutes. Cover the pot and maintain it at a simmer for 10 minutes. Stir polenta for 1 minute, cover, and cook 10 minutes more. Repeat the cycle 2 more times, so that total cooking time is about 40 minutes. Just before serving thoroughly stir up from the bottom and from the sides again.

WHEN THE POLENTA IS WITHIN 5 MINUTES OF BEING DONE, melt the butter in a 12-inch skillet or sauté pan over medium-high heat. Combine the flour with a pinch of salt and pepper to taste in a shallow bowl. Coat scallops with flour, shaking off the excess. Sauté the scallops in the butter, turning once, until very lightly browned but still slightly translucent in the middle, about 1 minute per side. Arrange a bed of polenta on each of 4 warmed plates and place the scallops over it. Toss nuts for a few seconds in the butter, then spoon over the scallops. Garnish with parsley.

Serves 4

pan-seared tuna
with sherry vinegar sauce

Pan-searing is a great way to prepare food if you are after a well-browned exterior but a rare center. It does require heavy-duty cookware that won't warp over higher-than-normal heat. Cast iron is a classic choice; enameled cast-iron or heavy-bottomed stainless are good choices when, as here, an acidic sauce is being made.

Both yellowfin and bigeye tuna are marketed as ahi in the Northwest, and are fabulously moist and flavorful. Albacore—the variety used for solid-pack canned tuna—has marvelously meaty flavor and firmer texture. Seafood markets in Oregon and Washington often have more than one variety at a time, so the kind to buy depends on your budget—albacore is always less money—and the appearance of the fish. Any of these tunas will be a good match with a Northwest Chardonnay. One that comes to mind is Evesham Wood, noted for the wines it produces—many of them unfiltered—from a few acres in the Eola Hills, northwest of Salem, Oregon. Filtering wines increases their clarity and makes it less likely that sediment will develop, but unfiltered wines tend to have a longer aftertaste, or finish. Evesham Wood's cellars are built into the hill and are therefore naturally cooled.

1½ pounds ahi or albacore tuna steaks, at least 1 inch thick,
    cut into 4 portions

Coarse salt

Freshly ground black pepper

1 cup chicken stock or low-sodium canned broth

¼ cup sherry vinegar

4 tablespoons (½ stick) butter, at room temperature

DRY THE TUNA STEAKS with paper towels and sprinkle with salt and pepper. Heat a heavy, nonreactive skillet large enough for the 4 steaks over medium-high heat for 2 to 3 minutes, until a bead of water dropped into the pan dances around pan rather than evaporating on contact. Place tuna steaks in the pan and sear until enough of a crust has formed that the steak can be loosened from the pan using a metal spatula, 2 to 3 minutes. Turn and sear the second side. Temperature on an instant-read thermometer should be about 100°F for a rare interior; 120°F will give you tuna mostly cooked through, with a grainier, drier texture. Transfer the steaks to warmed, but not hot, plates. Pour the stock and vinegar into the pan. Add the butter. Boil sauce down until it thickens a bit; large bubbles will start to appear when it is ready. Taste for salt, add pepper to taste, and spoon the sauce over the tuna. Serve at once.

Serves 4

salmon patties on lightly dressed mixed greens

Salmon is an icon for the North-west in the minds of many. Residents of Alaska, Washington, Oregon, and Idaho took the existence of salmon for granted for many years. Now certain salmon runs have seriously declined. Aquaculture has grown, however, and farm-raised salmon are available not only from U.S. waters, but also from Chile, Norway, and other sources. Still, there is no denying the excitement in the fish markets during certain seasons, such as the spring chinook run from Alaska's Copper River.

When the urge for salmon strikes, but you want something other than a fillet or steak, try making these patties and serve them with a Northwest Chardonnay. Cristom Vineyards, in the Willamette Valley's Eola Hills, makes wines from local grapes, and, like many other wineries, buys grapes from other regions. Its Columbia Valley Chardonnay is highly regarded. Cristom is also one of the few Oregon producers of Viognier.

1 pound fresh salmon fillet, preferably boneless tail pieces

1 cup (lightly packed) parsley leaves

4 scallions, cut into 1-inch pieces

1 tablespoon capers, rinsed and drained

1 large egg, beaten

1 teaspoon dried dill weed

¼ teaspoon coarse salt

Freshly ground black pepper

1 teaspoon Worcestershire sauce

½ teaspoon hot pepper sauce

½ cup cracker meal or medium-size, dry bread crumbs, plus
   2 tablespoons

DRESSING

2 teaspoons unseasoned rice vinegar

1 teaspoon Dijon mustard

¼ cup extra virgin olive oil

10 cups mixed lettuce greens or baby spinach

Coarse salt

Freshly ground black pepper

2 medium tomatoes, each cut into 12 wedges

2 tablespoons olive oil

½ cup Caper Tartar Sauce (see page 232) (optional)

REMOVE THE BONES from center-cut fillets using needle-nose pliers. Lay the fillets skin side down and use a sharp chef's or fillet knife to cut the flesh away from the skin, holding knife at an angle slightly toward the skin to prevent waste. Cut the fish into 1-inch pieces and set aside.

PUT THE PARSLEY in the work bowl of a food processor and mince. Add the scallions and the capers and process until they are minced. Add the salmon and pulse to chop it until it resembles coarsely ground meat. In a medium mixing bowl mix egg with dill, salt, pepper, Worcestershire sauce, hot pepper sauce, and cracker meal. Add chopped salmon mixture and use a rubber spatula to mix the patty ingredients thoroughly. Moisten your hands with water and make 4 round patties about ¾ inch thick. Set aside.

WHISK TOGETHER DRESSING INGREDIENTS in a large mixing bowl. Add lettuce greens, season with salt and pepper, and toss thoroughly. Divide among 4 serving plates, arranging 6 tomato wedges around the outside edge of the salad on each plate.

HEAT OIL in a 12-inch skillet, preferably nonstick, over medium heat. Place the remaining ½ cup of cracker meal in a shallow bowl. Lightly press salmon patties into cracker meal to coat on all sides and gently place them in frying pan. Sauté until browned, turn and brown other side. Total cooking time will be about 5 minutes. Place cooked patties in the center of the prepared plates. Top with 2 tablespoons of the Caper Tartar Sauce and serve immediately.

Serves 4

top ten oregon wine grapes

Oregon has more wineries than Washington, but its vineyards are smaller. A little less than eight thousand acres are planted, less than half the acreage of Washington. The top ten wine grapes in the vineyards in order of acres planted are:

Pinot Noir

Chardonnay

Pinot Gris

Riesling

Cabernet Sauvignon

Merlot

Gewürztraminer

Pinot Blanc

Müller-Thurgau

Sauvignon Blanc

Zinfandel

Pinot Noir, Chardonnay, and Pinot Gris together account for about 75 percent of Oregon's acreage.

chicken in turkish-style walnut sauce

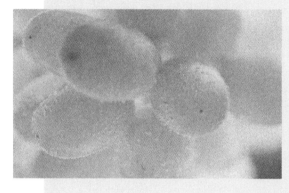

Some years ago we had the good fortune to be invited to a potluck dinner where the most memo-rable dish of the evening was Turkish chicken in walnut sauce, prepared by a woman who was born in the old country. The chicken had been shredded after cooking, mixed with a rich nutty sauce, and served at room temperature. We have created our own version of the dish, based on hers. You could open a chilled Chardonnay, as we did, in our case a 1.5 liter bottle of nonvintage Bonair Winery Yakima Valley Chardonnay, a good value from the small wine maker near Zillah, Washington.

1 whole chicken (3½ to 4½ pounds)

2 scallions

3 thick slices baguette-style bread

½ cup milk

3 tablespoons walnut oil

8 ounces walnut pieces, roasted and cooled (see page 69)

¼ teaspoon crushed saffron threads

¼ teaspoon cayenne pepper

1½ teaspoons coarse salt

1 teaspoon freshly ground black pepper

1 cup finely chopped onion

1 clove garlic, minced

1 cup (lightly packed) parsley leaves, very coarsely chopped

PUT THE CHICKEN IN A POT LARGE ENOUGH TO HOLD IT, and cover with cold water. Place the pot over medium-high heat, cover, and bring water to a simmer. Skim off the foam as it rises to the surface. Add scallions, and maintain water at a simmer until chicken legs move easily when wiggled with your hand, about 30 minutes after the water comes to a simmer. Lift the chicken out of the pot with tongs and a heavy spoon and place in a large bowl to cool. Set aside 2 cups of the broth for the sauce. (Extra broth may be boiled down to concentrate its flavor and used for other cooking. Refrigerate, covered, for up to 3 days or freeze.)

TEAR BREAD INTO COARSE PIECES and place in a medium mixing bowl. Pour the milk and walnut oil over the bread and allow to soak for 20 minutes. Place the walnuts in the work bowl of a food processor and chop until fine. Add soaked bread mixture and purée.

COMBINE THE BROTH, saffron, and cayenne in a 3-quart saucepan over medium-high heat. Bring to a simmer. Add the salt, pepper, onion, garlic, and walnut purée. Return to a simmer and cook for 5 minutes. Remove from the heat.

WHEN THE CHICKEN IS COOL ENOUGH TO HANDLE, pull the meat off the bones and shred it across the grain into ¼- to ½-inch strips. Toss the chicken with half of the walnut sauce in a large bowl. Arrange the chicken on a large platter or rectangular baking dish and top with remaining sauce. Garnish with parsley. Serve warm, or at cool room temperature.

Serves 6 to 8

veal scaloppine with
apple-brandy sauce

One of the commonly tasted flavor components of Chardonnay wines is apple. The subtle apple flavors that may be apparent in a wine can be quite good paired with a sauce that includes apple brandy. In this recipe veal scaloppine—thin slices, usually from the leg—are very quickly sautéed and kept warm while a fast pan-reduction sauce including apple brandy is made. The sauce is finished with diced apples. The key to success is to avoid overcooking the veal.

Clear Creek Distillery, in Portland, Oregon, ferments Hood River Valley fruit in small batches, then distills it into an intensely flavored apple brandy. It can sometimes be purchased in 50 ml miniature bottles, two of which are enough for this recipe.

1 medium-size crisp sweet-tart apple, such as Gala, Braeburn, Fuji, or Granny Smith

2 tablespoons fresh lemon juice

1 pound veal, thinly sliced

⅓ cup all-purpose flour for dredging

Coarse salt

Freshly ground black pepper

2 tablespoons unsalted butter

1 tablespoon vegetable oil

½ cup apple brandy

½ cup chicken stock or low-sodium canned broth

½ cup finely chopped red onion

½ cup whipping cream

½ cup (lightly packed) parsley leaves, coarsely chopped

PEEL AND CORE THE APPLE, then cut it into ¼-inch dice. Place in a small bowl. Add the lemon juice, and cold water to cover. If the scaloppine are thicker than about ³⁄₁₆ inch, put them between 2 sheets of plastic wrap and pound them thin using a flat meat pounder or the bottom of a small saucepan. Whisk together the flour, a pinch of salt, and pepper to taste in a small bowl, then transfer to a wide, flat plate. Just before you are ready to cook, dust the veal with flour, shaking off the excess and arranging the slices on a platter or baking sheet for quick access. Melt butter with oil in a heavy-bottomed 12-inch skillet or sauté pan over medium-high heat. When the foam subsides, place as many slices of veal as will fit into pan without crowding. Sauté quickly, 30 to 60 seconds per side; slices should still be pink in the center. Transfer the slices as they finish cooking to a warm platter and keep warm in a low oven.

POUR FAT FROM THE PAN. Add the apple brandy, scraping the pan to loosen any browned bits. Add the stock and onion. Drain the apple pieces in a wire strainer. Cook the sauce until reduced by half, then whisk in the cream. Taste for salt, and add pepper to taste. Add the apples. Arrange the veal in overlapping slices on 4 dinner plates, and spoon the sauce over them. Sprinkle with parsley and serve.

Serves 4

cold sliced pork tenderloin
with tuna mayonnaise

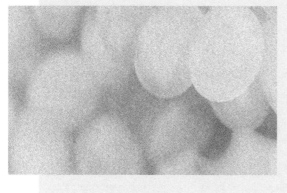

A variation on an Italian classic, vitello tonnato, *this dish makes use of affordable and tender pork tenderloin, rather than veal. It is meant to be served with the sauce between the pork slices, so that every bite is flavored with the tuna mayonnaise. It makes a terrific buffet presentation, is good cold or at cool room temperature, and may be prepared a day ahead of serving—and it will be even more flavorful if it is. A Chardonnay, whether crisp, fruity, or buttery, will be a welcome wine to sip with this richly flavored dish.*

Covey Run Vintners (once named Quail Run, before a lawsuit involving California's Quail Ridge winery) is on a high hill above Zillah, Washington. The winery offers a long list, with Chardonnays in various price ranges, including a single-vineyard wine from Celilo Vineyard near White Salmon, Washington.

¼ cup dry white wine, such as Chardonnay

2 cups chicken stock or low-sodium canned broth

1 small onion, sliced

2 cloves garlic, smashed

1 rib celery, thinly sliced

1 small carrot, thinly sliced

1 bay leaf

1 tablespoon chopped fresh tarragon or 1 teaspoon dried tarragon

½ teaspoon freshly ground black pepper

2 pork tenderloins (about 2 pounds)

1 cup mayonnaise

1 teaspoon anchovy paste

1 can (6 ounces) solid tuna, packed in vegetable oil

2 tablespoons capers, rinsed and drained

½ cup (lightly packed) parsley leaves, chopped

COMBINE THE WINE, stock, onion, garlic, celery, carrot, bay leaf, tarragon, and pepper in a nonreactive sauté pan at least 10 inches wide over medium heat and bring to a boil. Reduce the heat and simmer, covered, for 30 minutes. While broth cooks, trim the pork of its silvery gristle, if any, by inserting a sharp boning knife between the meat and the gristle, and with the knife angled slightly toward the gristle, cutting along the length of tenderloin to free the gristle.

WHEN THE BROTH HAS SIMMERED FOR 30 MINUTES, slide the tenderloins in, bring back to a bare simmer and cook, partially covered, until an instant-read thermometer inserted on an angle in the middle of the meat registers 140°F, 10 to 15 minutes. Remove the pan from the heat, uncover, and allow the pork to cool in the broth. Cover and refrigerate overnight in the broth.

PUT THE MAYONNAISE in the work bowl of a food processor. Add the anchovy paste and tuna, including its oil. Process to blend well. Or drain the tuna—reserving the oil—and chop by hand, then whisk the sauce together. Stir in capers.

DRY THE TENDERLOINS. The broth may be strained and used for other cooking. Slice the meat on a slight diagonal into ⅛- to ¼-inch slices. Fan the slices in a circular or oval pattern around a large platter, putting a dollop of tuna mayonnaise between each slice. Several layers may be placed on one platter, if necessary. Cover with plastic wrap and refrigerate until 30 to 60 minutes before serving. Garnish with parsley.

Serves 8 or more as part of a buffet or picnic

chardonnay

foods to pair with

sauvignon blanc

Parmesan-Stuffed Artichokes
Asparagus, Goat Cheese, and Walnut Salad
Gruyère Cheese and Green Bean Salad
Asparagus with Poached Eggs and Shaved Parmesan
Scallop and Broccoli Salad with Orange Vinaigrette
Sautéed Trout in Lemon Butter
Shrimp, Sage, and Butternut Squash Frittata
Rosemary-Sage Biscotti

the sauvignon blanc grape

The Sauvignon Blanc (SO-veen-yon BLONC) grape (also called Fume Blanc) is quickly increasing in popularity in the Northwest, because of its very dry, grassy, citrusy qualities that go so well with fish and shellfish, among other foods. The Northwest style in general is to make the wine straightforwardly lean, rather than to barrel ferment or age in oak, although there are exceptions to the rule.

Compared to the Willamette Valley, the Columbia Valley's climate seems to present fewer challenges to wine makers. That said, grapes from cooler climates can and do produce very appealing wines in skilled hands. Rex Hill Vineyards is one of Oregon's consistent producers, as is Laurel Ridge Winery. Washington icons Chateau Ste. Michelle and its cousin Columbia Crest Winery make good Sauvignon Blanc. The Spokane area's Arbor Crest Cellars Bacchus Vineyard is very well thought of, too.

Sauvignon Blanc's flavors and aromas include the grassy and citrusy notes mentioned already, as well as kiwi, pineapple, melon, green apple, and vegetal and herbaceous influences.

Since this is a grape that is less forgiving in the winery, owing to its lean characteristics, you can teach yourself something about the style of wines you prefer by buying three bottles of Sauvignon Blanc. Get one plain, with no oak at all, another aged in oak, and a third that has been barrel fermented. Taste all three at the same time and the same temperature. You'll likely enjoy them all, but you'll probably have a style preference that might influence you in purchasing other white wines, too.

Northwest Sauvignon Blanc's natural acidity makes it an easy match with mild vinaigrette dressings, dishes with lemon and other citrus, and fish and shellfish. Goat cheese is another classic match.

Serve slightly chilled, about 50°F.

parmesan-stuffed artichokes

Artichokes are grown in the Northwest, including around Tillamook, Oregon. The very tasty vegetable has gotten bad press because of the ill-conceived notion that it makes all wine taste bad. The tendency of an artichoke to make everything tasted after it seem sweeter is due to a naturally occurring chemical, but pairing the artichoke with an appropriate wine solves the problem before it begins. Very dry wines make sense, such as bone-dry sparkling wine. High-acid, low-tannin red wines are also complementary. And a classic match is a very dry Sauvignon Blanc—crisp, acidic, and assertive.

Caterina Winery, in Spokane, Washington, makes highly regarded Sauvignon Blanc from Columbia Valley grapes, which you could enjoy with these artichokes.

4 large artichokes

⅓ cup olive oil

2 cups fresh bread crumbs (see page 142)

¼ cup thyme leaves

1 cup oregano leaves

1 tablespoon sherry vinegar

½ cup imported parmesan or other hard grating cheese

¾ teaspoon coarse salt

Freshly ground black pepper

CUT OFF THE STEM END of each artichoke so that it will sit flat on a plate, then cut off the top inch. Tear off any small bottom leaves and use scissors or kitchen shears to snip off the sharp tips of the leaves. Bring 5 to 6 quarts of water to a boil in a pan large enough to hold the 4 artichokes at once. Drop them into the boiling water and cook for 10 minutes. Remove, turn upside down on a rack or towel to drain and cool slightly.

PREHEAT THE OVEN TO 350°F.

HEAT THE OIL in a 10-inch skillet or sauté pan over medium heat. Add the crumbs and stir and toss over the heat until the crumbs become lightly brown. Scrape out into a medium mixing bowl. Add the thyme, oregano, sherry vinegar, grated cheese, salt, and pepper to taste. Toss thoroughly.

GENTLY SPREAD THE TOP OUTER LEAVES of each artichoke. Grasp the thin inner leaves of the choke and pull out as many in 1 handful as you can. Use a small spoon to scrape out all the remaining fibers and small leaves. Spoon the seasoned crumbs into the center of each artichoke, reserving about ½ cup. Gently spread the leaves of each artichoke while sprinkling about 2 tablespoons crumb mixture over it.

PLACE CHOKES in a 9 x 13-inch baking dish, pour in about ½-inch hot water, and cover pan with an identical baking dish, inverted, to serve as a lid, or aluminum foil. Place on the middle oven rack and bake for 1 hour. Very gently remove from the pan using tongs while supporting the bottom with a metal spatula. Serve. May be served hot, cold, or at room temperature.

Serves 4

NOTE: TO MAKE FRESH BREAD CRUMBS The best crumbs come from the best bread, so make or buy a loaf with a firm texture, either white or with some whole wheat. Cut the bread into 1-inch cubes, and put the cubes into the work bowl of a food processor. Process until the bread is uniformly chopped into crumbs of the size you need. Or, chop bread by hand using a sharp chef's knife. (Store unused crumbs in a freezer bag in the freezer for up to 3 months.)

washington wine grapes

Washington wine grapes are different from other grapes even though they seem to be the same. The workhorse European-sourced wine grapes of the modern Northwest wineries *(Vitis vinifera)* are descended from grapes native to Middle Eastern and Mediterranean regions. The climate there is semiarid, and the grapevines there don't face particularly cold winters. South-central Washington, on the other hand, where 90 percent of the state's wine grapes are grown, is a world away in more than one respect. Unlike the Middle East (and Burgundy and Bordeaux in France), the Columbia Valley growing region faces winter temperatures well below 0°F. Grapevines can and sometimes do suffer serious winter damage, especially if a warm spell precedes a hard freeze. Also, the Columbia Valley's latitude is farther north than the latitude of its wine grapes' cousins in California, so the vines have fewer hours of daylight in fall, and more in summer. These kinds of variances in environment help make one wine different from another that is made from the same grapes, but ones that were grown around the bend in the road, or in another state, or across the Atlantic Ocean.

In other words, Washington wine makers—who love a challenge or they wouldn't be wine makers—are working with grapes from a more variable climate than their counterparts in California or France. Their raw material is at more risk, thanks to Mother Nature. More than twenty-five years of *Vitis vinifera* growing experience is paying off, however. Nearly seventeen thousand acres are now planted with grapevines in Washington, up from only about four hundred acres in the early 1970s. Washington State University's research extension center in Prosser—right in the heart of the Columbia Valley region—is constantly developing better ways to grow grapevines. The center's Dr. Sara Spayd, Food Scientist and Enologist, uses a short phrase to describe Washington-grown *Vitis vinifera* grapes: *"Vive la différence!"*

sauvignon blanc

asparagus, goat cheese,
and walnut salad

Asparagus is one of the kings of the vegetable world and, sadly, of shorter season and higher price than many of its produce market companions. Washington's Yakima Valley is an important region for asparagus production in the Northwest. Asparagus lovers can quibble about whether pencil-thin or thumb-thick stalks are better, but none will dispute the royalty of the vegetable. During its brief season, we serve it often, sometimes hot, other times cold. You might sip a Sauvignon Blanc, a wine that can be vegetal or fruity, with this salad. Either style would complement the flavors.

2 pounds asparagus, cut into 5- to 6-inch lengths, tips rinsed
Coarse salt

DRESSING

½ cup extra virgin olive oil
2 tablespoons freshly squeezed lemon juice
½ teaspoon coarse salt
Freshly ground black pepper to taste
⅓ cup minced chives

1 large head leaf lettuce, or 8 to 10 cups mixed salad greens
Freshly ground black pepper

6 ounces soft goat cheese, crumbled

1 cup walnut pieces, roasted (see page 69)

IF ASPARAGUS IS THICK, peel it from just under the tips to the bases using a vegetable peeler. Cook asparagus in boiling salted water until crisp-tender, 4 to 5 minutes for thick stalks. Drain, plunge into cold water for 5 minutes, drain again, and dry. Whisk together the dressing ingredients and place in a 9 x 13-inch glass baking dish. Add the asparagus and toss with your fingers to coat. Cover and refrigerate for 1 hour.

REMOVE THE ASPARAGUS TO A PLATE. Tear the salad greens into large bite-size pieces and put in a large mixing bowl. Add dressing from the baking dish, sprinkle with salt and pepper to taste, and toss. Arrange the greens on 4 salad plates. Top with asparagus, crumbled cheese, and walnuts.

Serves 4

gruyère cheese
and green bean salad

The late food writer James Beard, who was born and raised in Oregon, included a salad made with gruyère cheese in his book Theory and Practice of Good Cooking. We enjoyed it, but our instinct told us that we might prefer it made with a little less cheese and a few more incidental ingredients. In our gruyère salad, the intense flavor of the cheese is balanced by green beans, toasted almonds, and black olives. The crisp, citrus-like flavors often found in Sauvignon Blanc wines cut the richness of the cheese, we think, and pair off handsomely against the beans and almonds.

Barnard Griffin Winery, in the Columbia Valley near Richland, Washington, makes (among other wines) white wines that are mostly barrel-fermented, which results in wines with more intense oak notes. We enjoyed a Barnard Griffin Fume Blanc with this cheese salad.

8 ounces green beans, trimmed

½ cup sliced almonds, roasted (see page 104)

8 ounces gruyère cheese, shredded

½ cup jumbo ripe olives, sliced

½ cup (lightly packed) parsley leaves, chopped

DRESSING

½ cup extra virgin olive oil

2 tablespoons champagne vinegar or white wine vinegar

1 teaspoon Dijon mustard

1 large shallot, halved and thinly sliced

Coarse salt

Freshly ground black pepper

1 head red leaf or green leaf lettuce

4 medium tomatoes, each cut into 8 wedges

STEAM THE BEANS or boil them in salted water until tender. They may be crisp-tender after 5 to 7 minutes. Sometimes beans will need much longer to cook and will lose their bright green color, regardless of how good they looked when purchased. Try one every couple of minutes until they are tender enough to suit you. Drain the beans, and plunge them into ice water for 5 minutes. Drain again, and pat the beans dry. Toss together the almonds, beans, cheese, olives, and parsley. In a small bowl or jar, whisk together dressing ingredients and pour over the bean mixture. Toss thoroughly. Taste for seasoning, adding salt or pepper to taste. Arrange the lettuce leaves on 4 plates, top with the bean mixture, and arrange tomato wedges as a border. Serve cold or at cool room temperature.

Serves 4

asparagus with poached eggs and shaved parmesan

This simple dish depends on three ingredients for its quality: asparagus, eggs, and imported parmesan cheese. The asparagus might well come from the Yakima Valley, which produces lots of it on land very near the vineyards that supply Washington's wineries with grapes. The glass of Sauvignon Blanc that will go so well with the dish could come from Shafer Vineyard Cellars, near Forest Grove, Oregon, in the northern Willamette Valley hills. Round out the dish by serving it with a rustic loaf of crusty bread.

2 pounds asparagus, cut into 5- to 6-inch lengths, tips rinsed

Coarse salt

1 tablespoon extra virgin olive oil

Freshly ground black pepper

8 large eggs

1 cup (lightly packed) parsley leaves, chopped

1 small piece imported parmesan, at room temperature, for shavings

IF THE ASPARAGUS STALKS ARE THICK, peel them from just under the tip to the base using a vegetable peeler. Cook the asparagus in boiling salted water until just crisp-tender, 4 to 5 minutes for thick stalks. Drain, toss with olive oil and salt and pepper to taste, divide among 4 dinner plates, and keep warm.

BRING ABOUT 1½ INCHES OF WATER TO A SIMMER in a 12-inch skillet or sauté pan over medium-high heat. Reduce the heat to a simmer and crack one egg at a time into a small ramekin or bowl and slide the egg gently into the simmering water. Repeat until all eggs are in water. Cook until the whites are just set. Remove them with a slotted spoon in the same order they went into the pan and place two on top of each asparagus portion; dab with a paper towel to soak up any visible water. Sprinkle with parsley. Pull a cheese planer across the top of the piece of parmesan to produce wide shavings. Or use a vegetable peeler on a narrower edge of cheese to get thinner shavings. Arrange several shavings around each plate. Serve at once.

Serves 4

scallop and broccoli salad
with orange vinaigrette

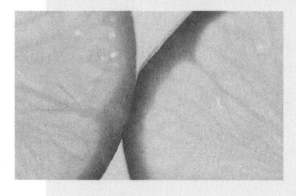

Scallops are a Northwest favorite, both in restaurants and at home. Sea scallops should be cooked until they are opaque on the outside and still slightly translucent in the center. At that point, they will yield gently to the tooth, with no suggestion of the rubberiness they exhibit when overcooked. Enjoy this salad with a Northwest Sauvignon Blanc, such as an Autumn Wind. Tom and Wendy Kreutner founded this Yamhill County, Oregon winery in the mid 1980s, and focus on affordable wines made with care.

DRESSING

2 oranges

¾ cup extra virgin olive oil

½ teaspoon coarse salt

Freshly ground black pepper

1 pound sea scallops

10 to 12 ounces broccoli florets (about 5 cups)

4 very thin slices of red onion

24 tiny cherry tomatoes or 12 larger cherry tomatoes

About 2 cups torn lettuce pieces, from inner leaves

1 cup (lightly packed) parsley leaves, very coarsely chopped

½ cup (lightly packed) basil leaves, very coarsely chopped

2 heads butter lettuce, or 1 large head leaf lettuce

1 firm-ripe avocado, halved, pitted, peeled and thinly sliced
(see page 121)

Freshly ground black pepper

GRATE THE ZEST OF THE ORANGES, then squeeze them. Bring ⅔ cup of the orange juice to a boil in a 1-quart non-reactive saucepan over medium heat and cook until it has reduced to ⅓ cup. Remove the pan from the heat, and whisk in the orange zest, olive oil, salt, and pepper to taste.

STEAM THE SCALLOPS until opaque outside, but a little translucent in the center, about 3 minutes. Set aside to cool. Line 4 dinner plates with large lettuce leaves, and tear remaining lettuce in pieces. Trim broccoli florets to between the size of a quarter and a fifty-cent piece. Steam until crisp-tender, about 4 minutes. Set aside to cool. Separate the onion slices into individual rings and put in a large mixing bowl. Add the scallops, broccoli, tomatoes (cut them in half if they are not the tiny kind), lettuce pieces, parsley, and basil. Whisk dressing ingredients again and add all but ¼ cup to salad. Add pepper to taste and toss well. Spread the salad on top of the lettuce-lined plates. Arrange avocado slices over the salad, drizzle with the remaining dressing, and serve.

Serves 4

sautéed trout in lemon butter

West of the Cascade Mountains most of the glory in fish markets goes to ocean varieties of fish and shellfish. Luckily, one common freshwater inclusion is rainbow trout. They're farm-raised, of course, usually in Idaho, and nearly always white-fleshed rather than having the pink or orange flesh of their wild relatives. Their flavor is quite mild, allowing gentle seasoning. This classic butter and lemon sauce adds a little richness and a little acidity to the fish. The fish are nice served with simple steamed or boiled baby potatoes and a green vegetable, and a Sauvignon Blanc.

One of the most unusual Sauvignon Blanc wineries in the Northwest is Cavatappi Winery, built in the basement of Cafe Juanita near Kirkland, Washington. There Peter Dow, cafe owner and wine maker, crafts and sells a very respected Sauvignon Blanc whose grapes come from Sagemoor Vineyard, on the banks of the Columbia River north of Pasco.

¼ cup all-purpose flour for dredging

4 rainbow trout, preferably boneless

2 tablespoons unsalted butter

SAUCE

6 tablespoons (¾ stick) unsalted butter

½ cup minced shallot or red onion

¼ cup fresh lemon juice

¼ teaspoon coarse salt

Freshly ground black pepper

½ cup (lightly packed) parsley leaves, minced

PUT THE FLOUR IN A DRY PLASTIC BAG. Shake the trout, one at a time, in the bag, holding the bag closed, to coat the fish with the flour. Melt 2 tablespoons butter in a 12-inch or larger skillet, preferably nonstick. When the pan is hot add the fish, all at once if they fit, or cook two at a time if necessary. Brown on one side, about 4 minutes, then carefully turn using 2 spatulas. Brown on second side, about 4 minutes more. Transfer fish to 4 warmed dinner plates and keep warm. Pour off the cooking butter.

TO MAKE THE SAUCE, melt 6 tablespoons butter in the pan and add the minced shallot. Cook, stirring, for about 1 minute. Stir in the lemon juice, salt, pepper to taste, and parsley. Spoon equally over the fish and serve.

Serves 4

shrimp, sage, and
butternut squash frittata

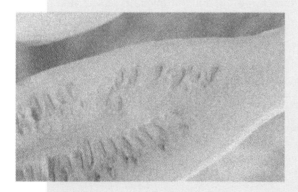

A frittata, a kind of dry omelet of Italian origin, is made by pouring beaten eggs into a hot pan that already contains the filling. When the eggs have partially cooked, the frittata is run under a broiler to lightly brown and puff the top. Cooked vegetables, meat, fish, or poultry can all go into a frittata. In this case, pieces of shrimp mingle with fresh sage leaves and sweet butternut squash cubes to produce a frittata that has substance but is not heavy. The fresh sage in this frittata could be appealing with a Sauvignon Blanc, a distinctly aromatic wine. One of the producers of Sauvignon Blanc is Hogue Cellars, the second-largest family-owned winery in the Northwest. Its reputation for quality is longstanding, and a visit to its tasting room in Prosser, Washington, should be on your agenda when you are in the Yakima Valley.

1 pound butternut squash, peeled, seeded, and cut into ½-inch dice

8 ounces rock shrimp (sold peeled and deveined)

2 tablespoons unsalted butter

½ cup finely chopped onion

About 18 large fresh sage leaves, chopped

6 large eggs

¼ teaspoon hot pepper sauce

¼ teaspoon coarse salt

½ teaspoon freshly ground black pepper

PUT THE SQUASH in a 10-inch nonstick ovenproof skillet. Add ⅓ cup of water and bring to a boil over medium heat. Reduce the heat and simmer, covered, until squash is almost tender, about 8 minutes. Add the shrimp and steam 2 minutes more. Drain immediately in a colander.

PREHEAT THE BROILER.

RETURN THE PAN TO THE HEAT and melt the butter in it. Add the onion and sage and sauté for 2 minutes. Return the squash and shrimp to the pan, spreading them out evenly. Beat the eggs with the hot pepper sauce, salt, and pepper. Pour over the squash and shrimp. Cook slowly over medium-low to medium heat without stirring, until the sides appear to be puffing up somewhat, but the top is still a bit jiggly, about 8 minutes. Place under the broiler until the top is lightly browned and egg mixture just barely set, about 2 minutes. Cut into 4 wedges and serve at once. Frittatas are also good served at room temperature.

Serves 4

rosemary-sage biscotti

If you grow your own herbs or live near a market that sells fresh herbs, try these savory biscotti with your favorite Sauvignon Blanc. Arbor Crest Winery, near Spokane, Washington, produces a highly regarded Sauvignon Blanc, as well as an assortment of other wines.

6 tablespoons olive oil

3 large eggs

⅛ teaspoon hot pepper sauce

2¼ cups bleached all-purpose flour

¼ cup cornmeal

2½ teaspoons baking powder

1 tablespoon sugar

¾ teaspoon salt

¼ teaspoon freshly ground black pepper

2 tablespoons chopped rosemary leaves

2 tablespoons chopped sage leaves

PREHEAT THE OVEN TO 350°F. Line a baking sheet with parchment paper or aluminum foil.

COMBINE THE OLIVE OIL, eggs, and hot pepper sauce in a large mixing bowl or the bowl of an electric mixer and beat until well mixed. In a medium bowl, combine the flour, cornmeal, baking powder, sugar, salt, pepper, rosemary, and sage. Whisk together thoroughly. Add the egg mixture and beat just until the dough comes together.

TURN OUT THE DOUGH onto a work surface and form into 2 log-shape pieces about 7 inches long. Place the shaped dough on the baking sheet. Bake for 20 minutes. Remove from the oven and allow to cool for 5 minutes. Use a sharp serrated knife to cut the dough into approximately ½-inch slices. Lay the slices out flat on the baking sheet and return to the oven for 15 minutes. Turn and bake for 15 minutes more. Cool on a rack.

Makes about 30 biscotti

foods to pair with

riesling

Oysters on the Half Shell with Asian Dipping Sauce
Dungeness Crab Cakes with Spicy Corn Relish
Chicken Soup with Green Curry and Coconut Milk
Vietnamese-Style Noodle Bowl with Pork
Roast Turkey Breast with Apricot-Nut Dressing
Chicken in Spicy Asian Peanut Sauce
Turkey Sandwiches with Cranberries and Baked Onions

the riesling grape

The Riesling (REES-ling) grape produces some of the most food-friendly wines in the Northwest. Both the cool moistness of western Oregon and the hot days–cool nights of the irrigated Columbia Valley result in grapes with enough acid to balance Riesling's inherent roundness. Riesling has good mouth feel even at a low alcohol level. It is the classic grape of Germany, and in the Northwest the wine is made in three distinct styles—dry, off-dry, and sweet.

Like Sémillon and Gewurztraminer, Riesling is subject to botrytis, or noble rot, which shrivels and dehydrates the grapes on the vine. If that happens the resulting wines are sweet as a result of the concentrated sugars in the grapes. Riesling grapes are also sometimes caught in a freeze during harvest, and made into so-called ice wine, a sweet and intensely flavored dessert wine.

High-quality Rieslings are made all over the Northwest, including Idaho. Those made in the hot, dry Columbia Valley tend to be mouth-filling versions with definite apricot or peach aromas, while those from cooler climates are typically lighter and more floral. Many consumers are under the impression that all Rieslings are either sweet or off-dry, but the fact is that many wineries produce quite dry, crisp wines which make a fine addition to the dinner table. Check to see if the label lists the residual sugar content; you want that number to be 1 percent or less if you are seeking a dry wine. Foods that are highly spiced or include Asian seasonings usually pair well with Riesling, as do cold roast meats, crab, and lobster, among other dishes.

Among the many Riesling makers are the giants Chateau Ste. Michelle and Columbia Winery, as well as Hogue Cellars, Washington's largest family-owned winery. Also in the game are Idaho's Ste. Chapelle Winery, and Oregon's Elk Cove Vineyards and Edgefield Winery.

Serve lightly chilled, about 50°F, or 40° to 45°F for dessert Rieslings.

oysters on the half shell
with asian dipping sauce

Even a dry Riesling has a roundness of flavor that provides a nice
foil for spicy foods. Here is a dipping sauce for oysters with just a
little spicy bite, which will take
you all of about three minutes to
stir together. It goes well with any of the many types of oysters available in
the Northwest, from Pacific oysters such as Quilcene and Hamma Hamma,
raised in southern Puget Sound, to European flats such as those from Westcott Bay in the San Juan Islands. Interestingly enough, the only oyster that is
native to the Northwest is the tiny Olympia, highly prized for its coppery
taste and diminutive size. Unfortunately, it was harvested nearly to extinc-
tion by the end of the nineteenth century. A comeback is occurring, though
Olympias are still not as easy to purchase as other oysters.

Many Northwest wineries make Riesling, among them Edgefield Winery, located on the grounds of the old Multnomah County Poor Farm in
Troutdale, Oregon, on the Columbia River Gorge. Part of the McMenamin
microbrewery empire, Edgefield offers a restaurant, pub, bed-and-breakfast
rooms, a theater, conference center, and winery, all on the same grounds.

SAUCE

1 quarter-size slice unpeeled ginger, minced

3 small scallions, white parts only, minced

3 tablespoons dry white wine

1 teaspoon unseasoned rice vinegar

¼ teaspoon Asian hot chili paste or sauce

riesling

12 to 16 oysters, shucked

STIR ALL THE SAUCE INGREDIENTS TOGETHER. Place in a small bowl in the middle of a platter. Arrange oysters on the half shell around the sauce and serve.

NOTE: Persons with compromised immune systems should never eat raw oysters.

Serves 4

cooking with asian ingredients

LEMONGRASS

Very light green stalks, about a foot long. Lemongrass has an appealing citrusy flavor. Strip away the tough outer layer, cut into pieces if long, and smash with the butt of a knife handle. Since the stalks are rather woody in texture, they are used for flavoring, then usually removed.

FISH SAUCE

Made from fermented, salted anchovies. Fish sauce packs a salty pungency that will probably not smell good to you, but judicious use adds depth of flavor.

RICE STICKS

Dried noodles made from rice flour, which should be listed on the label. The exact Asian name, as well as length and thickness, varies from one manufacturer to another. For our recipes, look for flat noodles about the size of linguine. Soak them for 15 minutes in hot water, then add to stir-frys or soups 1 or 2 minutes before the dish is finished cooking.

dungeness crab cakes
with spicy corn relish

Crab of one variety or another is prized along all the coastal regions of the United States. In the Pacific Northwest, Dungeness is the variety most often brought to market, and Dungeness crab cakes are among the most popular restaurant menu items. These cakes are simple, lightly seasoned, and rely mostly on the sweetness of the crabmeat for their appeal. Crabmeat is usually sold by the pound or in prepackaged containers at markets where crab is sold.

Riesling grapes grown in the Northwest produce wines that are dry, off-dry, or late-harvest sweet, depending on the whims of the wine maker and Mother Nature. Increasingly popular are Rieslings at the dry end of the scale. We find them appealing, and suggest you try one with your crab cakes, perhaps Idaho's Ste. Chapelle Dry Johannisberg Riesling.

SPICY CORN RELISH

2 cups frozen petite corn kernels, thawed in a single layer on
    paper towels

½ red bell pepper, cut into ¼-inch dice

¼ cup diced (¼ inch) onion

1 firm-ripe small avocado, halved, pitted, and cut in ¼-inch dice
    (see page 121)

1 jalapeño, seeded, and cut into tiny dice

1 medium tomato, seeded, and cut in ¼-inch dice

½ cup (lightly packed) cilantro leaves, chopped

½ teaspoon coarse salt

Freshly ground black pepper

½ cup mayonnaise

Clea~

1 pound crabmeat, bits of shell and cartilage removed, then shredded
   or coarsely chopped

8 scallions, halved lengthwise, and sliced crosswise very thinly

2 cups (lightly packed) parsley leaves, chopped

½ teaspoon coarse salt

Freshly ground black pepper

¼ cup mayonnaise

¼ teaspoon hot pepper sauce

3 egg whites

1 cup cracker meal or dry bread crumbs, for coating

Olive oil, for sautéing

TO MAKE THE SPICY CORN RELISH: Combine the corn, red pepper, onion, avocado, jalapeño, tomato, and cilantro in a medium mixing bowl. Sprinkle with the salt and pepper to taste, and toss thoroughly. Add mayonnaise, and toss again to mix well. Refrigerate until ready to serve.

TO MAKE THE CRAB CAKES: Combine the crabmeat, scallions, parsley, salt, and pepper to taste in a large mixing bowl and toss to blend. Add the mayonnaise and hot pepper sauce and mix again. In a medium mixing bowl, beat the egg whites until they hold soft peaks but are not stiff. Use a rubber spatula to fold them into the crab mixture. Wet your hands and form 8 patties ½ to ¾ inch thick. Spread the cracker meal on a plate or in a shallow bowl. Press each crab cake into the crumbs, coating all sides. Heat ¼ cup olive oil in a 12-inch skillet or sauté pan over medium heat. Sauté the cakes until they are golden brown on each side, about 4 minutes per side, adding more oil when turning them.

Spoon some corn relish on each of 4 plates, top with 2 crab cakes, and serve.

Serves 4

riesling

chicken soup with green curry and coconut milk

Curries can star with a spicy Gewürztraminer, as well as with a crisp, dry Riesling. Riesling pairs off well against chilies, coconut milk, lemongrass, and lime. Accompanying this Thai-style soup with a Chateau Ste. Michelle 1996 Columbia Valley Dry Riesling was a marriage made in heaven. Better supermarkets usually sell an assortment of Thai-style seasonings and at least one brand of unsweetened coconut milk; if you live near an Asian market your selection will be even wider.

2 cans (14½ ounces each) low-sodium chicken broth

1 stalk lemongrass

1½ chicken breasts, skinless and boneless (¾ to 1 pound)

1 can (13½ ounces) unsweetened coconut milk

2 tablespoons fresh lime juice

2 teaspoons bottled green curry paste

2 tablespoons fish sauce

2 medium leeks, white part only, split, rinsed between layers, and cut crosswise in ¼-inch slices

1 red bell pepper, cut into ½-inch dice

1 pound red or white potatoes, peeled, and cut into ½-inch dice

2 cups frozen petite peas

1 cup (lightly packed) basil leaves, shredded

STRIP AWAY THE TOUGH OUTER LAYER of the lemongrass, then cut it into 3-inch lengths and smash the pieces with the butt of a knife handle. Set aside.

COMBINE THE CHICKEN BROTH, 1 can of water, and the lemongrass in a 3-quart or larger saucepan or pot and bring to a boil over medium-high heat. Slide the chicken pieces into the liquid. Regulate the heat so that the liquid simmers but does not boil. Cook until an instant-read thermometer inserted on an angle into the center of a breast registers 150°F, or until juices run clear when meat is pricked with a sharp knife, about 9 minutes. Remove from broth and set aside.

STIR THE COCONUT MILK, lime juice, curry paste, and fish sauce into the broth. Add the leeks and red pepper, and simmer 5 minutes, covered. Add the potatoes and simmer, covered, until they are just barely tender, about 5 minutes. Slice the chicken lengthwise in half, then crosswise into ½-inch slices. Taste broth for salt, adding more if necessary. Use tongs to remove the lemongrass pieces. Add sliced chicken and peas and simmer for 1 minute. Ladle into 4 warmed soup bowls and top with the basil. Serve at once.

Serves 4

vietnamese-style noodle bowl with pork

Among the diverse ethnic populations in the Northwest are the Vietnamese. In urban areas their Pho (pronounced fah*) restaurants have become meccas for noodle lovers. Pho parlors are busy because they offer lots of tasty food for not a lot of money, serving forth huge bowls of piping hot broth teeming with everything from shrimp to meatballs. Raw vegetables are often served on the side, to add to the noodle bowl as desired. Our bowl of noodles contains several ingredients that may be unusual to many cooks but are now often found in better markets. The flavors are bright, fresh, and mildly spicy, well matched with dry or off-dry Riesling's refreshing floral or fruity flavors. Argyle Winery, in Dundee, Oregon, is noted for its sparkling wines in particular, but also makes an excellent dry Riesling.*

1 stalk lemongrass

¾ pound ground pork

1 tablespoon vegetable oil

4 scallions, white and light green parts minced, green tops
   thinly sliced

2 large cloves garlic, minced

4 quarter-size slices unpeeled ginger, minced

2 cups water

4 cups chicken stock or low-sodium canned broth

¼ cup fresh lime juice

¼ cup fish sauce

1 teaspoon Asian hot chili paste or sauce

Coarse salt

Freshly ground black pepper

1 cup bean sprouts

4 medium tomatoes, cut into 8 wedges each

½ cup (lightly packed) cilantro leaves, chopped

8 ounces rice stick noodles, soaked in hot water for 15 minutes

STRIP AWAY THE TOUGH OUTER LAYER of the lemongrass, then cut it into 3-inch lengths and smash the pieces with the butt of a knife handle. Set aside.

SAUTÉ THE PORK in a 4-quart or larger saucepan over medium heat, breaking up lumps and scraping the bottom of the pan, until the pork is lightly browned. Use a slotted spoon to transfer the pork to a plate and pour off accumulated fat. Return the pan to the heat, add the oil, minced scallions, garlic, and ginger and sizzle for 1 minute, without burning the garlic. Add 2 cups water, the stock, and the lemongrass, and bring to a boil. Reduce the heat and simmer, covered, for 15 minutes. Use tongs to remove the lemongrass pieces. Add the lime juice, fish sauce, and hot chili paste or sauce. Taste for salt and pepper. Add cooked pork.

DIVIDE THE SLICED SCALLION TOPS, bean sprouts, tomatoes, and cilantro among 4 large soup or pasta bowls. Drain the rice sticks and stir into the soup. Cook for about 1 minute, then ladle soup into the prepared bowls. Use a spaghetti fork or pasta tongs to help divide the noodles.

Serves 4

riesling

roast turkey breast with apricot-nut dressing

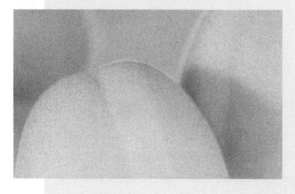

In this recipe the breast of turkey is roasted while sitting directly on the dressing, so that turkey juices drip into the dressing and add their own extra flavor. The apricots in the dressing will highlight the apricot aroma in many fuller-style Northwest Rieslings. The Columbia Valley's weather tends to result in wines with full, ripe flavor, and white wines which often have peach and apricot notes.

2 cups dried apricots

4 cups bread cubes (½ inch) cut from baguette-style bread

4 cups bread cubes (½ inch) cut from multigrain or whole wheat bread

4 tablespoons (½ stick) unsalted butter

1 medium onion, finely chopped

4 ribs celery, peeled and cut into ¼-inch slices

½ teaspoon dry mustard

2 cups walnut pieces, roasted (see page 69)

1 cup (firmly packed) oregano leaves, chopped

2 cups (lightly packed) parsley leaves, chopped

2 large eggs, lightly beaten

1¾ cups chicken stock or low-sodium canned broth

1 teaspoon coarse salt

Freshly ground black pepper

1 turkey breast roast (about 6 pounds), thawed if frozen

PREHEAT THE OVEN TO 350°F.

SOAK THE DRIED APRICOTS in boiling water to cover for 30 minutes. Drain and chop them. Set aside.

SPREAD THE BREAD CUBES on a large baking sheet and dry them out in the oven, until they are quite firm on the outside, but not browned, about 15 minutes. Melt the butter in a 10 to 12-inch frypan over medium heat. Add the onion and celery and sauté until soft but not brown, about 5 minutes. Stir in the mustard. Put the bread cubes, walnuts, and apricots in a very large mixing bowl. Add the onion-celery mixture, oregano, and parsley. Beat the eggs into the stock and add to the bowl. Add the salt and pepper to taste. Toss thoroughly. Spoon into a greased 9 x 13-inch baking pan. Place the turkey breast on top. Bake until the turkey is done, 160°F when measured with an instant-read thermometer, about 2 hours.

Serves 8

chicken in spicy asian peanut sauce

This is our variation on a classic Chinese dish variously known as Pang Pang Chicken or Bang Bang Chicken. The chicken-cooking technique is classic Asian; it produces amazing results and leaves you free to do something else while the bird cooks. The cooked chicken is arranged on a bed of translucent, very thin noodles often known as cellophane noodles. Made of mung bean starch, cellophane noodles are also called bean threads and slippery noodles, and have a milky white appearance until they are soaked. Since they have practically no taste they absorb the flavors of the other ingredients in a dish, like the spicy peanut sauce in this one. Rieslings go awfully well with spicy foods.

Montinore Vineyards, near Forest Grove, Oregon, makes Rieslings suitable for drinking with the main course, and others for after-dinner appreciation. The vineyards went in on the property after the eruption of Mount St. Helens in 1980 dropped enough volcanic ash on the land to bankrupt the farmer then leasing the land.

2 quarter-size slices unpeeled ginger

2 whole scallions

1 whole chicken (about 3½ pounds)

SAUCE

6 large cloves garlic, minced

4 quarter-size slices unpeeled ginger, minced

½ cup creamy peanut butter, preferably a nonhomogenized, unsweetened, and unsalted variety, at room temperature

5 tablespoons soy sauce

2 tablespoons Chinese black vinegar or Worcestershire sauce

1 tablespoon hot chili oil or 1½ teaspoons Asian hot chili paste

2 tablespoons sugar

2 packages (1.75 ounces each) cellophane noodles, softened in a bowl of hot water for 30 minutes

1 tablespoon vegetable oil

1 tablespoon Asian sesame oil

4 scallions, thinly sliced on the diagonal

1 English cucumber, peeled, halved lengthwise, seeded, and cut into large matchstick-size pieces

½ cup (lightly packed) cilantro leaves, chopped

FILL A 10-QUART OR LARGER STOCKPOT to within 2½ inches of the top with hot water. Add the ginger and whole scallions, and bring to a boil, covered, over medium-high to high heat. Remove any giblets from the cavity of the bird. When the water is at a rolling boil, submerge the chicken in the water, wings down. Cover the pot, turn off the heat, and let stand for 1½ hours. Do not uncover the pot to peek—you will lose valuable heat. After 1½ hours, lift the bird from the water to a plate or baking dish, and allow to cool until it can be handled. Remove the skin, pull the chicken off the bones completely, and refrigerate the chicken for 30 minutes to firm it. Cut into large matchstick-size pieces. Chicken should be at cool room temperature when served.

TO MAKE THE SAUCE, place all the sauce ingredients in the work bowl of a food processor and blend. Or stir together in a medium bowl. Allow to rest for 1 hour or refrigerate for later use.

TEST TENDERNESS OF NOODLES. They should be slightly crunchy, not rubbery. If they are still not quite tender, drop them into boiling water for 1 or 2 minutes, then drain through a wire strainer. Shake off all moisture, and toss with the vegetable oil, sesame oil, and sliced scallions. Spread on a large serving plate. Arrange the cucumber around the outside, then mound the chicken in the center. Drizzle half of the sauce over the chicken and noodles and serve the remainder on the side. Garnish with cilantro.

Serves 4

top ten idaho wine grapes

Although Idaho's wine industry is small, some very good wines are made by the state's eighteen wineries, which harvest grapes from about six hundred and fifty acres. Here are the top ten wine grapes of Idaho, in order of acres planted:

Riesling

Chardonnay

Merlot

Cabernet Sauvignon

Pinot Noir

Sauvignon Blanc

Gewürztraminer

Chenin Blanc

Cabernet Franc

Lemberger

Riesling and Chardonnay combined make up about 70 percent of Idaho's plantings.

turkey sandwiches with cranberries and baked onions

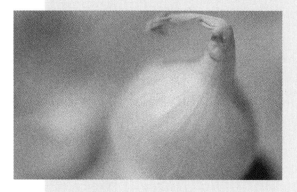

The roundness and fruitiness of dry Riesling wine are very appealing with this kind of combination. The richness of the cream cheese mixed with sweet-tart cranberries and the bite of a little horseradish set the stage for good eating and drinking. The sandwich is not served hot, but the onions are baked in advance and can be used warm if desired. The particularly sweet onions from Washington's Walla Walla region would be a very good choice.

1 large unpeeled onion, halved crosswise, root and top ends left on

1 tablespoon vegetable oil

4 ounces tub-style regular cream cheese

¼ cup minced chives

8 slices multi-seed or multigrain bread

24 very thin slices peeled cucumber

½ cup whole cranberry sauce, homemade or canned

12 to 16 ounces sliced turkey, light or dark meat, or a combination

4 lettuce leaves

4 tablespoons cream-style horseradish sauce

PREHEAT THE OVEN TO 400°F. Line a baking pan with foil or use a nonstick pan.

MAKE 2 CROSS-SHAPED CUTS in the root and top ends of the onion to vent steam in the oven. Dry the cut ends with a paper towel, then rub with the oil. Place onions, flat side down, on the pan. Bake onions for 30 minutes. Remove from oven and allow to cool until they can be handled.

BLEND THE CREAM CHEESE with the chives using a rubber spatula or fork. Spread on 4 slices of the bread. Top each slice with 6 slices of cucumber, 2 tablespoons cranberry sauce, and ¼ of the turkey.

SQUEEZE THE COOKED ONION out of the peel and discard peel. Mash or coarsely chop and spread on top of the turkey. Top with a lettuce leaf. Spread horseradish sauce on remaining slices of bread and close the sandwiches. Serve.

Serves 4

pacific rim flavors

For well over one hundred years, the Northwest has been home to people whose roots are somewhere on the other side of the Pacific Ocean. The immigrants arriving from such countries as China, Japan, Korea, the Philippines, Vietnam, Laos, Cambodia, and Thailand have brought with them a craving for the foods of their homelands. The resulting proliferation of Asian food markets has given many Northwesterners the opportunity to easily obtain the ingredients necessary to create a classic Pad Thai plate of noodles, to buy a special soy sauce for a Chinese "red cooked" braised beef, to purchase Philippine lumpia wrappers for a crisp-fried spring roll, and to stock up on stalks of lemongrass for a Vietnamese Pho bowl.

A large, well-stocked Asian market carries dried mushrooms of several kinds, dried fish and shrimp, fresh produce both common and uncommon, tofu of several consistencies, pungent bottled fish sauces, sake and mirin wines, seasoned and unseasoned rice vinegars—the list of dried, fresh, bottled, and canned goods available from Pacific Rim countries is nearly endless. The best of these stores may also carry strikingly fresh (and often live) whole fish, shellfish, and crustaceans. Highest quality sashimi-grade cuts of tuna, salmon, and other fish can be had for those willing to pay the price.

Cooking and eating opportunities in the Northwest have been dramatically expanded by Asian influences. Asian dishes are now common on the menus of many upscale Northwest restaurants, and it is not unusual to find an offering like steamed fish in a lightly curried broth on the same page with a hamburger and house-made french fries. Because Asian foods vary tremendously in flavor intensity, in spiciness, and in body, no one wine suits every Asian meal. But one thing is certain: Northwesterners are lucky to be able to choose from many quality Gewürztraminers and Rieslings, because those wines pair so well with so many Asian foods.

foods to pair with

gewürztraminer

Spaghettini with Spicy Scallops
Lobster with Caramelized Walla Walla Onions
Spicy Rice Noodle Bowl with Beef and Spinach
Garlic-Sesame Ahi over Sesame Noodles
Curried Chicken in Lettuce Leaves
Pizza with Thai-Style Shrimp and Peanut Topping

the gewürztraminer grape

Gewürztraminer (ge-VURTZ-tra-meener) grapes are made into wine by a huge list of Northwest wineries, because the wine-buying public likes the result of their efforts. A specialty of the Alsace region of France and in Germany, Gewürztraminer wines are famous for their spiciness, and their packed-full-of-fruit flavors. It isn't surprising, then, that they are often served with Asian foods to match with the spiciness that is often present in them.

Gewürztraminer is made in three distinct styles—dry, off-dry, and late harvest. Both dry and off-dry make excellent dinner wines. People favoring dry wines are often surprised at how well an off-dry wine can accompany a spicy meal. One of the Gewürztraminer dessert wines is so-called ice wine, made from grapes that are pressed while still partially frozen as the result of an early frost. Much of the water is tied up in ice crystals, so the juice that runs from the press is super concentrated and makes marvelously intense sweet wine. It is unique but expensive. Gewürztraminer can also become a dessert wine when the grapes are attacked by the botrytis mold, which shrivels them and concentrates the sugar. In either event, the wine-maker's skill can turn what looks like disaster into liquid gold.

Flavor components in Gewürztraminer include ginger, cinnamon, nutmeg, cardamom, honey, grapefruit, and a flavor note not thought of by many Westerners—litchi. Litchi, once experienced in a wine, seems to show up with regularity in wines not usually regarded as spicy by many consumers, such as Chardonnay.

One of the famous vineyards in the Northwest is Kiona Vineyards and Winery, on Red Mountain in Benton City, Washington. The Red Mountain growing area has produced so many memorable wines, both red and white, that it may well be a legally recognized growing region before long. Kiona produces an excellent late harvest Gewürztraminer.

Serve dry and off-dry Gewürztraminer slightly chilled, about 50°F, sweet wines a little cooler, 40° to 45°F.

spaghettini with spicy scallops

Sea scallops are large enough to make an impression on the plate, even in concert with pasta. Their creamy flavor works well with several white wines, but the spicy character of this dish suggests a Gewürztraminer. Umpqua, Oregon, near the world-famous trout fishing river of the same name, is the home of Henry Estate Winery, whose 1996 Gewürztraminer we savored with this meal.

Coarse salt

1½ pounds sea scallops

2 tablespoons unsalted butter

2 large onions, coarsely chopped or diced

2 cloves garlic, minced

4 jalapeños, halved, seeded, and thinly sliced

2 bottles (7 or 8 ounces each) clam juice

2 cups whipping cream

1 pound spaghettini or vermicelli

2 tablespoons vegetable oil

Freshly ground black pepper

1 cup (lightly packed) parsley leaves, chopped

8 medium tomatoes, peeled, seeded, and diced

BRING 6 QUARTS WATER TO A BOIL in a large pot over high heat. Add 1 tablespoon salt, reduce to a simmer, and cover. Slice the scallops into coin shapes about ¼ inch thick. Set aside.

gewürztraminer

MELT THE BUTTER in a 12-inch sauté pan over medium heat. Add the onions, garlic, and jalapeños. Sauté until the vegetables are soft but not browned, 5 to 10 minutes. Add the clam juice and cream. Bring to a boil, reduce to a simmer, cover, and cook for 10 minutes.

RETURN THE PASTA WATER TO A BOIL, add the spaghettini, and cook until al dente. Drain, return to the pan, and toss with the vegetable oil. Divide among 4 soup plates or pasta bowls, and keep warm.

TASTE THE SAUCE FOR SALT, add pepper to taste, and the parsley. About 2 minutes before serving add the tomatoes and scallops. When the scallops are opaque on the outside and slightly translucent in the middle, ladle the sauce over the noodles and serve.

Serves 4

lobster with caramelized
walla walla onions

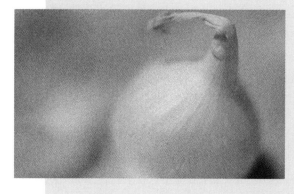

Because Gewürztraminer wine has what many people detect as spicy notes, it stands to reason that it would go well with a dish that includes some spice, such as this Indian-inspired dish meant to go over rice or pasta. Visit an Indian or Asian market to pick up garam masala, a dried spice mixture, or make your own (recipe follows). Serve with a dry Gewürztraminer, perhaps from Elk Cove Vineyards, near Gaston, south of Forest Grove, Oregon. Elk Cove Vineyards was first planted in 1976, making it one of the oldest Northwest wineries. It is a short distance from Kramer Vineyards, known for a variety of grape wines as well as for several berry wines.

4 lobster tails (about 7 ounces each)

2 large sweet onions

¼ cup vegetable oil

4 quarter-size slices unpeeled ginger, minced

4 teaspoons ground cumin

2 teaspoons ground mild paprika

2 teaspoons garam masala (see page 185)

Freshly ground black pepper

2 teaspoons hot pepper sauce

½ teaspoon coarse salt

1 cup crushed or diced tomatoes in purée

¾ cup plain yogurt

¾ cup whipping cream

1 cup (lightly packed) cilantro leaves, chopped

1 cup (lightly packed) parsley leaves, chopped

Cooked rice or noodles, for serving

THAW LOBSTER TAILS in the refrigerator for 24 hours, or place them in a medium bowl set in the sink and let cold water run slowly over the tails to thaw them in 1 to 2 hours. Use small kitchen scissors to snip lengthwise through the shell on top and the membrance on the bottom of each tail. Pull the shell away from the meat. Cut crosswise into ¼-inch slices.

SLICE ABOUT AN EIGHTH off one of the onions, mince the piece, and set aside. Coarsely chop the remaining piece of onion and the whole onion. Heat 2 table-spoons of the oil in a 12-inch skillet or sauté pan over medium heat. Add the chopped onion and cook, stirring occasionally, as the onion softens. When it begins to color stir more often. Moisture will evaporate and the onions will turn a very dark brown, almost black, 30 to 45 minutes, depending on the heat and how much water is in the onions. They should be dry and crispy. Set aside and prepare sauce.

HEAT THE REMAINING OIL in a 3-quart saucepan over medium heat. Add the minced onion and ginger and sauté until soft, about 3 minutes. Add the cumin, paprika, garam masala, black pepper, hot pepper sauce, and salt. Cook, stirring, for 2 minutes. Add tomatoes and bring to a boil. Reduce heat, cover, and simmer for 5 minutes. Add yogurt and whipping cream and return to a bare simmer. Stir in the cilantro, parsley, and lobster. Cook, without boiling, just until the lobster is opaque, 2 to 3 minutes. Spoon over rice or noodles, sprinkle with caramelized onion, and serve.

Serves 4

northwest food & wine

garam masala

You will find many uses for this aromatic spice blend.

2 teaspoons cardamom seeds

1 teaspoon whole cloves

2 teaspoons ground nutmeg

3 sticks cinnamon

1 tablespoon coriander seeds

PUT THE CARDAMOM, cloves, nutmeg, cinnamon, and coriander in a small heavy skillet and set the pan over medium heat. Toast the spices, shaking the pan now and then, until they color, 2 to 4 minutes. Transfer to a plate and let cool thoroughly. When cooled, grind to a powder in a spice grinder or with a mortar and pestle. (Garam masala may be stored in a tightly covered jar in a cool dark place for several months.)

Makes about ¼ cup

spicy rice noodle bowl
with beef and spinach

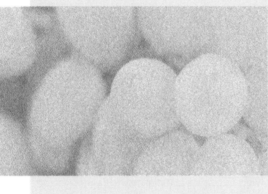

Southwest of Portland, on a hillside above the small town of Amity, Myron Redford makes wine at Amity Vineyards. Known as an experimenter, Redford is a wine maker willing to try new techniques and explore uncharted territory with grape varieties not common to the region. Amity Vineyards gets respect for wines made from Gamay Noir, Pinot Blanc, Pinot Noir, and Riesling. It also gets plenty of respect for its Gewürztraminers. Gewürztraminer is often made into delectable late-harvest dessert wines. The same grape, harvested earlier and fermented under different conditions, can make a sturdy and thoroughly dry white wine that complements spicy dishes, including those with red meat. An Amity Vineyards Dry Gewürztraminer would be a welcome accompaniment to this bowl of slippery rice noodles, with thinly sliced beef.

1 stalk lemongrass

¾ pound boneless rib-eye steak, preferably choice grade

4 cups chicken stock or low-sodium canned broth

2 sticks cinnamon

1 teaspoon anise seed

¾ pound rice stick noodles

2 tablespoons vegetable oil

4 cloves garlic, minced

6 scallions, white and light green parts minced, green tops
   thinly sliced

4 quarter-size slices unpeeled ginger, minced

1½ teaspoons Asian chili sauce or paste

3 tablespoons soy sauce

4 cups (lightly packed) spinach leaves, washed, dried, and cut into
   1-inch strips (about 5 ounces)

1 cup (lightly packed) cilantro leaves, chopped

STRIP AWAY THE TOUGH OUTER LAYER of the lemongrass, then cut into 3-inch lengths and smash the pieces with the butt of a knife handle. Set aside. Using a sharp chef's knife or boning knife, trim the fat and gristle from the steak. Set the trimmings aside. Cut the steak lengthwise into 3 strips, then cut each strip crosswise in 1-inch pieces. Give each piece a quarter turn and cut across the grain into slices about ⅛ inch thick. Brown the beef trimmings on all sides in a 3-quart or larger heavy saucepan over medium heat. Add the stock, lemongrass, cinnamon, and anise seed. Bring to a boil, reduce the heat and cook at a bare simmer, covered, for 30 minutes. Meanwhile, put rice stick noodles in a large bowl or pot, cover with hot water, and soak for 15 minutes.

POUR THE STOCK through a strainer into a fat separator, if available, or into a heatproof mixing bowl if not. Skim the fat from the surface of the bowl using a large serving spoon. Drain the noodles, arrange lengthwise on a cutting board, and cut them crosswise into thirds.

BRING 4 QUARTS OF WATER TO A BOIL in a large pot over high heat. In another large saucepan, wok, or Dutch oven, heat the vegetable oil over medium heat. Add the garlic, minced scallions, and ginger. Let sizzle for 30 to 60 seconds, taking care not to burn them. Add the strained and defatted stock, chili sauce, 4 cups water, and soy sauce. Bring to a simmer and cook for 5 minutes. Cook the noodles in the boiling water for 30 to 60 seconds. Drain the noodles and divide among 4 bowls. Arrange the spinach strips over the noodles. Stir the beef strips into the stock and cook for 15 seconds, then stir in the cilantro and scallion tops. Ladle over the noodles and serve at once.

Serves 4

gewürztraminer

garlic-sesame ahi
over sesame noodles

Northwest fish markets usually have glistening fresh tuna available from Pacific waters. Whether bigeye ahi, yellowfin ahi, or albacore, tuna is a fish to savor. This is an attractive plate of tuna slices laid over a noodle bed, the noodles themselves resting on light green romaine leaves. The tuna's spiciness is subtle, and it is wonderfully meaty in flavor. The tuna is served warm, sliced over cool, room-temperature noodles for an intentional temperature contrast. The chilies and garlic in the marinade make the dish Gewürztraminer-friendly, and Covey Run's Celilo Vineyard Gewürztraminer is a wine of good reputation. The grapes are grown across the Columbia River from Hood River, Oregon, near White Salmon, Washington.

Coarse salt

8 ounces dried spaghetti

½ cup vegetable oil

1 tablespoon Asian sesame oil

2 teaspoons unseasoned rice vinegar

3 scallions, thinly sliced on the diagonal

Freshly ground black pepper

MARINADE

1 tablespoon soy sauce

1 teaspoon unseasoned rice vinegar

1 teaspoon hot chili oil, preferably sesame oil based
1 clove garlic, minced

*

¾ pound ahi tuna steaks, about 1 inch thick

*

2 heads romaine
Coarse salt
Freshly ground black pepper
1 cup (lightly packed) parsley leaves, chopped

BRING 6 QUARTS OF WATER TO A BOIL in a large pot. Add 1 tablespoon coarse salt. Stir in the spaghetti and cook, stirring frequently, until al dente. Drain and rinse under cold water to stop the cooking. Drain thoroughly. Toss with the vegetable oil, sesame oil, rice vinegar, scallions, ¼ teaspoon salt, and pepper to taste. Cover and refrigerate until 1 hour before serving. Toss with a little extra vegetable oil before serving if noodles become dry during refrigeration.

BLEND THE MARINADE INGREDIENTS TOGETHER in a shallow bowl or plate just large enough to hold the fish in a single layer. Lay the tuna in the marinade and turn to coat all sides. Let stand for 30 minutes, turning once.

REMOVE THE OUTER ROMAINE LEAVES and save for another use. Separate the inner, light-colored leaves, and wash and dry thoroughly. Arrange them in a sunburst pattern on each of 4 dinner plates, with the tips extending just beyond the edge of the plates. Toss the pasta and arrange in center of plates. Dry the tuna on paper towels. Heat a heavy skillet large enough to hold the tuna in a single layer over medium-high heat. When the pan is very hot cook the tuna so that each side browns nicely but the center remains rare, about 2 minutes per side. Allow tuna to rest about 3 minutes, then cut into ¼-inch slices. Arrange the slices on the spaghetti. Sprinkle with salt and pepper, garnish with parsley, and serve.

Serves 4

gewürztraminer

curried chicken
in lettuce leaves

The larger cities west of the Cascades in Oregon and Washington have many Asian markets that stock an amazing variety of unfamiliar packaged, dried, fresh, and frozen foods. Several of them are used in this recipe and are featured in this book. The spicing in this chicken makes it a nice match with Gewürztraminer. Yakima Valley's Hogue Cellars, in Prosser, Washington, is well known for quality, variety, and value. Its 1996 Gewürztraminer didn't let us down.

6 medium dried shiitake mushrooms (about ½ ounce)

2 heads romaine, leaves separated, washed, and dried

1¼ to 1½ pound skinless and boneless chicken thighs

¼ cup vegetable oil

6 scallions thinly sliced, white and light green parts kept separate
    from green tops

1 serrano chili, minced

1½ tablespoons Thai curry paste

½ cup canned unsweetened coconut milk

3 tablespoons soy sauce

1 medium carrot, shredded

1 small apple, such as Gala, Braeburn, Fuji, or Granny Smith, peeled,
    cored, and diced

1 cup frozen petite peas

Freshly ground black pepper

3 tablespoons cornstarch mixed with 3 tablespoons cold water

1 cup (lightly packed) fresh basil leaves, chopped

SOAK THE MUSHROOMS in 1 cup hot water for 30 minutes. Lift the mushrooms from the soaking liquid and rinse the gills under running water. Lay the mushroom tops on a cutting board, pull the tops in the opposite direction from the stems, and trim off. Discard the stems. Thinly slice the tops. Strain the soaking liquid through a paper towel–lined strainer, reserving ½ cup of the liquid.

REMOVE THE OUTER ROMAINE LEAVES and save for another use. Arrange crisp inner leaves around a 1-quart serving bowl set on a serving platter. Trim chicken thighs of excess fat, if any. Cut them into ¼-inch dice or use a food processor to coarsely chop them.

HEAT 2 TABLESPOONS of the oil in a large wok or sauté pan over medium-high heat. Add the chicken and stir-fry until it has lost all pink color. Transfer the chicken to a large plate or medium bowl.

ADD THE REMAINING 2 tablespoons oil to the pan. When hot, add the white and light green parts of the scallions and the serrano chili, and stir-fry about 1 minute. Add the curry paste, reserved mushroom liquid, coconut milk, and soy sauce and bring to a boil. Reduce the heat and simmer for about 3 minutes. Add the carrot, apple, peas, mushrooms, and pepper to taste. When the liquid returns to a simmer add cooked chicken. When the chicken simmers, mix the cornstarch slurry, and stir in about a third of it. Wait for the cornstarch to thicken the curried chicken. Add more of the slurry if necessary; sauce should be neither runny nor dry. It will thicken somewhat as it cools. Add the basil and scallion tops. Turn into the serving bowl and serve. Spoon a little curried chicken onto a lettuce leaf, roll, and eat with your fingers.

Serves 4 to 6 as a main dish, or more as part of a buffet

gewürztraminer

pizza with thai-style shrimp and peanut topping

Thai food has established itself as one of the Northwest's favorite styles of Southeast Asian cooking. This interesting twist on pizza uses several ingredients often found in Thai dishes, all of which go nicely with Gewürztraminer. The pizza is designed to pair with a dry or off-dry style of Gewürztraminer, either as an appetizer or as dinner. Cook the pizza on an outdoor grill if you like, following the directions on page 194.

DOUGH

1 cup warm water (about 105°F)

Pinch of sugar

1 tablespoon or 1 package active dry yeast

1 teaspoon coarse salt

3 tablespoons vegetable oil

3 cups unbleached all-purpose flour, or more if needed

Cornmeal for dusting pan

⅓ cup creamy peanut butter, preferably nonhomogenized, unsweetened, and unsalted, at room temperature

1½ tablespoons soy sauce

1 large clove garlic, minced

1 large jalapeño, seeded and minced

¼ cup unsweetened canned coconut milk

3 Roma tomatoes, peeled, seeded, and coarsely chopped

4 ounces small shrimp, peeled and deveined

4 scallions, thinly sliced

1 cup (lightly packed) cilantro leaves, chopped

TO MAKE THE DOUGH, place the water and sugar in a small bowl or 2-cup glass measure. Stir in yeast. When the mixture bubbles vigorously, about 5 minutes, whisk in the salt and oil.

THE DOUGH CAN BE MADE BY HAND (see page 68), or in a food processor (see page 40). To mix the dough in a stand mixer, pour the yeast mixture in the mixer's bowl, and add the flour. Fit the mixer with the dough hook. Run on medium-low speed. Mix until a dough ball forms on the hook, then continue to knead for 5 minutes. If the dough does not clean the bottom of the bowl, add extra flour a little at a time. Place dough in a large well-oiled bowl and cover with plastic wrap. Allow to rise until doubled in bulk, about 1 hour.

PREHEAT THE OVEN TO 500°F and adjust the rack to the middle level. Liberally sprinkle a 12- to 14-inch pizza pan or other round baking sheet with cornmeal and set aside.

BLEND PEANUT BUTTER, soy sauce, garlic, jalapeños, and coconut milk in a small mixing bowl.

DEFLATE THE DOUGH and pull into a ball with your hands. Roll out on a lightly floured surface in a round about 1 inch wider than the pan. Lightly flour the top of the dough, using your hands to spread the flour. Roll the dough around a rolling pin, then unroll over the top of the pan. Use your hands to nestle the dough into the pan, folding the extra edges over to form a thicker crust around the edge.

SPREAD THE PEANUT BUTTER MIXTURE OVER THE DOUGH. Arrange the tomatoes, shrimp, scallions, and cilantro on top. Bake until the edges of the crust are a dark golden brown, 10 to 12 minutes. Cut into 4 wedges and serve.

Serves 4

gewürztraminer

grilling pizza

Grilling a pizza is an adventure worth trying, especially if you are enter-taining outdoors. Prepare a medium charcoal fire or preheat a gas or elec-tric grill. Build your pizza sized to fit your grill; you may need to make 2 small ones. Liberally dust a bread peel or thin baking sheet without sides with cornmeal and place pizza on it. It should slide around on your peel when you jerk it. Position the peel on the part of grill you are using and jerk it out from under the pizza. Grill until the edges are nicely browned, checking to make sure the bottom is not burning from too much heat. Use the peel and a large spatula to remove the pizza from the grill.

foods to pair with

pinot blanc

Oysters on the Half Shell with Shallot Wine Sauce
Potato Soup with Crisp Bacon
Smoked Trout Salad with Small Potatoes and Fresh Fennel
Fresh Sturgeon Salade Niçoise
Fish Tacos with Avocado and Lime
Shellfish Risotto
Mussels Steamed in Pinot Blanc
Northwest Seafood Stew
Smoked Trout Hash
Sautéed Pork Chops over Creamy Cabbage
Artisan Bread Tuna Melt with Northwest Cheddar

the pinot blanc grape

Wine makers in Oregon's Willamette Valley are famous for their Pinot Noir and Pinot Gris, and now there is a third Pinot grape beginning to make news—Pinot Blanc (PEE-no BLONC). It is a grape suitable for growing in a cool, moist climate like Oregon's, and it is increasingly finding a willing audience among people who appreciate a lighter, crisper wine reminiscent of Chardonnay.

The list of Pinot Blanc producers is still relatively small, since the grape's history in Oregon is short. Myron Redford was an Oregon wine pioneer of the 1970s, founding Amity Vineyards in Amity, Oregon, and getting raves for dry Rieslings and dry Gewürztraminers. He is known for shaking things up and is one of the modern-day Pinot Blanc pioneers. A few miles north, near Yamhill, WillaKenzie Estate wine-maker Laurent Monthelieu, formerly with Bridgeview Vineyard in southern Oregon, is making Pinot Blanc of notable style. South of Corvallis at Tyee Wine Cellars, Barney Watson, enology professor at Oregon State University, makes well respected Pinot Blanc. Look for other labels on store shelves now and many more in upcoming years.

Pinot Blanc's appeal lies in its appley, buttery flavors, and in its crisp nature, which is lighter than some Chardonnays. Try it with artichokes, asparagus, cheeses, dishes with olives and herbs, simple chicken dishes, white fish species, crab, and scallops. Pinot Blanc wines are usually drinkable at bottling. Bigger versions ought to have a life of two or three years, but it's probably not a good idea to forget them in your cellar.

Serve slightly chilled, about 50°F.

oysters on the half shell
with shallot wine sauce

The farm-raised oyster that con-stitute most of the Northwest's supply is the Pacific oyster, Cras-sostria gigas, with origins in Japan and China. Some Euro-pean flats are also raised in the Northwest. Oysters' trade names (Willapa Bay, Quilcene, Umpqua, Pearl Point, Westcott Bay, etc.) refer to the area where they are grown. An oyster is a filter feeder, processing more than 200 gallons of water a day in search of the diatoms that are its primary food. The intertidal waters of the Northwest vary in salinity and the presence of minerals such as copper, iron, and iodine. So the flavor of the oyster you eat is very much related to water con-ditions where it was raised, just as the flavor of wine is related to the soil in which the grapes were grown.

Since most Northwest oysters are farm-raised and have been geneti-cally altered to prevent their spawning, the old "r" month rule (eat oysters only during months that have an "r" in the name) no longer automatically applies. Eat your cultivated oysters year-round. Store them, if you must, on ice, cupped side down. Never store them in a closed plastic bag, since they will suffocate.

SAUCE

    1 tablespoon minced shallots

    ¼ cup dry white wine

    2 teaspoons unseasoned rice vinegar

    ¼ teaspoon hot pepper sauce

pinot blanc

Freshly ground black pepper to taste

1 tablespoon minced parsley

~~~

12 to 16 oysters, shucked

MIX SAUCE INGREDIENTS TOGETHER. Place in a small bowl in the middle of a platter, surrounded with oysters on the half shell.

NOTE: Persons with compromised immune systems should never eat raw oysters.

Serves 4

artisan bakeries

At about the same time the winery population of Oregon and Washington was beginning to explode, Northwesterners were developing an appetite for freshly baked breads of character. Into the breach stepped small, newly founded artisan bakeries dedicated to the production of rustic, European-style loaves. Long, thin baguettes, oval ciabattas, round sour ryes, and loaves dotted with cured olives and fresh herbs soon became available. These breads had a depth of flavor quite unlike the squishy-soft, sliced white sandwich bread common at that time.

Today's artisan bakeries usually use slow-rising doughs because of the superb texture and flavor that results. A "poolish" bread comes from a freshly made starter used with a little baker's yeast to produce full-flavored loaves without the tang of sourdough. A "levain" bread is made from a sour starter that has been kept alive for an indefinite period of time; the bread tastes a bit acidic as a result. The eggs, milk, flavorings, fats, and fillers common to mass produced breads are mostly absent. Artisan bread doughs are often quite wet, difficult to handle, mostly formed by hand, and baked in shapes other than the traditional sandwich loaf. The slow-rising, wet dough tends to produce bread with large interior holes and full flavor. Steam-injected, brick-lined ovens encourage a last quick rise called oven-spring, which gives the exterior of the bread its characteristic crustiness.

Artisan bakeries have established themselves in many neighborhoods in Northwest metropolitan areas. In Seattle, Grand Central Bakery, Macrina Bakery, The Essential Baking Co., La Panzanella, and A la Française are among the best choices. In Portland, Grand Central Bakery, Marsee Baking, and Pearl Bakery are standouts. In Eugene, Metropol and Eugene City Bakery provide breads of distinct quality.

potato soup with crisp bacon

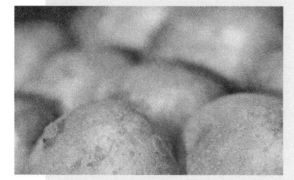

The whole world knows that Idaho produces potatoes, but both Oregon and Washington are major potato-growing states as well. The same brown, pebbly skinned russet potatoes that make great french fries also make great mashed potatoes—and soup. This hearty soup is appealing with a wine that is a bit crisp and lightly fruity. That describes lots of Northwest Pinot Blancs. Oregon's Willamette Valley is the source of most of the production, with Amity, Cameron, Erath, Tyee, and WillaKenzie among the wineries now bottling this wine. Serve the soup with a loaf of rustic bread for a simple dinner.

8 ounces bacon strips, preferably apple wood–smoked, cut
   crosswise into 1-inch pieces

1 jumbo onion, coarsely chopped or diced

3 pounds russet (baking) potatoes, peeled, and cut into
   1½-inch pieces

2 teaspoons dried dill weed

½ teaspoon freshly ground black pepper

6 cups chicken stock or low-sodium canned broth

½ cup whipping cream

Coarse salt

½ cup (lightly packed) parsley leaves, chopped

FRY THE BACON in a 4-quart saucepan or a Dutch oven over medium heat until it renders its fat and becomes crisp. Use a slotted spoon to transfer bacon to a paper towel–lined plate. Pour off all but about 2 tablespoons of the fat and add the onion to the pan. Sauté until soft but not browned. Add potatoes, dill, pepper, and stock and bring to a boil. Reduce the heat and simmer, covered, until the potatoes are tender when pierced with a fork. Pour the soup through a strainer into a large bowl. Purée the solids with some of the broth in a blender or food processor. Return the purée and broth to the pan. Stir in the cream, reheat if necessary, and taste for seasoning. Divide among 4 soup bowls, sprinkle bacon into each bowl, and garnish with the parsley. Serve.

Serves 4

smoked trout salad with small potatoes and fresh fennel

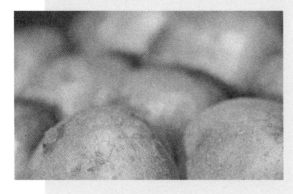

Rainbow trout is one of the great game fish of the world, drawing fishermen from all corners of the globe to the cold, swift mountain streams of the Northwest. Luckily for the rest of us, rainbow and golden trout are commercially raised, especially in Idaho. Smoked rainbow trout is sometimes available in fish markets, but using your charcoal or gas grill to do the job is not at all difficult. Smoking an uncured trout results in a fish with a buttery texture and no added salt. The fish is perishable, though, so you should use it within a couple of days. If you have any left over, use it to make Smoked Trout Hash (page 216).

Fresh, fruity, and crisp are all descriptions applied to the Pinot Blanc grape, which makes wine often described as Chardonnay-like, but lighter on the tongue and more delicate in the nose. We were lucky enough to find a bottle of Adelsheim 1996 Pinot Blanc, which made for good drinking and good label viewing. The female faces on Adelsheim labels are Ginny Adelsheim's drawings of some of her acquaintances.

2 rainbow trout, cleaned and preferably boneless (10 to 12 ounces each)

10 small white potatoes, scrubbed

2 heads butter or leaf lettuce, leaves separated, washed, and dried

2 bulbs fennel (anise), stems discarded, bulbs halved and very thinly sliced

4 medium tomatoes, cut in 8 wedges each

8 very thin slices of red onion

2 cups (lightly packed) parsley leaves, coarsely chopped

Fresh ground black pepper

DRESSING

1 cup mayonnaise

6 tablespoons skim milk

4 teaspoons unseasoned rice vinegar

5 tablespoons Dijon mustard

2 teaspoons sugar

4 teaspoons celery seeds

½ teaspoon freshly ground black pepper

1 teaspoon coarse salt

TO SMOKE THE TROUT on an outdoor grill, place about 1 cup dry wood chips (such as oak, maple, alder, apple) in the center of a 12-inch square of aluminum foil. Fold the foil over the chips to make a square envelope. Use a two-tined fork or metal skewer to punch holes all over the top of the foil packet, to allow smoke to escape easily. If you are using a charcoal grill, build a medium fire on one side and place foil packet directly on the burning coals. If using a gas grill with 2 burners, place foil on the lava rocks or metal burner shield of the lighted burner. Place fish on a small oiled cake rack or perforated grill rack, and place the rack on the side of the grill opposite the heat source, and close the grill cover. After a few minutes the foil packet will begin to issue smoke, which will flavor the fish. After awhile the smoke will subside. When smoke dies down turn grill to low; on a charcoal grill add a few briquets as necessary to maintain a low fire. Timing will vary depending on your grill and the outside temperature. Ours was done in 1½ hours, with a final temperature of 120°F on an instant-read thermometer. If you prefer a drier-textured fish, cook it to 140°F. Remove fish from grill and refrigerate unless serving within 2 hours.

STEAM OR BOIL THE POTATOES until they are barely tender when poked with a wire cake tester or toothpick, about 25 minutes. Allow them to cool somewhat while preparing the salad. Arrange 3 or 4 of the large lettuce leaves on each of 4

dinner plates. Put the fennel, tomatoes, onion slices, parsley, and a few torn lettuce leaves in a large mixing bowl. Whisk together the dressing ingredients. Pour
about 1 cup into the vegetable mixture, add pepper, and toss thoroughly. Arrange
on top of the lettuce liners. Cut the potatoes into 4 wedges or slices each, and
arrange in 2 rows on each plate, leaving space for the fish between the rows.
Remove skin and carefully bone the fish, leaving fillets intact as much as possible.
Lay 1 fillet between the potato rows on each plate. Drizzle more dressing from
side to side on each plate, creating an attractive pattern with dressing. Serve.

Serves 4

cougar gold

One of the Northwest's more unusual cheeses is Cougar Gold, a sharp white cheddar with an interesting history. Produced at a creamery on the grounds of Washington State University, in Pullman, Washington, Cougar Gold comes packaged in cans. Once opened, the cheese must be refrigerated, and it will continue to develop sharper flavors and become more crumbly over time.

Cougar Gold was developed in the 1940s, when the school was involved in a packaging research program between the federal government and the American Can Company. At that time, plastic was not available as a packaging material for cheeses, and traditional wax coatings were not sturdy enough to withstand shipping. Cans seemed a good alternative, but it was necessary first to create a cheese that did not produce gases after it was processed, which would cause the can to bulge. The result of the research was a group of cheeses, the most famous of which is Cougar Gold, named after Dr. N.S. Golding, one of the researchers.

Aged for at least one year, Cougar Gold has a unique flavor reminiscent of both Gouda and Swiss cheeses. About 160,000 cans of Cougar Gold are produced annually at WSU's creamery. Sister cheeses include American Cheddar (an orange cheddar aged for at least one year), a smoked version of American Cheddar, and a handful of other, softer cheeses.

Cheeses from the WSU creamery are available at Ferdinand's, the creamery retail outlet, as well as by mail order. Specialty retailers often carry one or more of the cheeses.

fresh sturgeon salade niçoise

The Columbia River system is home to white sturgeon, an ancient fish with cartilage instead of bone, like shark. It can live to be more than one hundred years old and reach lengths of twenty feet. It prowls the river bottoms, and those who fish for it must throw back catches over sixty inches to ensure that adult females survive to spawn. The commercial season is limited to brief periods during the spring and fall, when Columbia River sturgeon appear in fish markets. Their flesh is a bit pearlescent, with streaks of yellow. It has a meaty texture, moist flesh, and mild flavor.

Sturgeon grills exceedingly well, and cooks who grill regularly know the value of cooking more than one meal's worth at a time. This salad is a variation of the classic salade niçoise. We paired the salad with a WillaKenzie Estate Oregon 1996 Pinot Blanc. Former Bridgeview wine-maker Laurent Monthelieu is in partnership in this new, very handsome Yamhill Valley winery, whose first vintage was 1995.

1 pound green beans, trimmed (see Note)

1 pound small white or red potatoes, scrubbed

1 large head romaine, leaves separated, washed, and dried

DRESSING

¾ cup extra virgin olive oil

3 tablespoons fresh lemon juice

2 teaspoons anchovy paste

¾ teaspoon coarse salt

½ teaspoon freshly ground black pepper

1 cup (lightly packed) parsley, chopped

18 sprigs fresh thyme, leaves only, chopped

1 medium cucumber, peeled, halved lengthwise, seeded, and
    cut crosswise into ⅛-inch slices

2 medium tomatoes, cut into 8 wedges each

4 hard-cooked eggs, peeled and sliced

¾ pound cooked, chilled sturgeon, cut across the grain in
    1 x ¼-inch slices

STEAM OR BOIL GREEN BEANS until just tender. Cool for 5 minutes in ice water, drain, dry, and refrigerate until ready to use. Steam potatoes until barely tender when tested with a wire cake-tester or a toothpick, 25 to 30 minutes. Set aside to cool slightly, leaving the peels on.

TO MAKE THE DRESSING, whisk together all the ingredients. Arrange outer romaine leaves as liners on 4 dinner plates. Tear romaine hearts into bite-size pieces. Put them in a large bowl, add cucumber slices and 2 tablespoons of the dressing, and toss. Arrange on top of the lettuce. Cut the warm potatoes into 4 to 6 wedges each and arrange around the outside edge of the plates. Arrange the beans, tomatoes, egg slices, and sturgeon slices on top of the salad. Drizzle with the remaining dressing and serve.

NOTE: Frozen petite beans may be substituted for fresh beans. Cook them in boiling salted water until just tender, about 6 minutes, drain them, and plunge into a large bowl filled with ice water. Let stand for 5 minutes, drain, dry, and refrigerate.

Serves 4

fish tacos with avocado and lime

One way to make tacos is with fresh corn tortillas using a roll-your-own technique at the table. You will be able to appreciate the fine flavor of fresh tortillas wrapped around fish with traditional taco condiments. It's quite a revelation. A Northwest Pinot Blanc, such as Tyee Wine Cellars near Corvallis, Oregon, would be a fine accompaniment to your tacos.

16 corn tortillas

2 medium tomatoes, cut in half crosswise, seeded, and diced

2 cups shredded cabbage

6 scallions, thinly sliced

2 firm-ripe avocados, halved, pitted, peeled (see page 121), and diced

¼ cup fresh lime juice

SAUCE

⅓ cup mayonnaise

¼ cup sour cream

3 tablespoons fresh lime juice

¼ teaspoon hot pepper sauce

¼ teaspoon sugar

Pinch of coarse salt

1 pound white-fleshed fish fillets, such as halibut, rockfish, ling cod, black cod (sable fish), shark, or sturgeon, cooked and cut into strips or cubes

PREHEAT THE OVEN TO 175°F. Place the tortillas in a covered container, such as a tortilla warmer or shallow casserole with lid. Place in the oven to warm.

PUT THE TOMATOES, cabbage, and scallions in separate small serving bowls. Toss the avocado with 1 tablespoon of the lime juice, and put in a serving bowl.

MIX THE SAUCE ingredients and place in a serving bowl.

REWARM FISH if it was cooked in advance. Place the fish on a warmed plate or in a bowl. Each person takes a tortilla, spreads it with a dollop of sauce, adds a little fish, tops with the vegetable garnishes, rolls, and eats.

Serves 4

shellfish risotto

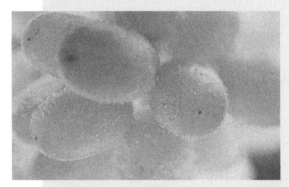

This risotto dish uses classic Northwest shellfish such as crab and bay scallops, as well as an easy, homemade fish stock as the liquid moistening the rice. If you can find Arborio rice, an Italian import, use that. If not available, use California Pearl rice. A properly made risotto is creamy, and has a special firmness of bite in the center of the rice grains. In fact, the creaminess of the finished dish—there is no cream in it— pairs off well against Pinot Blanc. Oregon pioneer wine-maker Dick Erath makes Pinot Blanc that reflects his longtime reputation for bottling quality at an approachable price.

FISH STOCK

1 tablespoon unsalted butter

6 scallions, coarsely chopped

3 to 3½ pounds fish trimmings such as heads, collars, and belly strips, from a non-oily fish such as halibut, sole, or rockfish

3 cloves garlic, smashed

1 cup dry white wine

6 black peppercorns

1 bay leaf

12 sprigs thyme

1 cup (lightly packed) parsley leaves

½ cup (lightly packed) fresh tarragon leaves

RISOTTO

⅓ cup olive oil

⅓ cup chopped onion

4 cloves garlic, minced

2 cups imported Arborio or California Pearl rice

⅓ cup dry white wine

4 ounces rock shrimp

4 ounces crabmeat

4 ounces bay scallops

Coarse salt

Freshly ground black pepper

½ cup (lightly packed) parsley leaves, chopped

TO MAKE THE FISH STOCK, melt the butter in a 4-quart or larger nonreactive saucepan over medium heat. Add the scallions and sauté until soft, 2 to 3 minutes. Add 10 cups water and the remaining ingredients and bring to a boil over medium-high heat. Reduce the heat and simmer, partially covered, for 40 minutes. Pour through a fine strainer and discard the solids. (The stock will keep, covered, for 2 days in the refrigerator. Freeze for longer storage.)

TO MAKE THE RISOTTO, pour the stock into a small saucepan over medium-high heat and bring to a boil. Reduce the heat and keep at a bare simmer. Heat the olive oil in a 4-quart or larger saucepan over medium heat. Add the onion and garlic, and sauté until soft, about 3 minutes. Add the rice and stir to coat with oil. Add the wine and cook until it is reduced to a syrup. Add ½ cup of the stock, stirring often, until it has been almost completely absorbed by the rice. Repeat the process until the rice grains have swollen and lost their opaque centers and raw taste, but still have a bit of bite in the center, 20 to 25 minutes. You may not need all of the fish stock. Add the shrimp, crabmeat, and scallops. Add salt and pepper to taste. Stir in enough stock, if necessary, so that the rice is the consistency of very soft mashed potatoes. Divide among 4 warmed soup plates, garnish with the parsley, and serve immediately.

Serves 6

mussels steamed in pinot blanc

A walk along a rocky beach or on a pier in the Northwest often means a view of colonies of mussels, bivalves that attach themselves to pier supports and rocky outcroppings with a few thin, tough strands of protein called a "beard." At least five mussel varieties are available in Northwest markets at one time or another, including the Puget Sound blue mussel, the Pacific Ocean mussel, the Mediterranean mussel, the East Coast blue mussel, and the New Zealand green-lipped mussel. Most that are sold commercially are farm raised, like Northwest oysters. Meats range in color from bright orange to green-tinged to gray. Removing a mussel's beard is not required, it is just a cosmetic exercise. But mussels cannot survive once bearded, so do that just before cooking them. Pinot Blanc is the cooking liquid for these mussels, and, in concert with some butter, garlic, and parsley, makes a flavorful and simple sauce.

4 pounds mussels

2 cups dry white wine, such as Pinot Blanc or Pinot Gris

2 large cloves garlic, minced

1 tablespoon unsalted butter

1 cup (lightly packed) parsley leaves, chopped

BEARD THE MUSSELS, if you like, by grasping the shell in one hand and the beard in other, and pulling firmly toward the end of the shell. Discard the beard in the garbage, not down a garbage disposal. Rinse the mussels, discarding any that are unusually heavy (possibly filled with sand or mud) or that do not close when tapped if they are open. In a 6-quart or larger low, wide pan with a lid, combine the wine, garlic, and butter. Add the mussels and bring to a boil over medium-high heat. Cover and cook until the shells have opened, about 5 minutes, then for 2 minutes more to steam the meats. Shake the pan to encourage all mussels to open. Use tongs or a large slotted spoon to transfer mussels to warmed serving bowls, discarding any that have not opened. Add parsley to broth and ladle over the mussels. Serve right away, with warm, crusty bread.

Serves 4 as a first course, or 6 as an appetizer

northwest seafood stew

The sheer variety of creatures from the sea available in Northwest markets can be astonishing. Combining several kinds of seafood in one bowl of flavorful broth allows the cook to pick the best of the market on any given day. This recipe suggests various types of shellfish and fin fish, but you should make your choice when you get to the market. Firmer-fleshed fish like halibut, tuna, swordfish, marlin, and shark—as well as salmon and sturgeon—work well in stews without falling apart.

Picking the best Pinot Blanc to serve with the stew could be a difficult but enjoyable task, since the number of wineries producing the wine is growing. We enjoyed the stew with a Rex Hill 1996 Willamette Valley Pinot Blanc. The well-known winery is southwest of Portland, just outside of Newberg, in a handsome building on a terraced hillside dotted with picnic tables. It is often the site of weddings and other social events.

2 tablespoons unsalted butter or chicken fat

2 cloves garlic, minced

1 medium-size sweet onion, such as Walla Walla, quartered and cut into thin slices

6 cups chicken stock or low-sodium canned broth

1 bottle (7 or 8 ounces) clam juice

½ cup dry white wine, such as Pinot Blanc

12 sprigs thyme, leaves only

½ teaspoon hot pepper sauce

1 red bell pepper, cored, seeded, and opened up to lie flat

Coarse salt

8 to 10 ounces waxy white potatoes (Yukon Gold, White Rose, or Yellow Finn), peeled and cut into ½-inch dice (about 1½ cups)

8 to 10 ounces butternut squash, peeled, any seeds removed, and cut in ½-inch dice (about 1½ cups)

12 clams

12 mussels, beards pulled off, if any

10 ounces salmon fillet, skinned and boned, cut into ½-inch dice

10 ounces sturgeon steak, skinned, boned, cut in ½-inch dice

8 ounces medium shrimp, peeled and deveined, tails left on

½ cup whipping cream

Freshly ground black pepper

½ cup (lightly packed) parsley leaves, coarsely chopped

MELT THE BUTTER in a 5- to 6-quart Dutch oven over medium-low heat. Add the garlic and onion, stir, cover, and cook 5 minutes. Add the stock, clam juice, wine, thyme, and hot pepper sauce. Bring to a boil. Reduce the heat and simmer, covered, 15 minutes. Blacken the skin of the pepper over a gas flame or under the broiler and place in a plastic bag for 10 minutes. Scrape the skin off with a paring knife (don't rinse), then cut into ½-inch dice. Taste broth and add salt if necessary. Add the potatoes and squash and cook for 5 minutes. Add the clams and mussels and cook 3 minutes. Add the salmon, sturgeon, shrimp, diced red pepper, and cream. Cook for 2 minutes. Add pepper to taste. Divide the stew evenly among 4 shallow soup bowls. Garnish with parsley. Have a bowl on the table for the empty shells and shrimp tails.

Serves 4

smoked trout hash

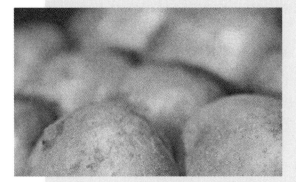

This hash is a good way to make a little smoked trout go a long way. It contains both celery and celery root, which give it a refreshing twist. It is a good excuse to open another bottle of Pinot Blanc.

You could do worse than to dust off a bottle from Oregon's Bethel Heights Vineyard, one of the oldest vineyards in the Eola Hills near Salem. Nearly everything here is estate bottled by a wine maker who allows grapes to ripen longer than most, his theory being that later-picked grapes result in more flavorful wines. Known especially for Chardonnay and Pinot Noir, Bethel Heights makes several other wines, among them the 1996 Pinot Blanc we drank with this dish.

HASH

2 large russet (baking) potatoes, peeled, and cut into ¼- to ½-inch dice

1 celery root, trimmed, peeled, and cut into ¼- to ½-inch dice

2 ribs celery, cut into ¼- to ½-inch dice

1 large onion, cut into ¼- to ½-inch dice

1 tablespoon thyme leaves, chopped

1¼ teaspoons coarse salt

½ teaspoon freshly ground black pepper

1 cup (lightly packed) parsley leaves, coarsely chopped

4 tablespoons (½ stick) unsalted butter

10 to 12 ounces smoked trout, carefully boned, and broken into small pieces

TOSS ALL THE HASH INGREDIENTS TOGETHER in a large mixing bowl. Melt the butter in a 12-inch heavy skillet or sauté pan, preferably nonstick, over medium heat. Add the hash, cover, and cook for 5 minutes. Remove the cover and continue to cook, stirring up from the bottom every few minutes using a flat-edged wooden spatula or similar utensil. The hash is done when the potatoes no longer taste raw, and the mixture is browned to your liking. Raise the heat if the hash tastes cooked, but browning is not occurring. Stir the trout into the hash just before serving, to preserve its moistness. Divide among 4 warmed plates and serve immediately.

Serves 4

six great-value wineries of the northwest

Chateau Ste. Michelle, Woodinville, Washington

Columbia Crest Winery, Paterson, Washington

Erath Vineyards, Dundee, Oregon

Hogue Cellars, Prosser, Washington

Sokol Blosser Winery, Dundee, Oregon

Willamette Valley Vineyards, Turner, Oregon

sautéed pork chops
over creamy cabbage

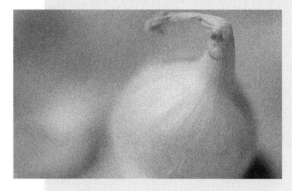

Cooking with friends is always fun, even if the talk in the kitchen sometimes causes someone to forget a step or two in a recipe. So it was one night when we were joined by Mary Evely,

Chef at California's Simi Winery and author of The Vintner's Table Cookbook. *Pork chops were the main course, and things went perfectly well until it was time for the pan to go into a preheated oven—which had not even been turned on. Luckily, a slight adjustment in timing produced a good meal. Steamed baby potatoes are a good accompaniment to this dish. A crisp Pinot Blanc is a nice wine to match with the creamy, dill-flavored slaw, as well as the pork chops.*

2 tablespoons unsalted butter

1 medium onion, sliced

1 small to medium head green cabbage (1½ to 2 pounds), cored, and
    medium sliced

1 cup whipping cream

1 teaspoon dried dill weed

Coarse salt

Freshly ground black pepper

1 tablespoon vegetable oil

4 boneless pork loin chops (about 8 ounces each)

PREHEAT THE OVEN TO 450°F.

MELT THE BUTTER in a 12-inch sauté pan with a lid over medium heat. Add the onion and cook, stirring, until slightly softened, about 3 minutes. Add the cabbage, cream, dill weed, and salt and pepper to taste. Reduce the heat to medium-low, cover, and simmer until the cabbage is cooked, about 10 minutes.

HEAT A 12-INCH HEAVY-BOTTOMED OVENPROOF SKILLET over medium-high heat until very hot. Add the oil, swirling to coat the pan, then add the chops, sprinkling with salt and pepper. Cook for 2 minutes, turn using a thin-blade metal spatula, and season the second side. Cook for 2 minutes on the second side, then place the pan in the oven. Bake for 4 minutes, until an instant-read thermometer inserted in a chop on an angle registers 145°F, then remove the pan from the oven using a heavy mitt or potholder. Taste the cabbage for seasoning, then arrange a bed of cabbage on each plate. Top with a pork chop and serve.

Serves 4

artisan bread tuna melt
with northwest cheddar

Here is a true Northwest tuna melt sandwich, built on local artisan bread, and served open face with a Northwest cheddar melted over the top. Serve it with thickly sliced, lightly salted potato chips and a glass of Northwest Pinot Blanc, such as Ken Wright Cellars, made in Carlton, Oregon.

3 cans (about 6 ounces) solid tuna in vegetable oil, well drained

1 rib celery, finely diced

½ cup finely diced onion

½ cup (lightly packed) parsley leaves, chopped

1 tablespoon chopped fresh thyme leaves or 1 scant teaspoon dried thyme leaves

1 teaspoon dried dill weed

2 tablespoons capers, rinsed and drained

Freshly ground black pepper

½ cup mayonnaise, or more as needed

2 tablespoons Dijon mustard

8 slices of bread, from a country-style loaf

6 ounces medium cheddar cheese, such as Cougar Gold or Bandon

PREHEAT THE OVEN TO 400°F.

FLAKE THE TUNA with a fork in a medium mixing bowl without mashing it. Add the celery, onion, parsley, thyme, dill weed, capers, and black pepper to taste. Toss well. Mix together the mayonnaise and mustard in a small bowl. With a rubber spatula, blend the mayonnaise mixture into the tuna salad. If it seems too dry, add a bit more mayonnaise.

ARRANGE THE BREAD SLICES on a baking sheet. Spread with the tuna salad. Top with slices of cheddar. Bake until the cheese is bubbly, about 5 minutes. Serve at once.

Serves 4

food shopping in the northwest

Specialty markets, artisan food producers, and truly fresh foods are a hall-mark of Northwest living. This phenomenon is part of neighborhood culture, as a visit to even one of the ever more upscale supermarkets in Oregon or Washington will reveal. The in-store bakery might not quite live up to artisan standards, and the fish case might not look like a dockside fish market, but you'll be able to pick out and bag your own fruits and vegetables—like fresh asparagus from the Yakima Valley, onions from Walla Walla, and chanterelle mushrooms from a forest nearby—in a well-stocked and clean produce department that likely also has an organic section. You may have a choice of certified, possibly organic meats to choose from. Regional dairies will probably have their products on display. And the word "local" on the strawberry, raspberry, and blueberry signs means you can expect the best the Northwest has to offer. Even in the world of supermarkets, the Northwest is a special place.

foods to pair with

pinot gris

Crostini with Sun-Dried Tomato Tapenade
Mixed Nut Pesto Pasta
Deep-Fried Oysters with Caper Tartar Sauce
Caper Tartar Sauce
Grilled Garlic Shrimp on Warm Cabbage Slaw
Grilled Ahi with Sun-Dried Tomato Sauce
Basil-Coated Grilled Swordfish with Eggplant
Grilled Salmon with Rosemary Fettuccine
Baked Potatoes Stuffed with Dungeness Crab
Northwest Vegetable and Tuna Sandwich

the pinot gris grape

The Pinot Gris (PEE-no GREE) grape (also called Pinot Grigio or Tokay d'Alsace) is on a roll in Oregon, now being the third most planted grape in the state. Washington's plantings have tripled in four years, though the acres planted remain few. But the popularity of Pinot Gris is soaring, and choices on the shelf are going to  multiply. Heavy-hitter labels like Argyle, Columbia Winery, The Eyrie Vineyards, King Estate Winery, Ponzi Vineyards, Silvan Ridge—to name just a few—are testimony to the future that Northwest wineries see in Pinot Gris.

The grape makes wine that can be described as generally medium-bodied, with definite citrus overtones and light acidity. It is dry but appealingly fruity. Common flavors and aromas include green apple, honey, and spice. Pinot Gris wines pair marvelously well with shellfish, fish, pork, and poultry, among other dishes.

Wine makers vinifying Pinot Gris are doing so in a variety of ways. The grape makes quite nice wine when fermented and stored in stainles-steel tanks and brought to market a few months after the harvest. It also makes wonderful wine when given some barrel age, which makes it more complex and mouth filling. A specialty of the Alsace region of France for a long time, the grape is also grown in Italy (and California) as Pinot Grigio.

Serve slightly chilled, about 50°F.

crostini with sun-dried tomato tapenade

The crispness of Pinot Gris balances the meatiness of the cured olives in this tapenade. Kathleen's sister, Marianne Barber, created this recipe, which we used as an appetizer preceding a dinner of Roast Quail with Barley, Prune, and Hazelnut Stuffing (see page 80) and Cranberry-Pear Chutney (see page 27). It was a memorable meal, thanks in no small part to this flavorful spread, as well as to a Pinot Gris from Willamette Valley Vineyards. Located several miles south of Salem, Oregon, and offering a nicely varied list of wines, Willamette Valley Vineyards was unusual in its use of public stock offerings to quickly raise start-up funds.

2 cups pitted cured black olives, such as kalamata

6 oil-packed anchovy fillets

2 large cloves garlic

2 tablespoons fresh lemon juice

¼ teaspoon cayenne pepper

2 tablespoons extra virgin olive oil

1½ ounces sun-dried tomatoes (dry, not oil-packed), soaked in hot water for 30 minutes and drained

CROSTINI

20 thin (¼-inch) slices of baguette-type bread

Olive oil

COMBINE THE OLIVES, anchovies, garlic, lemon juice, cayenne, and olive oil in the work bowl of a blender or food processor and blend. Scrape down the bowl once or twice, making certain that all ingredients are consistently blended. Transfer to a small mixing bowl.

PAT THE SOAKED TOMATOES DRY using paper towels, then cut them into small dice. Stir into the olive mixture. Transfer to a small bowl.

PREHEAT THE OVEN TO 400°F. Lightly brush both sides of the bread with olive oil, and arrange on a baking sheet. Bake for about 4 minutes on each side, or until bread is lightly browned.

PLACE THE BOWL OF TAPENADE in the center of a large platter and arrange the crostini around it. Provide a small spreader or butter knife for guests to serve themselves. (The tapenade will keep, covered, for 2 weeks in the refrigerator.)

Makes 20 slices

dick erath

In the early 1960s a young San Francisco–based electrical engineer named Dick Erath sipped his first glass of good wine while on a photography trip to Big Sur in northern California. His interest in photography and music led to his appreciation of wine making as both an artistic and scientific undertaking, and he started making wine as a hobby.

The Pinot Noir grape captured Erath's imagination, and he believed that it could thrive in the cool and damp climate of Oregon's Willamette Valley. In 1968 Erath moved to Beaverton, Oregon, where he went to work for a major electronics manufacturer. Some days he spent his lunch hour in a plane flying above the hills in the northern Willamette Valley, looking for land that might produce quality Pinot Noir grapes. Erath also put thousands of miles on an old station wagon, searching for property suitable for a vineyard. He eventually found two plots totaling sixty-one acres of land, for five hundred dollars an acre. In early 1969 Erath optimistically planted several acres of Pinot Noir, Riesling, and Gewürztraminer grapes on land where walnut trees had grown.

The twig borers that had resided in the walnut trees attacked Erath's new plantings, and before the fall was over an ice storm layered heavy ice on the weakened vines, causing many to break. In spite of a rough beginning, Erath Vineyards survived and prospered. A partnership in the early 1970s with businessman Cal Knudsen (now a partner in Argyle Winery) lasted well over a decade, during which time the Knudsen-Erath label become the top Pinot Noir producer in the nation. In 1974 Erath made friends with Russian-born André Tchelistcheff, legendary wine maker at Beaulieu Vineyards in the Napa Valley, who was then consulting with the early Washington State wine makers.

Erath's winery now produces about 35,000 cases a year. Estate-grown Pinot Noir is the premier product, and the winery also produces many other wines, including Chardonnay, Pinot Blanc, and Pinot Gris.

pinot gris

mixed nut pesto pasta

The crispness of flavor in Pinot Gris happens to nuzzle up nicely to the nuts and herbs and oil that coat the noodles in this dish. Perhaps one of the reasons it tastes so good is that the hazelnuts almost certainly come from Oregon's Willamette Valley, the same land that nurtures most of the Pinot Gris grapes in the Northwest.

While Washington has not been as prolific as Oregon in Pinot Gris production, several of its wines merit tasting. Otis Vineyard, north of Grandview in the Yakima Valley, has long been a source for Cabernet and Chardonnay. It also now produces some Pinot Gris, planted on a northwest-facing plot, to take advantage of the grape's ability to ripen in cooler surroundings. Columbia Winery, in Woodinville, Washington, buys the grapes and makes a Pinot Gris of excellent quality.

¼ cup hazelnuts (filberts), roasted and skinned (see page 110)

¾ cup walnut pieces

¼ cup pine nuts

¼ cup shelled pistachios

2 large cloves garlic

1 cup (firmly packed) basil leaves

½ cup (lightly packed) parsley leaves

¾ to 1 cup extra virgin olive oil

1 cup grated imported pecorino romano cheese

Coarse salt

Freshly ground black pepper

1 pound dried pasta, such as fettuccine

PLACE THE NUTS, garlic, basil, and parsley in the work bowl of a food processor or a blender. Chop the mixture. With the machine running, add ¾ cup oil in a thin stream. Add the cheese, ½ teaspoon salt, and pepper to taste, and process for a few seconds. The pesto should be a moist paste. If it seems dry, add remaining oil. Refrigerate, covered, until needed.

WHEN READY TO SERVE, bring the pesto sauce to room temperature. Bring 6 quarts of water to a boil in a large pot over high heat. Add 1 tablespoon salt. Add the pasta and cook, stirring often, until al dente. Drain, reserving ½ cup of the pasta water. Return the pasta to the pot and toss with 1¼ to 1½ cups of the pesto sauce. If the mixture seems too thick, add a tablespoon or more of the pasta cooking water. Divide among 4 warmed plates or pasta bowls and serve immediately. Pass additional cheese at the table.

Serves 4, with about half the pesto left for another meal

deep-fried oysters
with caper tartar sauce

Willapa Bay is separated from the Pacific Ocean by Long Beach Peninsula, and is famous as one of the sources of oysters along the Northwest coast. The small town of Oysterville is rich with the history of boom and bust times in the oyster trade. First-time visitors are amazed to see huge piles of oyster shells outside packing plants, not to mention the shells used as paving on some of the private roads near the water. Modern methods of aquaculture have returned the Northwest oyster industry to prosperity, and reversed the decline that towns like Oysterville suffered in decades past.

The extra richness deep-frying imparts makes these oysters a nice match for a crisp, fruity Pinot Gris. Lange Winery, in the Red Hills near Dundee, Oregon, makes a Pinot Gris that tends to be richly flavored, thanks to barrel fermentation. Stangeland Winery in the Eola Hills also produces Pinot Gris, from vineyards established in 1978 by Larry and Kinsey Miller.

6 to 8 cups corn or peanut oil

2 jars (10 ounces each) shucked oysters, small or extra-small size preferred

1 cup all-purpose flour

1 cup ale or beer

1 to 1½ cups cracker meal or dry bread crumbs

Coarse salt

Caper Tartar Sauce (see page 232)

northwest food & wine

FILL A WOK or large Dutch oven with 1½ to 1¾ inches of oil. Fasten a deep-fry thermometer to the side of the pan with the probe beneath the surface of the oil. About 10 minutes before you want to cook, turn the heat to medium-high and bring the oil to 375°F, or until a cube of bread sizzles instantly when dropped into the oil. Regulate the heat so the temperature is maintained.

DRAIN OYSTERS. Whisk together the flour and ale to make a batter. Add oysters and mix gently. Place cracker meal in a shallow bowl. Roll the battered oysters, one at a time, in the meal, then set aside on a baking sheet or plates. Allow to rest, uncovered, for 15 minutes. Line a baking sheet with 2 layers of paper towels for draining cooked oysters.

WITH SPRING TONGS GENTLY DROP OYSTERS, one by one, into hot oil without crowding the pan. Use a bamboo chopstick or other heatproof tool to prevent the oysters from sticking together. Fry them until they are lightly browned, about 2 minutes. Using a skimmer or other heatproof strainer, lift the oysters out of the oil and onto the baking sheet. Sprinkle with salt. Repeat until all the oysters are cooked. Serve with the tartar sauce.

Serves 4

caper tartar sauce

Tartar sauce, which is both creamy and piquant, makes a flavorful addition to fish or shellfish dishes. This version uses both sweet-hot mustard and capers, and makes a wonderful accompaniment to deep-fried calamari or oysters, as well as salmon patties.

1 cup mayonnaise

2 tablespoons skim milk or buttermilk

1 tablespoon sweet-hot mustard

1 tablespoon capers, drained, coarsely chopped

1 cup (lightly packed) parsley leaves, chopped

½ teaspoon dried dill weed

Freshly ground black pepper

MIX TOGETHER all the ingredients in a small mixing bowl. Transfer to a small serving bowl. (Extra tartar sauce will keep, covered, for 1 week in the refrigerator.)

Makes about 1½ cups

grilling in the northwest

More than half the households of America now prepare food on an outdoor grill on a regular basis. Nowhere is that more true than in the Northwest. Thanks to the mild climate, especially west of the Cascade Mountains, most Northwesterners can cook outdoors through most of the year, if a little rain is of no concern.

Properly done, grilling adds a robust, smoky flavor to the food being cooked, allowing the cook to keep the rest of the meal simple. Because grilling gives meats, poultry, and seafood an added heartiness, they don't necessarily require sauces. Vegetables can be grilled alongside to create a common theme in the meal and perk up taste buds tired of the same old accompaniments.

Store shelves groan with bottled marinades, sauces, bastes, and the like, many, undoubtedly, fine products. To make grilling less dependent on purchased flavorings and more of a last-minute possibility, keep the following in mind:

- Dry the surface of whatever is being grilled.
- Brush on a light coating of olive or vegetable oil; sprinkle with salt and freshly ground pepper.
- Sprinkle the food with finely chopped herbs before grilling and after.
- Keep the grill covered during cooking to trap the smoke produced by food juices dripping onto hot coals or lava rocks—that is where most grilling flavor comes from.
- Use an instant-read thermometer to judge when meat, poultry, or seafood is cooked to your requirements. The difference between succulence and sawdust is just a few degrees too much heat. (Example: A fillet of salmon at 120°F is juicy and not flaked yet; at 140°F it is a little drier, and flaking; at 160°F it will be dry, and overcooked for many people.)
- If you add a sauce during cooking and that sauce contains sugar (as most do), add it just a few minutes before finishing the cooking to avoid having the sauce burn.

grilled garlic shrimp
on warm cabbage slaw

Tiny coldwater shrimp, also known as baby shrimp or salad shrimp, are harvested along the Northwest coast and are a popular addition to salads. Larger shrimp are used for grilling, a cooking technique that lends the shellfish a robust flavor. Spot prawns, netted in Northwest waters and often brough to market with the heads still on, would work especially well in this dish. Served with quickly sautéed cabbage, these grilled shrimp are slightly crunchy, sweet, briny, and smoky. Pinot Gris is a fine choice for an accompanying wine.

Ponzi Vineyards, a pioneer Oregon winery founded in Beaverton in 1970 by Dick Ponzi, an engineer who once designed amusement park rides for Disney, is now nearly surrounded by the growing city. The Ponzi family has built a long-standing reputation of quality. We savored these shrimp with their 1996 Oregon Pinot Gris.

1 to 1¼ pounds large shrimp, peeled and deveined, tails left on

1 large garlic clove, minced

4 scallions, white and light green part, minced

1 tablespoon fresh lime juice

¼ cup extra virgin olive oil

Coarse salt

Freshly ground black pepper

SLAW

  1 head green cabbage (about 1½ pounds)

  2 tablespoons extra virgin olive oil

  2 cloves garlic, minced

  4 scallions, thinly sliced on the diagonal

  1 medium carrot, shredded

  1 tablespoon fresh lime juice

  Coarse salt

  Freshly ground black pepper

IN A LARGE MIXING BOWL TOSS THE SHRIMP with the garlic, scallions, lime juice, olive oil, and salt and pepper to taste. Allow to stand for 30 minutes.

PREPARE A HOT CHARCOAL FIRE or preheat a gas or electric grill.

TO PREPARE THE SLAW, cut the cabbage in half top to bottom, then cut each half in half again. Trim the core out of each piece, then slice crosswise into thin shreds. Just before grilling, drain the shrimp, reserving the marinade. Heat the olive oil in a 12-inch sauté pan over medium-high heat. Add the garlic and sauté for a few seconds. Add the cabbage, scallions, and carrot. Toss the mixture in the pan using tongs or a couple of wooden spoons. When the cabbage starts to soften just a little, about 2 minutes, add the lime juice, shrimp marinade, and salt and pepper to taste. Toss the mixture again, then divide among 4 warmed plates. Keep warm while you grill the shrimp for 2 to 3 minutes on each side, until they are barely translucent in the center. Arrange shrimp in a pinwheel pattern on top of the cabbage and serve.

  Serves 4

grilled ahi with
sun-dried tomato sauce

Bill Blosser and Susan Sokol married in 1966 and by 1971 had grapevines planted in the hills above Dundee, Oregon. They were in what is often called the second wave of wine makers (coming just after the pioneers of the late 1960s and early 1970s), who believed in the wine-making potential of the Willamette Valley. Their winery, Sokol Blosser, has operated since 1977, and they raised their children on the property. Sokol Blosser produces about 30,000 cases of wine a year, and Pinot Gris is now among the offerings. Pinot Gris accompanies this tuna dish, setting off the sweetness of the tomatoes nicely.

If you have the good fortune to live near a quality fish market, as many of us in the Pacific Northwest do, you may be offered fresh tuna fairly often. Tuna goes by various names in different parts of the world. Ahi is a name often used in the Northwest to refer to yellowfin as well as bigeye. Both tuna have steaks of dark color and fine flavor. Bigeye is slightly more translucent, and is especially prized for preparing sashimi, a Japanese style of very thin slices of raw fish. Ahi tuna is nothing short of extraordinary when briefly cooked over very high heat, whether in a hot skillet or on a charcoal grill. Drinking a worthy wine with the tuna enhances the eating experience.

BARLEY

1 cup pearl barley

2 cups chicken stock or low-sodium canned broth

1 teaspoon coarse salt

½ red bell pepper, cored, seeded, and cut in ¼-inch dice

Freshly ground black pepper

TUNA

2 cups chicken stock or low-sodium canned broth

1 medium onion, finely chopped

1 teaspoon anchovy paste

1 cup oil-packed sun-dried tomatoes

¼ teaspoon hot pepper sauce

Freshly ground black pepper

4 ahi tuna steaks, 1 to 1½ inches thick (1¼ to 1½ pounds)

½ cup (lightly packed) parsley leaves, chopped

COMBINE THE BARLEY and stock in a 2-quart saucepan and bring to a boil over medium-high heat. Add the salt and bell pepper. Reduce the heat and simmer, covered, until the raw taste is gone but the barley has just a hint of bite in the center, 35 to 40 minutes. Remove from the heat, add pepper to taste, and set aside, covered.

PREPARE A HOT CHARCOAL FIRE or preheat a gas or electric grill.

COMBINE THE CHICKEN STOCK, onion, and anchovy paste, and bring to a boil over medium-high heat. Cook, uncovered, until the liquid has reduced to 1 cup. Purée the sun-dried tomatoes, including the oil, in a blender or food processor. Add the purée to the pan. Add the hot pepper sauce and black pepper to taste. Sauce should be the thickness of thin oatmeal; add a little water to thin it out, if necessary. Grill the tuna for 3 to 4 minutes per side to medium rare, 100° to 120°F on an instant-read thermometer. Spread some barley on each of 4 warmed plates. Place the tuna half on, half off barley bed. Stir parsley into sauce and ladle over the part of the tuna steaks not on barley bed. Serve.

Serves 4

pinot gris

basil-coated grilled swordfish with eggplant

Swordfish in the eastern Pacific Ocean is found from southern California to Chile. It is justifiably popular in Northwest markets. Because of its meaty texture and mild flavor, it makes a fine companion for a full-bodied Pinot Gris.

Long popular in Europe (and called Pinot Gris everywhere except in Italy, where it is known as Pinot Grigio), Pinot Gris was not in commercial production in this country before being planted at The Eyrie Vineyards near Dundee, Oregon. It is now a very popular grape, with Oregon production growing rapidly.

½ cup olive oil

1 large sweet onion, such as Walla Walla, halved, and sliced about
  ¼ inch thick

Coarse salt

1 tablespoon sherry vinegar

2 cups (lightly packed) fresh basil leaves, chopped

Freshly ground black pepper

1 medium eggplant, unpeeled, cut crosswise in 1-inch slices

2 swordfish steaks about 1 inch thick (about 1½ pounds)

Sun-Dried Tomato Tapenade (see page 225), optional

PREPARE A HOT CHARCOAL FIRE or preheat a gas or electric grill.

HEAT 2 TABLESPOONS OF THE OLIVE OIL in a 12-inch skillet or sauté pan over medium heat. Add the onions and cover pan for 5 minutes. Uncover the onions and sauté, stirring occasionally, until onions are limp and beginning to turn a light brown color, about 10 minutes more. Sprinkle with salt, stir in the vinegar, and remove from the heat. Cover to keep warm.

COMBINE THE BASIL, 2 tablespoons of the olive oil, and salt and pepper to taste in a medium mixing bowl. Spread the mixture on both sides of the swordfish steaks. Lay the eggplant slices on a large platter or baking sheet, lightly brush with olive oil, and sprinkle with salt and pepper on both sides.

GRILL THE SWORDFISH and eggplant together. Turn the fish after 3 or 4 minutes. Cook the fish until an instant-read thermometer inserted in the center of the fish registers 120°F for moist texture, 140°F if you prefer a firmer texture. Grill eggplant until it is browned on both sides, and cooked through without being mushy. To serve, cut each steak in half, spread some onions on each of 4 plates, and set the swordfish on top of them. If using, spread a light coating of the tapenade on top of each eggplant slice. Arrange the eggplant on each plate and serve.

Serves 4

grilled salmon with rosemary fettuccine

Pinot Gris has a special affinity for salmon, a fish well endowed with flavorful oil. This recipe is quick to prepare and relies on the simple goodness of the fresh fish for its appeal. You could pick up a very nice Pinot Gris at the Argyle tasting room in Dundee, Oregon. Argyle wines, made by the Dundee Wine Company, come from a partnership between Australian Brian Croser and Oregon grape-grower Cal Knudsen, who was in partnership with Dick Erath when their winery was known as Knudsen-Erath in the 1970s and 1980s.

Coarse salt

1 tablespoon vegetable oil

1 pound salmon fillet, pin bones, if any, removed with
   needle-nose pliers

Freshly ground black pepper

½ cup extra virgin olive oil

2 tablespoons anchovy paste

2 tablespoons chopped rosemary leaves

2 cups (lightly packed) parsley leaves, chopped

¾ pound dried fettucine or 1 pound fresh fettuccine

BUILD A MEDIUM-HOT CHARCOAL FIRE or preheat a gas or electric grill.

BRING 6 QUARTS or more of water to a boil in a large pot over high heat. Add 1 tablespoon salt. Rub vegetable oil on both sides of the fish to lightly coat it. Sprinkle with salt and pepper on the flesh side.

COMBINE THE OLIVE OIL, anchovy paste, rosemary, parsley and pepper to taste in a small mixing bowl and whisk until well blended. Set aside.

PLACE THE FISH ON THE GRILL skin side down. Cook until an instant-read thermometer registers 120°F, or 140°F if you prefer your salmon somewhat drier and flakier. If cooking the tail portion of the fillet, do not turn the fish, just gently lift it from the grill using 1 or 2 large metal spatulas. If cooking the thicker end, gently turn the fish after 4 or 5 minutes, then check often for doneness.

IF YOU ARE USING DRY PASTA begin cooking it, stirring frequently, as soon as the salmon is on the grill. If you are cooking fresh fettuccine, begin cooking it when the salmon is about half cooked. Cook pasta until al dente. Drain, and return to the pot. Whisk the herb mixture again and toss with the pasta. Divide among 4 warmed dinner plates. Remove the salmon skin if it did not stick to the grill. Cut the fish into 4 portions and nestle each one on top of the fettuccine. Serve immediately.

Serves 4

baked potatoes stuffed
with dungeness crab

Dungeness crab, the Northwest's favorite crustacean, yields famously sweet meat, especially when picked fresh from the shell. For a dish such as this, however, it's easier to buy crabmeat already picked; it may cost more, but it will save both time and work. Crabmeat and herbs make an unusual filling for twice-baked potatoes. The result is a fine match for a Pinot Gris; sparkling wines also pair wonderfully with these. Serve with a simple salad of baby greens.

4 large russet (baking) potatoes

About 1½ cups whipping cream

2 tablespoons finely diced onion

1 medium tomato, seeded and finely diced

¼ cup chopped fresh tarragon

¼ cup chopped parsley leaves

8 ounces Dungeness crab meat, picked over for shell and cartilage, and coarsely chopped

Coarse salt

Freshly ground black pepper

2 tablespoons grated imported parmesan

PREHEAT THE OVEN TO 400°F.

SCRUB THE POTATOES, pierce with a fork in the center to vent steam while cooking, and bake for 1 hour. Remove and let cool until you can handle them without burning your hands. Increase the oven heat to 450°F.

CUT THE TOP THIRD OFF EACH POTATO lengthwise. Scoop out the pulp, leaving the skins intact. Save the tops for another use. Mash the potatoes in a medium mixing bowl. Blend in as much cream as needed to make the mixture spoonable but not runny. Add the onion, tomato, tarragon, parsley, crabmeat, and salt and pepper to taste.

SPOON THE POTATO MIXTURE back into the potato shells. Sprinkle grated cheese on top. Place the potatoes on a baking sheet and return to the oven for 15 minutes. Serve at once.

Serves 4

northwest vegetable and tuna sandwich

The arrival in the Northwest and other parts of the country of high-quality rustic breads— European-style loaves with real crusts, large interior holes, and a chewy texture—has given rise to higher sandwich expectations. Ciabatta, an Italian loaf, is usually wider and flatter than a French baguette, and therefore a good choice for this sandwich since it provides more space for layering ingredients. Pinot Gris being the noble grape it is, it is only fair to ask that the sandwich accompanying it be made of quality ingredients.

Near Hillsboro, Oregon, is Oak Knoll Winery. One of the earliest of the Willamette Valley wineries, Oak Knoll's first vintage was 1970. It makes several wines, including a very respected raspberry wine. Oak Knoll Pinot Gris is also well respected, and would make an appetizing accompaniment to this sandwich.

1 pound oblong rustic loaf, such as ciabatta or French batard

2 tablespoons extra virgin olive oil

2 cloves garlic, minced

1 tablespoon anchovy paste

2 tablespoons Sun-Dried Tomato Tapenade (see page 225)

1 can (about 6 ounces) solid white tuna in vegetable oil, drained

2 tablespoons salted or brined capers, rinsed

2 large eggs, hard-cooked and sliced

1 small onion, thinly sliced

1 large red bell pepper, roasted, skinned, and thinly sliced

2 medium tomatoes, sliced

SLICE THE BREAD HORIZONTALLY FROM END TO END. Mix the olive oil and garlic and brush onto the cut side of sandwich bottom. Brush anchovy paste onto the cut side of sandwich top, then brush with the tomato tapenade. Flake the tuna, toss with capers, and spread on sandwich bottom. Top with egg, onion, red pepper, and tomato. Place top on sandwich, cut in half, and wrap each half thoroughly in plastic film. Place the sandwiches in a 9 x 13-inch baking dish or similar container. Weight the sandwiches down by putting something heavy on them, such as another baking pan or a small cutting board with several cans of foods on top. Refrigerate overnight.

REMOVE FROM THE REFRIGERATOR about 1 hour before serving. Cut each piece in half again and serve.

Serves 4

risk takers

The history of Northwest wine making is filled with trial and error, as vineyard owners struggle to grow just the right mix of grapes that their soil and microclimate will support, and the wine makers strive to make the finest wines they can with the grapes they are able to obtain. Then they must try to sell them to the public, which sometimes thinks the only two wines in the world are Chardonnay and Cabernet Sauvignon (or Merlot, in Washington). Consequently, the introduction of a wine from a new varietal can be risky for both the vineyard owner, who must put some land and several years' expense into getting vines to bear fruit, and for the winery owners, who must convince the public that the new wine is worth trying.

Enter two wine makers, at opposite ends of Washington State. Both are committed to making fine wine from grapes originally from the Rhône Valley of France, such as Syrah and Grenache. Rusty Figgins (Glen Fiona Winery) and Doug McCrea (McCrea Cellars) are staking their wine-making reputations on a grape new to most Northwesterners, Viognier. The grape exhibits flavors and aromas of apricot, litchi, and peach, combined with low acidity and slightly higher than normal alcohol for a white grape. The result is an elegant, rich-feeling, very food-friendly wine, one that complements sweeter shellfish like crab, lobster, and scallops; Asian dishes that are not extremely hot; and smoked chicken and turkey, among others.

Glen Fiona Winery, just east of Walla Walla, hopes to produce Viognier in 1998 or 1999, a complement to the Syrah and Grenache that winemaker Rusty Figgins makes in his very young winery. McCrea Cellars hopes to release its first Viognier in 1998.

foods to pair with

late harvest
wines

Fresh Peach Pie
Prune and Hazelnut Tart
Strawberry Hazelnut Tartlets with White Chocolate
Lemon Cream Cake with Mascarpone
Hazelnut-Espresso Shortbread
Homemade Whole Wheat Fig Bars

Late harvest wines include wines made from several different grapes, both red and white. The Northwest is fortunate to have the kind of climate that every so often provides the wine maker with the opportunity to make a lucious, sweet wine from the same grapes that are usually vinified as dry wine. In Washington and Oregon the grapes used are most often Gewürztraminer, Riesling, and Sémillon (SEM-mee-yon).

Sweet or dessert wines have residual sugar of about 3 percent or more, and it is perceived as sweetness as soon as the wine is sipped. That sweetness gets there in several different ways. In some cases—especially when nights are cool, mornings damp or foggy, and afternoons warm—the grapes are attacked by a mold called *Botrytis cinerea,* or noble rot. The mold causes the grapes to shrivel as water evaporates from damaged skins, and this concentrates the grape juice. This extra-sweet juice gives the wine maker a chance to stop the fermentation before all the sugar is converted to alcohol and carbon dioxide, and to leave some sweetness in the wine.

In other cases there is a freeze during harvest, and the ripe grapes arriving at the crusher contain ice crystals. During the pressing, concentrated grape juice runs off, but some water remains inside the skins, trapped as ice, and is discarded. The result is concentrated sugars in the juice, giving the wine maker an opportunity to turn what would have been dinner wine into dessert wine instead.

Sweet wines come from Idaho, Oregon, and Washington. They tend to be expensive because it takes so many more grapes to make a bottle. If you've never tried a sipping a late harvest Gewürztraminer with a ripe peach, or a late harvest Sémillon with Roquefort cheese, or a late harvest Riesling with strawberry shortcake, then you have a treat in store. Also, in the following chapter you will find recipes for a Prune and Hazelnut Tart, Lemon Cream Cake with Mascarpone, and Fresh Peach Pie, among others. Avoid chocolate with these wines, since it tends to make the wine taste strange. Instead, pair chocolate with full-bodied red wines.

Serve late harvest wines chilled, about 40° to 45°F.

fresh peach pie

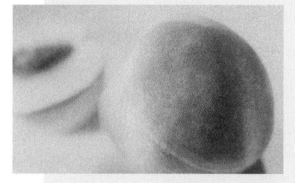

Peach is one of the flavors often detectable in wine, especially late harvest wine. Coincidentally, the warmer and drier regions in the Northwest's wine country support peach orchards along with vineyards. The Rogue Valley region near Medford, Oregon, is one such area. The Columbia Valley region from The Dalles north through Washington's Yakima Valley also produces the popular fuzzy fruit. Fresh, ripe, end-of-summer peaches are a natural companion to late harvest wines. This pie includes a small amount of a very full-flavored rum bottled under the Myers's label, and is topped with the coarse, loose-crystal, light-brown sugar called turbinado. It adds a nice crunch to the top crust.

CRUST

2½ cups all-purpose bleached flour, plus flour for dusting

1 teaspoon salt

2 tablespoons sugar

11 tablespoons (1 stick plus 3 tablespoons) unsalted butter, very cold

7 tablespoon solid vegetable shortening, frozen

7 tablespoons very cold water, or more if needed

FILLING

3½ to 4 pounds peaches

1 cup pecan pieces (about 4 ounces), roasted (see page 251)

½ teaspoon ground nutmeg

½ teaspoon salt

¼ cup Myers's dark rum

¾ cup (lightly packed) light or dark brown sugar

5 tablespoons quick-cooking tapioca

2 tablespoons very cold butter, cut into pea-size pieces

Clee

1 tablespoon milk

1 tablespoon turbinado sugar or 2½ teaspoons granulated sugar

TO MAKE THE CRUST, place the flour, salt, and sugar in the work bowl of a food processor and process for 5 seconds to blend. Cut butter and shortening into tablespoon-size pieces and place in the processor. Pulse until the butter pieces are no larger than a lima bean but no smaller than a pea. Add the 7 tablespoons water and quickly pulse a few more times to blend. Squeeze a little dough in your hand to see if it will barely hold together. If not, add a tablespoon more of cold water and pulse a few more times. Do not let a ball of dough form in the machine. Turn the dough out onto a lightly floured surface and squeeze with your hands to form a mass. Divide the dough into 2 pieces, one slightly larger than the other. Flatten each piece into a disk about 1 inch thick, wrap in plastic and refrigerate for at least 30 minutes but not more than 2 days.

PREHEAT THE OVEN TO 400°F with the rack in the middle level.

PEEL THE PEACHES using a swivel-action vegetable peeler or drop them in boiling water for 15 seconds to loosen the skins. Cut each peach into about 12 slices, freeing each slice from the stone. Place the slices in a 4-quart or larger mixing bowl. Add the pecans, nutmeg, salt, rum, brown sugar, and tapioca, and toss well.

ROLL OUT THE SMALLER OF THE PASTRY DISKS, which will become the bottom crust, on a lightly floured surface to 12 to 13 inches, sprinkling flour on the sur-face and dough as necessary. Roll the dough up around the rolling pin, then unroll the dough over a 10-inch pie pan. Gently press the dough into the pan. Cut off the dough around the outside edge of the pan and use pieces to patch any holes; just moisten with water, and then press together.

GIVE THE PEACH MIXTURE A FINAL TOSS, then spoon evenly into the pie shell. Dot the top of the filling with the small pieces of butter. Roll out the other piece of dough to 12 inches, roll around the pin, then unroll carefully over the top of the pie. Patch, if necessary, and crimp with a fork or pinch the bottom and top dough together at the edge of the pie, and trim the edge. Brush the top with enough milk to moisten, then sprinkle with the sugar. Use the tip of a knife to cut about 6 slits in the top crust to allow steam to escape during baking. Place the pie pan on a rimmed baking sheet to catch any drips.

BAKE 20 MINUTES, then reduce the heat to 350°F and bake until crust is golden brown, about 40 minutes more. Cool on a rack for at least 1 hour to allow juices to set.

Serves 8 to 10

to roast pecans

Preheat the oven to 350°F. Spread pecans on a baking sheet and roast for 10 minutes. Cool before chopping or grinding.

prune and hazelnut tart

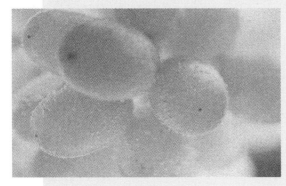

Hazelnuts make fabulous eating, as do prunes—together they are an extraordinary combination. Oregon's Willamette Valley is a major producer of both. Just as prunes have concentrated flavor resulting from evaporation of the water from plums, ice wines such as Chateau Ste. Michelle's 1995 Riesling Ice Wine Chateau Reserve also have concentrated flavor. This tart is terrific eating with an ice wine, which wineries produce only occasionally, when a freeze occurs during harvest. Ice crystals inside harvested grapes stay behind with the skins during crush, which concentrates the flavor of the juice. Since wine yields are lower from partially frozen fruit, expect to pay more by the time ice wine is bottled.

PASTRY

1¼ cups bleached all-purpose flour

1 tablespoon sugar

⅛ teaspoon coarse salt

6 tablespoons (¾ stick) unsalted butter, very cold, cut into ½-inch cubes

3½ tablespoons ice water, or more if needed

FILLING

1 pound pitted prunes

¼ cup granulated sugar

2 large eggs

1¼ cup crème fraîche (see page 15)

Zest of 1 large orange, finely chopped

½ cup hazelnuts (filberts), roasted, skinned, and coarsely chopped
(see page 110)

Powdered sugar for garnish

TO MAKE PASTRY, place flour, sugar, and salt in the work bowl of a food processor and process for 5 seconds to blend. Add the butter and pulse machine until the butter pieces are no larger than a lima bean and no smaller than a pea. Add the water and quickly pulse a few more times to blend. Squeeze a little dough in your hand to see if it will barely hold together. If not, add a tablespoon more of ice water and pulse a few more times. Turn dough out onto a lightly floured surface and form into a disk about an inch thick. Wrap in plastic and refrigerate at least 30 minutes but not longer than 2 days.

ROLL DOUGH OUT on a lightly floured surface to about 13½ inches. Flour the top of the dough circle very lightly, then roll the dough up around the rolling pin, and gently unroll over an 11- or 12-inch tart pan with a removable bottom. Nestle dough down into the pan. Gently roll the pin across the top of the tart pan and remove scraps of dough. Cover with plastic or foil and refrigerate for at least 30 minutes. Then, move the pan to the freezer for 30 minutes more.

PREHEAT THE OVEN TO 375°F.

PRESS A PIECE OF ALUMINUM FOIL down on top of the pastry shell and fill with aluminum pie weights or about 2 cups dried beans. Place tart pan on a rimmed baking pan, and bake for about 17 minutes. Remove foil and weights, and bake for 8 minutes more. Allow to cool.

MEANWHILE, place the prunes in a small, nonreactive saucepan, cover with water, and bring to a boil over medium heat. Reduce heat and simmer for about 30 minutes. Allow to cool.

PREHEAT THE OVEN TO 375°F.

DRAIN PRUNES IN A STRAINER. Place the sugar, egg, crème fraîche, and orange zest in the work bowl of a food processor and process to blend. Spread the prunes in the tart shell, sprinkle with the chopped nuts, and pour the crème fraîche mixture over. Place tart pan on a rimmed baking pan to catch any leaks. Bake for 25 minutes. Cool on a rack. Shake a little powdered sugar through a small strainer to dust top of tart before serving. Remove the rim of the tart pan and place the tart on a cake plate or serving platter.

Serves 8 to 10

what the sun does in vineyards

Grapevines, like people, are shaped by their environment. Also like people, they are adaptable as long as the basics are covered. One of the basics in vineyards is warmth.

In the spring of each year dormant vines, which have been pruned to the wine maker's specifications over the winter, lie in wait for things to warm up. When the average daily temperature reaches about 50°F, tiny shoots begin appearing as the sap flows through the vines. Around 60 days later, if the weather cooperates, flowers bloom. This is a dangerous time in Northwest vineyards, because rainstorms or late frost can prevent the flowers from setting fruit and thus reduce the vineyard yield tremendously. So long as Mother Nature cooperates, tiny grape buds develop and grow quickly on the vines, which are trained as they grow to gain maximum exposure to sunlight.

In order to ripen properly, wine grapes need a certain amount of cumulative warmth over their growing season. So vineyard owners keep track of Growing Degree Days (GDD). Since nothing much happens in the vineyard below 50°F, the GDD measurement system uses that temperature as its starting point. A single GDD is a day on which the average temperature is 51°F. If that day's temperature averages 70°F, then the grapes add 20 points to their heat memory bank. By harvest time the degree total may be well over 2,500 GDDs. Cooler years result in slower ripening grapes, later harvests, and risk of weather damage in the fall. The wines tend to be more acidic, thinner in body, more vegetal, and less fruity in flavor. Wine makers routinely spin the vineyard roulette wheel, hoping, as every day passes, that the grapes will ripen more and the rains or frost will hold off. No wonder wine makers don't get much sleep during harvest!

strawberry hazelnut tartlets
with white chocolate

Sweet, gooey desserts will over-power a late harvest wine, but this dessert is little more than a glorified hazelnut shortbread topped with a few strawberries and then gilded with white chocolate. In individual tartlet form, it is wonderful accompanied by a golden, late harvest Gewürztraminer.

Stewart Vineyards, near Sunnyside, Washington, makes a late harvest Gewürztraminer in some years. Wine makers at Stewart have included Mike Januik, now with Chateau Ste. Michelle, and Joel Tefft, who also owns and makes wine at Tefft Cellars.

CRUST

1¼ cups hazelnuts (about 5 ounces), roasted and skinned
   (see page 110)

⅓ cup granulated sugar

2 cups bleached all-purpose flour

Coarse salt

Grated zest of 1 small lemon

16 tablespoons (2 sticks) unsalted butter, very cold, cut into
   ½-inch cubes

2 large eggs

1 teaspoon pure vanilla extract

½ cup strawberry preserves or jam

1 pound fresh strawberries

Clem

1 tablespoon whipping cream

2 ounces quality white chocolate, such as Lindt

¼ teaspoon Frangelico (optional)

PLACE THE NUTS AND SUGAR in the work bowl of a food processor fitted with a metal blade and process until the nuts are finely ground. Add the flour, salt, and lemon zest. Pulse once or twice to blend the ingredients. Place butter cubes in the work bowl and process to the texture of coarse meal. Lightly beat the eggs with the vanilla, and, with the machine running, add to flour mixture. Stop just as it forms a ball of dough. Turn dough out onto a floured work surface and divide into 8 portions. Press each portion into a 4½-inch tart pan with a removable bottom. Prick each pastry in 4 or 5 places with a table fork. Cover and refrigerate for 30 minutes, then move to the freezer for at least 30 minutes, or overnight. Remove the tart pans from the freezer and place on 1 or 2 rimmed baking sheets.

PREHEAT THE OVEN TO 325°F. When the oven is ready, bake the tarts until the crusts are well browned and firm, about 40 minutes. Allow to cool on a rack.

MELT THE STRAWBERRY PRESERVES in a small saucepan over low heat. Brush on the cooled pastries. Rinse, hull, and dry strawberries. Cut in half or in quarters, depending on their size, and arrange them over the jam layer.

COMBINE THE WHIPPING CREAM AND WHITE CHOCOLATE in a small saucepan over very low heat. Stir just until the chocolate is melted. Remove from the heat, add the Frangelico, if desired, and allow to cool and thicken slightly. When slightly thickened, drizzle over the tartlets in a zigzag pattern. Tartlets can be served immediately or refrigerated for a few hours before serving. Using a thin-bladed knife, remove tartlets from pan bottoms before serving.

Serves 8

lemon cream cake
with mascarpone

This cake is a worthy accompaniment to a memorable Northwest late harvest white wine. Northwest dessert wines are most often made from Gewürztraminer, Muscat, and Riesling grapes, and can be unctuous and fruity-fresh at the same time. Be certain that the dessert wine you serve is slightly sweeter than the dessert, so that the wine does not come off as acidic in your mouth.

The mascarpone filling includes a bit of pear brandy. One to try is made by Steve McCarthy, owner of Clear Creek Distillery in Portland, using Hood River Valley fruit.

4 large eggs

1⅓ cups granulated sugar

¼ teaspoon pure vanilla extract

½ cup whipping cream

6 tablespoons (¾ stick) unsalted butter, melted

Grated zest of 2 lemons

¼ cup fresh lemon juice

2 cups cake flour

1 teaspoon baking powder

¼ teaspoon coarse salt

FILLING

    1½ cups mascarpone

    ½ cup whipping cream

    2 tablespoons powdered sugar

    2 teaspoons pear brandy

Berries, or grapes and Medjool dates

PREHEAT THE OVEN TO 350°F. Place the oven rack in the middle of the oven. Grease and flour two 9 x 5-inch loaf pans.

USING AN ELECTRIC MIXER, beat the eggs and granulated sugar until the mixture is pale yellow and soft ribbons form. Add the vanilla, cream, melted butter, lemon zest, and lemon juice. Beat briefly just to blend. Sift or whisk together the flour, baking powder, and salt. Add to the cake batter and mix very briefly just to blend. Pour batter into the pans. Bake until a wire cake-tester or toothpick comes out clean when inserted into the center of the cake, about 40 minutes. Allow cakes to cool 15 minutes, then run a knife or cake spatula around inside edges of pans to loosen cakes. Invert pans onto a cooling rack, remove pans from cakes, and cool cakes for 1 hour.

TO MAKE THE FILLING, whip together the mascarpone, cream, powdered sugar, and pear brandy. Use a bread knife to split cakes in half horizontally. Spread the bottom halves with the mascarpone filling and replace cake tops. Refrigerate, covered, until 30 minutes before serving.

TRIM THE ENDS of the cakes so they are square, then cut into 1-inch slices. Serve with fresh berries, or fresh grapes and Medjool dates.

Makes about 16 slices

hazelnut-espresso shortbread

This shortbread is made with two ingredients for which the Northwest has become famous— hazelnuts and dark-roast coffee. The combination is rich, deeply flavored, and not so sweet that it overpowers a dessert wine. One of the most unusual late harvest wines in the Northwest is made by Wade Wolfe at Thurston Wolfe Winery in Prosser, Washington. Sweet Rebecca is a blend of Chenin Blanc, Riesling, Sauvignon Blanc, and Sémillon. The winery makes other late harvest wines, as well.

¾ cup hazelnuts (3 ounces), roasted and skinned (see page 110)

1½ cups bleached all-purpose flour

½ cup rice flour

2 tablespoons finely ground espresso-roast coffee

½ cup sugar

¼ teaspoon salt

16 tablespoons (2 sticks) unsalted butter, at room temperature

PREHEAT THE OVEN TO 275°F.

PLACE THE NUTS IN THE WORK BOWL of a food processor and process until finely chopped. Add the all-purpose flour, the rice flour, ground espresso, sugar, and salt, and process to blend. Add the butter and process until mixture just gathers into a ball of dough.

PRESS THE DOUGH EVENLY into an 11- or 12-inch round cake, pie, or quiche pan. Use the tines of a fork to prick down into dough to mark the outline of 16 uniform wedges. Bake for 50 minutes. Increase the oven temperature to 300°F and bake for 15 minutes more. Cool in the pan.

Makes 16 pieces

oregon hazelnuts

Hazelnuts, also known as filberts, can be used anywhere on the menu, from soup to, well, nuts. Oregon is the source for nearly all the crop in the United States, and what little isn't grown there comes from not far across the Columbia River in Washington. Northwest hazelnuts are large and full flavored. The trees are descendants of European trees; trees native to the Northwest produce nuts that are smaller and in less demand. Hazelnut skins need to be removed to make them suitable for most cooking, a task most easily accomplished by oven-toasting them, which also intensifies their flavor.

homemade
whole wheat fig bars

These little fig bars have lots of moist, soft fruit, and a dough that includes whole wheat flour and sour cream. Flavor is what these bars are all about. Late harvest wines are bursting with flavor too.

Preston Premium Wines, north of Pasco, Washington, has made late harvest Riesling since 1977. Its first vineyard was planted with greenhouse starts on a 104°F day in July of 1972, well before the Washington wine country really blossomed. Early Preston wine-maker Rob Griffin, later of Hogue Cellars and now wine maker/owner of Barnard Griffin, put Preston on the map with respected wines, and for a time it was the largest family-owned winery in Washington. You could try your fig bar with a Preston Late Harvest Riesling.

FILLING

> 1½ pounds dried soft figs
>
> ½ cup honey
>
> ¼ cup fresh lemon juice
>
> 2 tablespoons water

DOUGH

> 1½ cups unbleached all-purpose flour
>
> 1½ cups whole wheat flour
>
> 1 teaspoon baking powder

½ teaspoon salt

8 tablespoons (1 stick) unsalted butter, at room temperature

¾ cup (firmly packed) brown sugar

1 large egg

¼ cup sour cream

FINELY CHOP THE FIGS in a food processor. Combine the figs, honey, lemon juice, and 2 tablespoons water in a small, nonreactive saucepan. Place over medium heat and bring just to a bare simmer, stirring now and then. Set aside to cool.

IN A MEDIUM BOWL, whisk together the all-purpose and whole wheat flour, baking powder, and salt. Set aside. Using an electric mixer fitted with the paddle attachment, beat the butter on medium speed until fluffy. Add the sugar and beat for about 1 minute. Add the egg and sour cream and beat until incorporated. Add the dry ingredients and beat on low until a uniform dough develops. Refrigerate dough 30 minutes.

PREHEAT THE OVEN TO 400°F.

LINE A BAKING SHEET with parchment paper or foil, or use a nonstick sheet. Divide the dough into 2 pieces. Roll out each piece of dough on a lightly floured surface into an oblong shape about 16 x 6 inches, and about ¼-inch thick. Spoon filling in a row down the center of each piece, leaving a ½-inch border all around. Use a long pastry spatula or a thin flat cookie sheet to slide under dough and fold the edges over to the center, overlapping the edges by ½ inch. Repeat with second piece of dough.

PLACE THE BARS ON THE BAKING SHEET. Bake until golden brown, about 18 minutes. Cool on a rack. Slice crosswise in 1-inch bars.

Makes about 30 pieces

other northwest wine grapes

The chapters in this book have been chosen because the grape variety on which each is based is currently or soon to be popular among Northwest wine consumers, and most likely will continue in popularity and, therefore, acres planted. There are other grapes from which wine is made in Idaho, Oregon, and Washington. Some of them are not well known to the wine-buying public, even though they may play a significant role in blending or as varietals on their own. Wine makers and vineyard owners experiment with grape varieties new to their area in a constant quest to find those that fit their particular microclimate, the volume needs of the winery, and the desire to make something different. Plantings of certain grapes inevitably increase, while others decline. Here is a quick overview of a few Northwest-grown grape varieties that are not found in separate chapters in this book.

Cabernet Franc
A red grape most often used for blending with Cabernet Sauvignon and Merlot but also made into a varietal wine of its own in Washington.

Chenin Blanc
Famous white grape of France's Loire Valley, a mainstay of Northwest wine production for a long time. Many wineries have approached it casually, to have something affordable to sell. A few, especially Hogue Cellars, have been putting more effort into their Chenin Blancs, making dry versions of greater than average quality.

Grenache
Famous Rhône-style light red grape, often blended with Syrah. Plantings have increased within the past five years.

Lemberger
An all-but-unknown grape to most of America. Performs predictably in varying vintages in Washington. A bright red, soft, berrylike, easy—and affordable—drinking wine.

Madeleine Angevine
Lightly planted white grape, mostly in western Washington's cool climate.

Mélon
A very close Pinot Blanc relative, used in Oregon to make dry, crisp white wines. Used for Muscadet in France.

Müller-Thurgau

A limited-production, early ripening white grape in the Northwest, a cross between Riesling and Silvaner. It is often described as musky as well as floral. These wines are often sweet, though dry versions exist, too.

Muscat

White grape produced mostly in the Willamette Valley. Can be very dry, sparkling, or dessert sweet. Orange aroma often evident.

Sangiovese

Famous grape of central Italy, including Chianti. A few wine makers in the Northwest are experimenting with it, sometimes for use in red blends, sometimes for bottlings that are full-fledged Sangiovese—and labeled as such.

Sémillon

The great white grape of France's Sauternes wine. Can make a very fine soft, dry wine. Often blended with Sauvignon Blanc.

Viognier

Famously aromatic white grape from France's Rhône Valley. Aromas of apricot, honeysuckle, litchi, and peach. Tends to be slightly higher in alcohol that most whites, and has pleasing viscosity. Several wine makers in Washington and Oregon are experimenting with Viognier, and small commercial releases of the wine have occurred recently. A grape with a Northwest future, most likely.

northwest wineries

Many wineries are not often open to the public and list only post office boxes, or list an out-of-state address. Call the winery for information on visiting and tasting policies, and for directions to the winery.

idaho wineries

BITNER VINEYARDS
16645 Plum Rd.
Caldwell, ID 83605
(208) 454-0086

CAMAS WINERY
110 S Main St.
Moscow, ID 83843
(208) 882-0214

CANA VINEYARDS
28372 Peckham Rd.
Wilder, ID 83676
(208) 482-7372

CARMELA VINEYARDS
795 W Madison
Glenns Ferry, ID 83623
(208) 366-2313

COCOLALLA WINERY
Hwy 95 North, MP 463
Athol, ID 83801
(208) 683-2473

**HEGY'S SOUTH
HILLS WINERY**
3099 East 3400 North
Twin Falls, ID 83301
(208) 734-6369
Fax (208) 733-7435

HELLS CANYON WINERY
18835 Symms Rd.
Caldwell, ID 83605
(208) 454-3300

**INDIAN CREEK
(STOWE) WINERY**
1000 N McDermott Rd.
Kuna, ID 83634
(208) 922-4791

KOENIG VINEYARDS
14744 Plum Rd.
Caldwell, ID 83605
(208) 454-5572

LIFE FORCE WINERY
531 S Main St.
Moscow, ID 83843
(208) 882-9158

PEND D'OREILLE WINERY
1067-B Baldy Industrial Park
Sandpoint, ID 83864
(208) 265-8545

PETROS WINERY
2303 Table Rock Rd.
Boise, ID 83712
(208) 346-6283

PINTLER CELLAR
13750 Surrey Lane
Nampa, ID 83686
(208) 467-1200

ROSE CREEK VINEYARDS
226 East Ave. North
Hagerman, ID 83332
(208) 837-4413

STE. CHAPELLE WINERY
19348 Lowell Rd.
Caldwell, ID 83605
(208) 459-7222

VICKERS VINEYARDS
15646 Sunny Slope Rd.
Caldwell, ID 83605
(not open to the public)

WESTON WINERY
16316 Orchard St.
Caldwell, ID 83605
(208) 459-2631

WOOD RIVER CELLARS
2606 San Marco Way
Nampa, ID 83686
(888) 817-7294

oregon wineries

**ABACELA WINERY &
VINEYARDS**
12500 Lookingglass Rd.
Roseburg, OR 97470
(541) 679-6642
Fax (541) 679-4455

ACADEMY OF WINES
18200 Hwy 238
Grants Pass, OR 97527
(541) 846-6817

ACME WINEWORKS
PO Box 48
Carlton, OR 97111
(503) 852-6969

ADELSHEIM VINEYARD
22150 NE Quarter Mile Lane
Newberg, OR 97132
(503) 538-3652
Fax (503) 538-2248

AIRLIE WINERY
15305 Dunn Forest Rd.
Monmouth, OR 97361
(503) 838-6013
Fax (503) 838-6279

ALPINE VINEYARDS
25904 Green Peak Rd.
Monroe, OR 97456
(541) 424-5851
Fax (541) 424-5891

AMITY VINEYARDS
18150 Amity Vineyards Rd. SE
Amity, OR 97101
(503) 835-2362
Fax (503) 835-6451

ANTICA TERRA
8535 SW 64th Ave.
Portland, OR 97219
(503) 221-7614

ARCHERY SUMMIT
PO Box 85
Dundee, OR 97115
(503) 864-4300
Fax (503) 864-4038

**ARGYLE WINERY/
DUNDEE WINE CO.**
PO Box 280
Dundee, OR 97115
(503) 538-8520
Fax (503) 538-2055

ASHLAND VINEYARDS
2775 E Main St.
Ashland, OR 97520
(541) 488-0088
Fax (541) 488-5857

AUTUMN WIND
VINEYARD
15225 NE North Valley Rd.
Newberg, OR 97132
(503) 538-6931

BEAR CREEK VINEYARDS
PO Box 609
Cave Junction, OR 97523
(541) 592-3727

BEAUX FRÈRES
VINEYARD
15155 NE North Valley Rd.
Newberg, OR 97132
(503) 537-1137
Fax (503) 537-2613

BELLE PENTE WINE
CELLARS
12470 Rowland Rd.
Carlton, OR 97111
(503) 852-6389
Fax (503) 852-6977

BELLFOUNTAIN CELLARS
25041 Llewellyn Rd.
Corvallis, OR 97333
(541) 929-3162
Fax (541) 929-6110

BENTON LANE WINERY
6126 Silverado Trail
Napa, CA 94558
(707) 944-2659
Fax (707) 944-9360

BERAN VINEYARDS, INC.
30088 SW Egger Rd.
Hillsboro, OR 97123
(503) 628-1298
Fax (503) 628-1298

BETHEL HEIGHTS
VINEYARD
6060 Bethel Heights Rd. NW
Salem, OR 97304
(503) 581-2262
Fax (503) 581-0943

BRICK HOUSE
VINEYARDS
18200 Lewis Rogers
Newberg, OR 97132
(503) 538-5136
Fax (503) 538-5136

BRIDGEVIEW VINEYARDS
PO Box 609
Cave Junction, OR 97523
(541) 592-4688
Fax (541) 592-2127

BROADLEY VINEYARDS
PO Box 160
Monroe, OR 97456
(541) 847-5934
Fax (541) 847-6018

CALLAHAN RIDGE
WINERY
340 Busenbark Lane
Roseburg, OR 97470
(541) 673-7901
Fax (541) 673-5580

CAMERON WINERY
PO Box 27
Dundee, OR 97115
(503) 538-0336
Fax (503) 538-0336

CARLO & JULIAN WINERY
1000 E Main St.
Carlton, OR 97111
(503) 852-7432

CHAMPOEG WINE
CELLARS
10375 Champoeg Rd. NE
Aurora, OR 97002
(503) 678-2144
Fax (503) 678-1024

CHATEAU BENOIT
6580 NE Mineral Springs Rd.
Carlton, OR 97111
(503) 864-2991
Fax (503) 864-2203

CHATEAU BIANCA
WINERY
17485 Hwy 22
Dallas, OR 97338
(503) 623-6181
Fax (503) 623-6230

CHATEAU LORANE
WINERY
27415 Siuslaw River Rd.
Lorane, OR 97451
(541) 942-8028

CHEHALEM/RIDGECREST
31190 NE Veritas Lane
Newberg, OR 97132
(503) 538-4700
Fax (503) 537-0850

COOPER MOUNTAIN
VINEYARDS
9480 SW Grabhorn Rd.
Beaverton, OR 97007
(503) 649-0027
Fax (503) 649-0702

CRISTOM VINEYARDS
6905 Spring Valley Rd. NW
Salem, OR 97304
(503) 375-3068
Fax (503) 391-7057

CUNEO CELLARS
9360 SE Eola Hills
Amity, OR 97101
(503) 835-2782
Fax (503) 835-6106

DENINO UMPQUA RIVER
ESTATE
451 Hess Rd.
Roseburg, OR 97470
(541) 673-1975

DOMAINE DROUHIN
OREGON
PO Box 700
Dundee, OR 97115
(503) 864-2700
Fax (503) 864-3377

DOMAINE SERENE
VINEYARDS (ADMIN.)
16235 Holdridge Rd.
Wayzata, MN 55391
(503) 852-7777

DOMAINE SERENE
VINEYARDS (WINERY)
338 W Main St.
Carlton, OR 97111
(503) 852-7777

DROBNEY VINEYARD, INC.
184 Missouri Flat Rd.
Grants Pass, OR 97527

DUCK POND CELLARS
PO Box 429
Dundee, OR 97115
(503) 538-3199
Fax (503) 538-3190

EDGEFIELD WINERY
2126 SW Halsey St.
Troutdale, OR 97060
(503) 665-2992
Fax (503) 661-1968

ELK COVE VINEYARDS
27751 Olson Rd.
Gaston, OR 97119
(503) 985-7760
Fax (503) 985-3525

EOLA HILLS WINE
CELLARS
501 S Pacific Hwy
Rickreall, OR 97371
(503) 623-2405
Fax (503) 623-0350

ERATH VINEYARDS
9009 NE Worden Hill Rd.
Dundee, OR 97115
(503) 538-3318
Fax (503) 538-1074

EVESHAM WOOD WINERY
3795 Wallace Rd. NW
Salem, OR 97304
(503) 371-8478
Fax (503) 371-8478

THE EYRIE VINEYARDS
PO Box 697
Dundee, OR 97115
(503) 472-6315
Fax (503) 472-5124

FIDDLEHEAD CELLARS
1667 Oak Ave., Ste. B
Davis, CA 95616
(916) 756-4550
Fax (916) 756-4558

FIRESTEED CELLARS
1809 Seventh Ave. #1108
Seattle, WA 98101
(206) 233-0683
Fax (206) 292-2780

FLERCHINGER
VINEYARDS
4180 Post Canyon Drive
Hood River, OR 97031
(541) 386-2882
Fax (541) 386-2882

FLYING DUTCHMAN
301 Otter Crest Loop
Otter Rock, OR 97369
(541) 765-2060
Fax (541) 765-2069

FLYNN VINEYARDS
2200 W Pacific Hwy
Rickreall, OR 97371
(503) 623-8683
Fax (503) 623-0908

FORIS VINEYARDS
WINERY
654 Kendall Rd.
Cave Junction, OR 97523
(541) 592-3752
Fax (541) 592-4424

GIRARDET WINE
CELLARS
895 Reston Rd.
Roseburg, OR 97470
(541) 679-7252
Fax (541) 679-9502

GOLDEN VALLEY WINERY
980 E 4th
McMinnville, OR 97128
(503) 472-2739
Fax (503) 434-8523

HELVETIA VINEYARDS
22485 NW Yungen Rd.
Hillsboro, OR 97124
(503) 647-5169

HENRY ESTATE WINERY
PO Box 26 Hwy 9
Umpqua, OR 97486
(541) 459-5120
Fax (541) 459-5146

HIGH PASS WINERY
24757 Lovell Rd.
Junction City, OR 97448
(541) 998-1447

HILLCREST VINEYARD
240 Vineyard Lane
Roseburg, OR 97470
(541) 673-3709

HINMAN VINEYARDS/
SILVAN RIDGE
PO Box 70303
Eugene, OR 97401
(541) 345-1945
Fax (541) 342-2695

HOLLEY BLUE VINEYARD
PO Box 1087
Corvallis, OR 97339
(541) 757-7777
Fax (541) 754-7605

HONEYWOOD WINERY
1350 Hines St. SE
Salem, OR 97302
(503) 362-4111
Fax (503) 362-4112

HOOD RIVER VINEYARDS
4693 Westwood Drive
Hood River, OR 97031
(541) 386-3772
Fax (541) 386-5880

HOUSTON VINEYARDS
86187 Hoya Lane
Eugene, OR 97405
(541) 747-4681
Fax (541) 345-7066

ISLAND PRINCESS WINES
4972 Cascade Hwy SE
Sublimity, OR 97385
(503) 769-4996

JOHN MICHAEL
CHAMPAGNE
1425 Humbug Creek Rd.
Jacksonville, OR 97530

KEN WRIGHT CELLARS
PO Box 190
Carlton, OR 97111
(503) 852-7070

KING ESTATE WINERY
80854 Territorial Rd.
Eugene, OR 97405
(541) 942-9874
Fax (541) 942-9867

KRAMER VINEYARDS
26830 NW Olson Rd.
Gaston, OR 97119
(503) 662-4545
Fax (503) 662-4033

KRISTIN HILL WINERY
3330 SE Amity-Dayton Hwy
Amity, OR 97101
(503) 835-0850

LA GARZA CELLARS
491 Winery Lane
Roseburg, OR 97470
(541) 679-9654
Fax (541) 679-3888

LA MERLEAUSINE
19143 NE Laughlin Rd.
Yamhill, OR 97148
(503) 662-3280
Fax (503) 662-4829

LANGE WINERY
PO Box 8
Dundee, OR 97115
(503) 538-6476
Fax (503) 538-1938

LAUREL RIDGE WINERY
PO Box 456
Forest Grove, OR 97116
(503) 359-5436
Fax (503) 359-0366

LAVELLE VINEYARDS
89697 Sheffler Rd.
Elmira, OR 97437
(541) 935-9406
Fax (541) 935-7202

LION VALLEY VINEYARDS
35040 SW Unger Rd.
Cornelius, OR 97113

MARQUAM HILL
VINEYARDS
35803 S Hwy 213
Mollala, OR 97038
(503) 829-6677

MCKINLAY VINEYARD
7120 NE Earlwood Rd.
Newberg, OR 97132
(503) 625-2534

MEDICI VINEYARDS
28005 NE Bell Rd.
Newberg, OR 97132
(503) 538-8298

MOMOKAWA SAKE LTD.
820 Elm St.
Forest Grove, OR 97116
(503) 357-7056
Fax (503) 357-1014

MONTINORE VINEYARDS
PO Box 490
Forest Grove, OR 97116
(503) 359-5012
Fax (503) 357-4313

MORGAN LAKE CELLARS
11975 Smithfield Rd.
Dallas, OR 97338
(503) 623-6420
Fax (503) 623-4310

MOUNTAIN VIEW
WINERY
22899 Alfalfa Market Rd.
Bend, OR 97701
(541) 388-8339

NEHALEM BAY WINE CO.
34965 Hwy 53
Nehalem, OR 97131
(503) 368-5300

NICOLAS ROLIN
VINEYARDS
2234 NE 50th St.
Portland, OR 97213
(503) 282-7542

OAK GROVE ORCHARDS
WINERY
6090 Crowley Rd.
Rickreall, OR 97371
(503) 364-7052

OAK KNOLL WINERY
29700 SW Burkhalter Rd.
Hillsboro, OR 97123
(503) 648-8198
Fax (503) 648-3377

OREGON CASCADE
WINERY
610 Jefferson
Oregon City, OR 97045
(503) 631-8426

OREGON ESTATES
WINERY
PO Box 417
Kerby, OR 97531
(541) 592-2825

PANTHER CREEK
CELLARS
455 N Irvine
McMinnville, OR 97128
(503) 472-8080
Fax (503) 472-5667

PONZI VINEYARDS
14665 SW Winery Lane
Beaverton, OR 97007
(503) 628-1227
Fax (503) 628-0354

RAINSONG VINEYARDS
WINERY
92989 Goldson/
Templeton Rd.
Cheshire, OR 97419
(541) 998-1786

RAPTOR RIDGE
29090 SW Wildhaven Lane
Scholls, OR 97123
(503) 628-3534

REDHAWK VINEYARD
2995 Michigan City Ave. NW
Salem, OR 97304
(503) 362-1596
Fax (503) 362-1596

REX HILL VINEYARDS
30835 N Hwy 99
Newberg, OR 97132
(503) 538-0666
Fax (503) 538-1409

SAGA VINEYARDS
30815 S Wall St.
Colton, OR 97017
(503) 824-4600
Fax (503) 824-4601

SALEM HILLS VINEYARD
& WINERY
7934 Skyline Rd. S
Salem, OR 97306
(503) 362-5250

SECRET HOUSE
VINEYARDS WINERY
88324 Vineyard Lane
Veneta, OR 97487
(541) 935-3774

SERENDIPITY CELLARS
WINERY
15275 Dunn Forest Rd.
Monmouth, OR 97361
(503) 838-4284
Fax (503) 838-0067

SEVEN HILLS VINEYARD
PO Box 21
Milton-Freewater, OR 97862
(541) 938-7710
Fax (509) 529-7198

SHAFER VINEYARD
CELLARS
6200 NW Gales Creek Rd.
Forest Grove, OR 97116
(503) 357-6604
Fax (503) 357-6604

SHALLON WINERY
1598 Duane St.
Astoria, OR 97103
(503) 325-5978

SOKOL BLOSSER WINERY
PO Box 399
Dundee, OR 97115
(503) 864-2282
Fax (503) 864-2710

SPRINGHILL CELLARS
2920 NW Scenic Drive
Albany, OR 97321
(503) 928-1009
Fax (503) 928-1009

ST. INNOCENT WINERY
1360 Tandem Ave. NE
Salem, OR 97303
(503) 378-1526
Fax (503) 378-1041

ST. JOSEF'S WINE CELLAR
28836 S Barlow Rd.
Canby, OR 97013
(503) 651-3190

STAG HOLLOW
VINEYARDS
7930 NE Blackburn Rd.
Yamhill, OR 97148-8501
(503) 662-4022
Fax (503) 662-4581

STANGELAND VINEYARDS
& WINERY
8500 Hopewell Rd. NW
Salem, OR 97304
(503) 581-0355
Fax (503) 540-3412

STARR WINERY
10610 NW St. Helens Rd.
Portland, OR 97231
(503) 289-5974

TEMPEST VINEYARDS
9342 NE Hancock Dr.
Portland, OR 97220
(503) 835-2600
Fax (503) 252-7059

TORII MOR WINERY
PO Box 359
McMinnville, OR 97128
(503) 434-1439
Fax (503) 434-5733

TROON VINEYARDS
1475 Kubli Rd.
Grants Pass, OR 97526
(541) 846-6562

TUALATIN VINEYARDS
Route 1 Box 339
Forest Grove, OR 97116
(503) 357-5005
Fax (503) 357-1702

TYEE WINE CELLARS
26335 Greenberry Rd.
Corvallis, OR 97333
(541) 753-8754

VALLEY VIEW VINEYARD
1000 Upper Applegate Rd.
Jacksonville, OR 97530
(541) 899-8468
Fax (541) 899-8468

VAN DUZER WINES
OF OREGON
501 Parducci Rd.
Ukiah, CA 95482
(707) 463-5350
Fax (707) 462-7260

WASSON BROTHERS
WINERY
41901 Hwy 26
Sandy, OR 97055
(503) 668-3124

WEISINGER'S OF
ASHLAND
3150 Siskiyou
Ashland, OR 97520
(541) 488-5989
Fax (541) 488-5989

WESTREY WINES
PO Box 386
Dundee, OR 97115
(503) 434-6357

WILD WINDS WINERY
9092 Jackson Hill Rd. SE
Salem, OR 97306
(503) 391-9991

WILLAKENZIE ESTATE
19143 NE Laughlin Rd.
Yamhill, OR 97148
(503) 662-3280
Fax (503) 662-4829

WILLAMETTE VALLEY
VINEYARDS
8800 Enchanted Way SE
Turner, OR 97392
(800) 344-9463
Fax (503) 588-8894

WINE COUNTRY FARM
6855 NE Breyman Orchards
Dayton, OR 97114
(503) 864-3446
Fax (503) 864-3109

WITNESS TREE
VINEYARD
7111 Spring Valley Rd. NW
Salem, OR 97304
(503) 585-7874
Fax (503) 362-9765

YAMHILL VALLEY
VINEYARDS
16250 SW Oldsville Rd.
McMinnville, OR 97128
(503) 843-3100
Fax (503) 843-2450

washington wineries

ALEXIA SPARKLING
WINES
c/o Matthews Cellars
620 NE 55th St.
Seattle, WA 98105
(206) 989-1156

ANDREW HILL CELLARS
12526 SW Bank Rd.
Vashon Island, WA 98070
(206) 463-3290

ARBOR CREST WINE
CELLARS
North 4705 Fruithill Rd.
Spokane, WA 99207
(509) 927-9894
Fax (509) 927-0574

BADGER MOUNTAIN
VINEYARDS
1106 South Jurupa
Kennewick, WA 99337
(509) 627-4986
Fax (509) 627-2071

BAINBRIDGE ISLAND
WINERY
682 State Hwy 305 NE
Bainbridge Island, WA 98110
(206) 842-9463

BALCOM & MOE WINERY
2520 Commercial Ave.
Pasco, WA 99301
(509) 547-7307
Fax (509) 547-4809

BARNARD GRIFFIN
WINERY
828 Tulip Lane
Richland, WA 99352
(509) 627-0266
Fax (509) 627-0266

BARON MANFRED VON
VIERTHALER WINERY
17136 Hwy 410 E
Sumner, WA 98390
(253) 863-1633

BIRCHFIELD WINERY
921-B Middle Fork Rd.
Onalaska, WA 98570
(360) 978-5224
Fax (360) 978-5225

BONAIR WINERY
500 S Bonair Rd.
Zillah, WA 98953
(509) 829-6027
Fax (509) 829-6410

BOOKWALTER WINERY
710 South Windmill Rd.
Richland, WA 99352
(509) 627-5000
Fax (509) 627-5010

CAMARADERIE CELLARS
335 Benson Rd.
Port Angeles, WA 98362
Fax (360) 452-4964

CANOE RIDGE VINEYARD
PO Box 684
Walla Walla, WA 99362
(509) 527-0885
Fax (509) 527-0886

CASCADE CLIFFS WINERY
PO Box 14
Wishram, WA 98673
(509) 767-1100
Fax (509) 767-1100
(call ahead)

CATERINA WINERY
North 905 Washington
Spokane, WA 99201
(509) 328-5069
Fax (509) 325-7324

CAVATAPPI WINERY
9702 NE 120th Place
Kirkland, WA 98033
(425) 823-6533
Fax (425) 823-8500

CHARLES REININGER
WINERY
Walla Walla Airport
Bldg. 805 C St.
Walla Walla, WA 99362
(509) 522-1994
Fax (509) 525-1201

CHATEAU GALLANT
South 1355 Gallant Rd.
Pasco, WA 99301
(509) 545-9570
Fax (509) 547-1768

CHINA BEND VINEYARDS
3596 Northport-Flat Creek Rd.
Kettle Falls, WA 99141
(509) 732-6123

CHINOOK WINERY
PO Box 387
Prosser, WA 99350
(509) 786-2725
Fax (509) 786-2777

CLAAR CELLARS
1081 Glenwood Rd.
Pasco, WA 99301
(509) 266-4449
Fax (509) 266-4444

COLUMBIA WINE
& SPIRITS
PO Box 1248
Woodinville, WA 98072
(425) 488-2776
Fax (425) 488-3460

COVENTRY VALE
PO Box 249
Grandview, WA 98930
(509) 882-4100
Fax (509) 882-5771

DELILLE CELLARS
PO Box 2233
Woodinville, WA 98072
(425) 489-0544
Fax (425) 402-9295

DI STEFANO WINES
1458 Elliott Way East
Seattle, WA 98119
(206) 282-6484
Fax (425) 452-1029

E.B. FOOTE WINERY
9354 4th Ave. S
Seattle, WA 98108
(206) 763-9928
Fax (206) 763-4271

EATON HILL WINERY
530 Gurley Rd.
Granger, WA 98932
(509) 854-2220

FACELLI WINERY
16120 Woodinville-
Redmond Rd., #1
Woodinville, WA 98072
(425) 488-1020
Fax (425) 488-6383

FAIRWINDS WINERY
1924 Hastings Ave. West
Port Townsend, WA 98368
(360) 385-6899

GLEN FIONA WINERY
PO Box 2024
Walla Walla, WA 99362
(509) 522-2566
Fax (509) 522-1008

GORDON BROTHERS
CELLARS
5960 Burden Blvd.
Pasco, WA 99301
(509) 547-6331
Fax (509) 547-6305

HEDGES CELLARS
(SALES & ADMIN.)
195 NE Gilman Blvd.
Issaquah, WA 98027
(206) 391-6056
Fax (425) 391-3827

HEDGES CELLARS
(WINERY)
53511 Sunset Rd. NE
Benton City, WA 99320
(509) 588-3155
Fax (509) 588-5323

HINZERLING WINERY
1520 Sheridan Ave.
Prosser, WA 99350
(509) 786-2163
Fax (509) 786-2163

HOGUE CELLARS
PO Box 31
Prosser, WA 99350
(509) 786-4557
Fax (509) 786-4580

HOODSPORT WINERY
North 23501 Hwy 101
Hoodsport, WA 98548
(360) 877-9760
Fax (360) 877-9508

HORIZON'S EDGE
WINERY
4530 East Zillah Drive
Zillah, WA 98953
(509) 829-6401

HUNTER HILL
VINEYARDS
2752 West McMannaman Rd.
Othello, WA 99344
(509) 346-2736
Fax (509) 346-2736
(call ahead)

HYATT VINEYARDS
2020 Gilbert Rd.
Zillah, WA 98953
(509) 829-6333
Fax (509) 829-6433

KIONA VINEYARDS
44612 North Sunset Rd.
Benton City, WA 99320
(509) 588-6716
Fax (509) 588-3219

KLICKITAT CANYON
WINERY
6 Lyle-Snowden Rd.
Lyle, WA 98635
(509) 365-2900

KNIPPRATH CELLARS
South 163 Lincoln St.
Spokane, WA 99204
(509) 624-9132

L'ECOLE NO.41 WINERY
PO Box 111
Lowden, WA 99360
(509) 525-0940
Fax (509) 525-2775

LATAH CREEK WINE
CELLARS
East 13030 Indiana Ave.
Spokane, WA 99216
(509) 926-0164
Fax (509) 926-0710

LEONETTI CELLAR
1321 School Ave.
Walla Walla, WA 99362
(509) 525-4006

LOPEZ ISLAND
VINEYARDS
Route 1, Box 1243-9B
Lopez Island, WA 98261
(360) 468-3644

LOST MOUNTAIN WINERY
3174 Lost Mountain Rd.
Sequim, WA 98382
(360) 683-5229
Fax (360) 681-8689

MARKET CELLAR WINERY
1432 Western Ave.
Seattle, WA 98101
(206) 282-6615

MATTHEWS CELLARS
18658 142nd Ave. NE
Woodinville, WA 98072
(425) 487-9810
Fax (425) 483-1652

MCCREA CELLARS
13443 118th Ave. SE
Rainier, WA 98576
(360) 458-9463
Fax (360) 458-9463
(call ahead)

MONT ELISE VINEYARDS
PO Box 28
Bingen, WA 98605
(509) 493-3001

MOUNT BAKER
VINEYARDS
PO Box 626
Deming, WA 98244
(360) 592-2300
Fax (360) 592-5753

MOUNTAIN DOME
WINERY
16315 East Temple Rd.
Spokane, WA 99207
(509) 922-2788
Fax (509) 922-8078

OAKWOOD CELLARS
40504 North Demoss Rd.
Benton City, WA 99320
(509) 588-5332
Fax (509) 588-5332
(call ahead)

OLYMPIC CELLARS
255410 Hwy 101
Port Angeles, WA 98362
(360) 683-9652
Fax (360) 683-9652

PASEK CELLARS
511 South 1st St.
Mount Vernon, WA 98273
(360) 757-1966

PATRICK M. PAUL
VINEYARDS
1554 School Ave.
Walla Walla, WA 99362
(509) 522-1127
Fax (509) 522-9404

PONTIN DEL ROZA
WINERY
35502 Hinzerling Rd.
Prosser, WA 99350
(509) 786-4449
Fax (509) 786-4449
(call ahead)

PORTTEUS WINERY
PO Box 1444
Zillah, WA 98953
(509) 829-6970
Fax (509) 829-5683

PRESTON PREMIUM
WINES
502 East Vineyard Drive
Pasco, WA 99301
(509) 545-1990
Fax (509) 545-1098

QUILCEDA CREEK
VINTNERS
5226 Old Machias Rd.
Snohomish, WA 98290
(360) 568-2389
Fax (360) 568-2389
(call ahead)

RANDALL HARRIS WINES
3051 42nd Ave. West
Seattle, WA 98199
(206) 283-7688
Fax (206) 283-7684

RICH PASSAGE WINERY
7869 NE Day Rd. West, Bldg. A
Bainbridge Island, WA 98110
(206) 842-8199
Fax (206) 842-8198

SAINTPAULIA VINTNERS
18302 83rd Ave. SE
Snohomish, WA 98296
(360) 668-8585

SALISHAN VINEYARDS
35011 North Fork Ave.
La Center, WA 98629
(360) 263-2713
Fax (360) 263-3675

SAMISH ISLAND WINERY
896 Samish Island Rd.
Bow, WA 98232
(360) 766-6086

SAN JUAN VINEYARDS
2000 Roche Harbor Rd.
Friday Harbor, WA 98250
(360) 378-9463

SETH RYAN WINERY
35306 Sunset Rd.
Benton City, WA 99320
(509) 588-6780
Fax (509) 588-6780
(call ahead)

SILVER LAKE SPARKLING
CELLARS
17721 132nd Ave. NE
Woodinville, WA 98072
(206) 486-1900
Fax (206) 483-3523

SOOS CREEK WINE
CELLARS
20404 140th Ave. SE
Kent, WA 98042
(253) 631-8775

STATON HILLS WINERY
71 Gangl Rd.
Wapato, WA 98951
(509) 877-2112
Fax (509) 877-3377

STIMSON LANE
VINEYARDS & ESTATES
PO Box 1976
Woodinville, WA 98072
(206) 488-1133
Fax (425) 488-4657

TAGARIS WINERY
PO Box 5433
Kennewick, WA 99336
(509) 547-3590
Fax (509) 547-8264

TEFFT CELLARS
1330 Independence Rd.
Outlook, WA 98938
(509) 837-7651
Fax (509) 839-7337
(call ahead)

TERRA BLANCA VINTNERS
34715 Demoss Rd.
Benton City, WA 99320
(509) 588-6082
Fax (509) 588-2634

THURSTON WOLFE
WINERY
3800 Lee Rd., Ste. C
Prosser, WA 99350
(509) 786-3313
Fax (509) 786-4580
(c/o Hogue Cellars)

TUCKER CELLARS
70 Ray Rd.
Sunnyside, WA 98944
(509) 837-8701
Fax (509) 837-8701
(call ahead)

VASHON WINERY
12629 SW Cemetery Rd.
Vashon Island, WA 98070
(206) 463-2990

WALLA WALLA VINTNERS
PO Box 1551
Walla Walla, WA 99362
(509) 525-4724
Fax (509) 525-4134

WASHINGTON HILLS
CELLARS (ADMIN.)
10604 NE 38th Place, Ste. 132
Kirkland, WA 98033
(206) 889-9463
Fax (425) 889-4581

WASHINGTON HILLS
CELLARS (WINERY)
111 East Lincoln Ave.
Sunnyside, WA 98944
(509) 839-9463
Fax (509) 839-6155

WATERBROOK WINERY
Route 1, Box 46
Lowden, WA 99360
(509) 522-1918
Fax (509) 529-4770

WHIDBEY ISLAND
VINEYARDS
5237 South Langley Rd.
Langley, WA 98260
(360) 221-2040

WHITE HERON CELLARS
PO Box 5245
George, WA 98824
(509) 785-5521

WIDGEON HILL WINERY
121 Widgeon Hill Rd.
Chehalis, WA 98532
(360) 748-0407
Fax (360) 736-2815

WILLOW CREST WINERY
55002 Gap Rd.
Prosser, WA 99350
(509) 786-7999

WILRIDGE WINERY
1416 34th Ave.
Seattle, WA 98122
(206) 325-3051
Fax (206) 447-0849

WIND RIVER CELLARS
PO Box 215
Husum, WA 98623
(509) 493-2324

WINEGLASS CELLARS
260 North Bonair Rd.
Zillah, WA 98953
(509) 829-3011

WOODWARD CANYON
WINERY
Rte. 1, Box 387
Lowden, WA 99360
(509) 525-4129
Fax (509) 522-0927

WORDEN'S WASHINGTON
WINERY
7217 West 45th Ave.
Spokane, WA 99204
(509) 455-7835
Fax (509) 838-4723

YAKIMA RIVER WINERY
143302 North River Rd.
Prosser, WA 99350
(509) 786-2805
Fax (509) 786-3203

index

m–o

p–r

index

index